Good Neighbourly Relations

Good Neighbourly Relations

*Jordan, Israel and the
1994–2004 Peace Process*

DONA J. STEWART

Tauris Academic Studies
LONDON • NEW YORK

Published in 2007 by Tauris Academic Studies,
an imprint ofI.B.Tauris & Co Led
6 Salem Road, London W2 4BU
175 Fifth Avenue, New York NY 10010
www.ibcauris.com

Library of Modern Middle Ease Studies 56

ISBN 978 1 8488 5970 8

A full CIP record for this book is available from the British Library
A full CIP record for this book is available from the Library of Congress

Library of Congress catalog card: available

Contents

List of Tables

List of Maps

Acknowledgements

This volume would not have been possible without the support of the Fulbright commission in Jordan. I would like to thank Alain McNamara, his family, and the Fulbright staff for the extensive support they provided to me and my family during our stay.

My understanding of the Jordanian-Israeli relationship benefited greatly from my association with the Amman Center for Peace and Development (ACPD), and its director General (Ret.) Mansour Abu Rashid. At ACPD I was able to participate in the process of making peace between Jordan and Israel amid great obstacles. I hope that this volume will, in some small way, contribute to that ongoing effort. I would like to thank Gen. Mansour both for his personal recollections of this last decade and for introducing me to the many Jordanians who shared their perspectives on the Jordanian-Israeli relationship.

I would like to thank a number of Israeli individuals and institutions for their assistance in understanding the Israeli view of the Israeli-Jordanian relationship, including: Samdar Shapira at the Perez Center for Peace, Ron Shatzberg of the Economic Cooperation Foundation, Yishay Sorak and Yitzak Gal at the Israeli-Jordan Chamber of Commerce, General (Ret.) Shlomo Brom of the Jaffee Center for Strategic Studies, General (Ret.) Dov Sedaka of the Economic Cooperation Foundation and Dr. Asher Susser at Tel Aviv University.

Comments by Dr. Robert Satloff (Washington Institute for Near East Policy) and Dr. Yoram Meital (Ben Gurion University) helped improve an earlier version of this manuscript. However, any omissions and errors remain my own.

Finally, I would like to thank Autumn Cockrell, who worked tirelessly to keep the Middle East Institute at Georgia State University running while I was on leave in Jordan, and Susanne Wilhelm for transforming this volume from a raw manuscript into its final formatted and copyedited form.

1

THE CHALLENGE TO CREATE 'GOOD NEIGHBOURLY RELATIONS'

On 26 October 1994, the Hashemite Kingdom of Jordan and the State of Israel signed a peace treaty in Wadi Araba (Arava), making Jordan the second Arab country—after Egypt—to conclude peace with Israel. By all accounts, the mood on that day was euphoric; in the words of King Hussein bin Talal it was 'a day like no other'.[1] Under tight security and scorching sun, Jordanian, Israeli and American officials, including President Bill Clinton, met at the Wadi Araba/Arava border crossing. There, a diverse crowd of 5,000 gathered on a former minefield:

> Israeli generals in combat fatigues mixing with Jordanians in red keffiyehs, diplomats in ties and farmers in open-necked shirts, former Prime Minister Yitzhak Shamir and elder statesman Abba Eban—and ordinary people, invited because they lost loved ones in the wars between the two countries now making peace.[2]

King Hussein had succeeded in brokering the treaty that brought decades of proscribed Jordanian-Israeli cooperation into the public spotlight. His partner in peace, Israeli Prime Minister Yitzhak Rabin, signed the historic accord for Israel, with his Jordanian counterpart Prime Minister Abdul-Salem Majali representing Jordan.

Ten years on, the mood in Jordan and Israel is decidedly less euphoric. The architects and main sponsors of the peace are both dead. Prime Minister Rabin paid the ultimate price for his willingness to make peace and was assassinated by a radical Jewish law student. His killer, Yigal Amir, deeply opposed the Oslo Agreement and had twice previously planned to kill the prime minister.[3] For many in Israel, Rabin's death, at a rally with 100,000 Peace Now supporters, was symbolic of the passing of the hope for Israel to reach peaceful relations with all its neighbours. His memorial in Tel Aviv remains a locus for public demonstrations, drawing 100,000 people on the anniversary of his death in 2003, but it has also been defaced as well as revered.[4] Rabin's death, only two years after the Jordan-Israel peace, highlighted deep divisions in Israeli society and reflected growing domestic discord in the post Oslo period. Lack of continued confidence in the Oslo process led to significant changes in Israel's ruling government, which has subsequently strained Jordanian-Israeli relations. With Rabin gone, King Hussein lost his 'partner in peace', and never had such close relations with another Israeli leader.

Five years after the peace, King Hussein succumbed to the cancer that had wracked his body even during the finalization of the treaty. His son, Abdullah bin Hussein, became the new monarch amid already apprehensive Jordanian-Israeli relations. Upon assuming the throne, King Abdullah affirmed the policies initiated by his father, including the peace with Israel.[5] In practical terms, however, the implementation of the peace, outside the key area of security and some economic cooperation, has scarcely moved forward. Support within Jordan for closer relations with Israel remains largely limited to the monarchy and the highest reaches of the government. Growing regional tension, including escalation of the Israeli-Palestinian conflict, further strain relations on all levels; as a result, many of the activities mandated by the treaty, especially those concerning relations between the countries' citizenry, remain unimplemented.

Approach of this Volume

This book is an attempt to understand the state of relations, or the 'progress of the peace', between Jordan and Israel over the last decade. It differs from many volumes dealing with the Middle East conflict, as the emphasis in not on the 'peace process', meaning the steps by which parties reach an agreement, but on the activities that take place once the agreement is signed. The title of this volume further reflects the viewpoint that the most crucial, and perhaps most challenging, part of the peace process takes place after the ink on the treaty has dried. Within the region, the only other example of a completed treaty is the Egyptian-Israeli peace, most often referred to as a 'cold peace'. In making peace with Jordan, Israel tried to avoid the disappointments of the peace with Egypt, which, three decades after the signing of the Camp David Accords, has failed to lead to significant economic or societal relations, resulting instead in a chilling of the official relationship. 'Cairo,' argues Meital, 'holds Israel mainly responsible for the deterioration in the peace process—primarily because of what the Egyptian public and leadership see as provocative policies by Israel's government.'[6] Though the two countries have diplomatic relations, the Egyptian ambassador to Israel left Tel Aviv after Prime Minister Ariel Sharon's visit to the Temple Mount and the start of the Al Aqsa *intifada* in November 2000.[7] Egypt also opposed the Washington Declaration (Common Agenda) between Jordan and Israel and prevented the formation of the Conference for Security and Cooperation in Europe-Middle East, a regional security structure called for in the Jordan-Israel peace treaty.[8] At the societal level, where 'normalization' was to take place between the two peoples, the situation is even worse: '…Egyptians burn the Israeli flag in pro-Palestinian demonstrations. "I hate Israel" was a hit song, and Egyptian state television aired a series based on the Protocols of the Elders of Zion, an anti-Semitic tract long ago discredited as a forgery….'[9]

Fifteen years after the Camp David Accords, the peace between Jordan and Israel was designed to be a 'warm peace', extending beyond formal government relations to include Israeli and Jordanian society.

An Unusual Treaty – Creating a 'Warm Peace'

Noting the distinctions between Israel's treaties with Egypt and Jordan, Satloff argues that the Israeli-Egyptian treaty was based on the concepts of 'respect' and 'security'; the document focused overwhelmingly on issues of security, recognition of each other's sovereignty and borders, and the composition of an international force for the Sinai peninsula.[10] Detailed annexes accompanied the highly legalistic document. Its tone, he further states, reflects the lack of trust between the two parties and their extended war experience.

By contrast, the Jordanian-Israeli peace treaty is based on the concepts of 'partnership' and 'cooperation'.[11] Indeed, the preamble to the treaty notes the 'desire to develop friendly relations and cooperation between them…' prior to its call for 'lasting security for both their States…'. The preamble also points out a major distinction between the Egyptian and Jordanian treaties, noting that the state of belligerence between Jordan and Israel had been terminated three months before, in July 1994, through the signing of the Washington Declaration. Therefore, the goal of the treaty signed at Wadi Araba/Arava was not to cease hostilities, but rather 'to establish peace between them'.

In this spirit, the treaty includes an article devoted to 'mutual understanding and neighbourly relations'.[12] It prohibits any discriminatory practices or expressions of hostility between the two parties. This approach is consistent with what has become known today as 'peace education' and places responsibility on both governments to remove hostile or inflammatory language from textbooks and government press. These measures, combined with plans for cultural and scientific exchange and joint projects in the areas of water resources, environment, and tourism, were designed to create a warm peace at the societal as well as governmental level.

The tone of the Jordanian-Israeli treaty also reflects the differing experiences of Jordan and Egypt with Israel. Only five short years had passed between the October 1973 War and the signing of the Camp David Accords; in contrast, Jordan and Israel had last fought 28 years before their treaty. Indeed, Jordan was a reluctant participant in the 1973 War; King Hussein had even tried to warn Israel of the impending attack by Egyptian forces.[13]

Evaluating the Jordanian-Israeli Peace

The goal of this book is not an overarching legalistic judgment of the treaty's success from the standpoint of fulfilling sections of the document, but rather to delve into the complex and nuanced relations between these two states who, as a result of the dictates of geography, share a destiny that necessitates a certain level of interdependence.

It is perhaps very revealing that academia has far more numerous measures and methods to assess conflict than to analyze 'peace'.[14] At a very basic level, peace is simply the absence of armed conflict. By that standard, Jordan and Israel have certainly achieved peace, though the Mish'al and Naharayim incidents (discussed in Chapter Four) shadow the record. However, Jordan and Israel not only set out to make peace, but to establish 'good neighbourly relations' between them. The peace treaty covered areas far beyond mere security considerations, such as tourism, and scientific and cultural exchange. Collaboration in these areas was designed to convey the peace down from the level of government and monarchy to the people themselves, and to create neighbourly bonds between the two societies.

For methodological reasons, the organization of this book largely parallels that of the peace treaty, addressing the major sections such as security, water and economic relations. Its emphasis is not primarily on assessing the implementation of each article or amendment from a technical standpoint,[15] but to assess at the overall relations in each area of the peace treaty. Through this broader approach, significant events in the bilateral relationship at both the governmental and societal level can be included. Conflict resolution practitioners have long recognized that, while treaties between states may formally end conflict, peace can only be created—and lived—by people. Commitment to this concept dramatically influenced the intent of the treaty, and therefore the approach of this volume.

The peace between Jordan and Israel was long in the making, and the meetings in Washington under the auspices of the Clinton Administration, though surprising to many at the time, were the culmination of a covert dialogue between the two countries, dating back at least 30 years.[16] Yet, the early 1990s finally seemed, from the point of view of King Hussein, the right time for a historic agreement with Israel. Chapter Two briefly examines the Jordanian-Israeli relationship in the second half of the twentieth century, focusing on the factors that led to the 1994 peace treaty. Such factors included the individual leadership of King Hussein of Jordan and Prime Minister Rabin of Israel, shared strategic concerns within both governments, the impact of the 1991 Gulf War on Jordan's relationship with the West, economic concerns in the Hashemite Kingdom and the onset of an unprecedented regional peace process beginning with the Madrid conference.

Security cooperation (Chapter Three) is the bedrock of the Jordanian-Israeli relationship and its most resilient aspect. Even when political and societal relationships reach their lowest point, cooperation on security issues, between military and security forces, continues in some form. Long-standing issues of shared concerns, such as border security, the potential use of territory by hostile groups, smuggling (including arms) and threats from regional actors, were a major factor in bringing both parties to formal peace negotiations and continue to drive cooperation today. The decades of secret security cooperation prior to the declaration of formal peace not only created the motivation for a treaty, but produced a sense of trust between the two parties.

Abrogation of this long-standing trust, the focus of Chapter Four, precipitated the most serious crises that have tested the agreement: the attempted assassination of a Hamas political leader by Israeli Mossad agents in Jordan, and the killing of seven Israeli schoolgirls by a Jordanian soldier on the 'peace island' in the Jordan River. The resolution of these crises required major concessions from both sides, but the bilateral security relationship ultimately prevailed and underscored the strength of the treaty. The other issue discussed in Chapter Four, the Israeli decision to open the Hasmonean tunnel, marks a significant turning point in the Jordanian-Israel relationship. This event also illustrates a strong belief held by Jordanians, even those that support the peace and are involved in the bilateral relationship that Israel fails to take into consideration the concerns of Jordan, or communicate with Jordan, on issues that will have significant domestic consequences in the kingdom.

The significance of water in the Middle East, and its potential role as a source of conflict has been mentioned so often (more precious than oil!) that it almost became a cliché. However, it would be hard to overestimate the importance of water to both Jordan's and Israel's survival and the centrality of this issue within the peace treaty. The treaty provided for the shared use of the Jordan and Yarmouk rivers and the ground water from Araba/Arava aquifers, and determined the specific allocations for each country. It also called for major bilateral projects to expand and better manage water resources. Unfortunately, the highly comprehensive Jordan-Israel peace treaty failed to anticipate a severe regional drought in 1999, triggering a crisis when Israel initially refused to deliver its required share of water to Jordan. The resolution of this conflict and an overview of the general state of Jordanian-Israeli cooperation on water resources is the focus of Chapter Five.

To overcome the Jordanian public's political sensitivities to peace with Israel, the government emphasized the economic benefits of the peace. This is the primary area where tangible gains have been realized, especially at the macro-level and through Jordan's new economic relationship the United States. The Qualified Industrial Zones (QIZ), which benefit from quota exemptions for export to the United States and require Israeli participation, have created strong export growth for Jordan. Perhaps the most significant economic impact is the US-Jordan Free Trade Agreement, which gives Jordanian products preferential access to the US market. Ironically, this agreement, signed in 2001, will reduce Jordanian dependency on the QIZ, and perhaps eliminate the need to work with Israeli partners.

However, economic benefits of the QIZ have generally not been felt at the micro-level and other economic projects have yet to be realized, leading to criticism that the peace has not delivered the expected dividend. Moreover, the Israeli economy dwarfs that of Jordan, prompting strong Jordanian concern that economic benefit is not accruing equally between the parties. In many cases, anticipated levels of economic cooperation between Jordan and Israel are forestalled by Israeli security concerns or bureaucracy, and little progress has been made on major projects called for in the treaty. Tension exists even within the successful QIZ projects over transportation issues between Jordan and Israel. Jordanian businesses are often frustrated in their relations with Israel and see Israeli recalcitrance as driven not only by security concerns, but a desire to protect Israeli business interests from any Jordanian competition. From the Israeli perspective, there is a feeling that no matter what they do, it simply will not be enough to satisfy Jordanians. Chapter Six explores the dynamics of Jordanian-Israeli economic cooperation.

Economic cooperation in the critical field of tourism has been hampered by rising violence following the breakdown of the Oslo process, the onset of the second Palestinian *intifada* in 2000, the increasingly harsh actions by the Israeli military, and the global slowdown in tourism as a result of 11 September 2001 and the Iraq War in 2003. Today, the situation on the ground is in marked contrast to the 1995 tourist season, which witnessed dramatic growth of Jordan's and Israel's tourism industry and raised expectations of a sustained, long-term growth in this sector. Chapter Seven examines the Jordanian tourism industry, which after a short-lived, post-peace boom has struggled to meet the cost of infrastructure created in anticipation of more extensive growth.

While most of the cooperation between Jordan and Israel takes place at the formal governmental level, non-governmental cooperation plays a key role in expanding the influence of the peace treaty beyond the official level (Chapter Eight). Because of political sensitivities to peace with Israel, cooperation by the very few Jordanian non-governmental organizations (NGOs) willing to work with Israelis is done very quietly and with discretion. They face numerous obstacles, including their own governmental bureaucracies, a lack of funding by governmental and international donors and differences in administrative capacity between most Jordanian and Israeli NGOs. Moreover, individuals and organizations inside Jordan, who participate in such projects, face criticism and sometimes severe punitive measures from the Jordanian 'anti-normalization' groups. Nonetheless, Jordanian and Israeli NGOs have been able to foster limited cooperation in areas of environment, education, religious dialogue and community development in border regions.

The peace with Israel remains a contested issue in Jordan; considerable resistance to normalization exists not only within political parties represented in parliament,[17] but also in the state bureaucracy, within the powerful professional unions (syndicates) and among the population. Though many Jordanians are quick to point out that they have no problems with Jews—who they consider religious brethren—only with the policies of the state of Israel, the result is serious resistance to any contact with Israelis. New survey research shows that for many Jordanians the Israeli-Jordanian relationship cannot be separated from the Israeli-Palestinian conflict. The lack of a comprehensive peace between Israelis and Palestinians and worsening conflict in the last five years has placed great strain on the potential for development of a 'warm peace'. The Jordanian and Israeli publics also hold divergent views of the benefits of the peace, creating a large 'perception gap' between the two societies. Ten years after the peace, there is a near total lack of contact between Jordanians and Israelis. Chapter Nine examines the societal challenges to normalization in Jordan and the government's attempt to manage internal opposition to its relations with Israel.

The Context of the Relationship

A number of issues, some related to domestic issues, as well as those created by external forces (such as the Israeli-Palestinian conflict), have affected the Jordanian-Israeli bilateral relationship. The peace treaty's environment, in which it was to survive and flourish, has worsened dramatically since the euphoric moments at Wadi Araba. While the significance of particular issues will be illustrated at appropriate points within the volume, it is useful to briefly introduce a set of issues that have influenced Jordanian-Israeli relations in the past ten years.

The Death of Rabin and Likud Political Dominance in Israel

Following the assassination of Yitzhak Rabin, the Likud party gained greater political control, central coalition partners also included hard-line and far right-wing elements in subsequent governments headed by Binyamin Netanyahu in (beginning 1996) and Ariel Sharon (beginning 2000). The inclusion of conservative religious parties in Netanyahu's coalition sent misgivings through the Arab world, which realized that Netanyahu would likely take a hard-line position on the Palestinians in order to maintain his coalition.[18] Though Jordan attempted to maintain a more reserved position amidst calls for a united Arab response to Netanyahu's 'aggressive and anti-peace' policies,[19] the personal connections between Rabin and Hussein that had under-girded the peace treaty were gone. By October 1996, King Hussein, who had urged his fellow Arabs to reserve judging Netanyahu early in his term, was severely criticizing his actions and warned that extremists were setting the agenda following Rabin's death.[20] Netanyahu's actions, especially towards the Palestinians, 'increased domestic and regional pressures upon him (Hussein) to take sides, which interrupted normalization and minimized ties in Israel'.[21] Jordan's relationship with Netanyahu's government was characterized, according to one observer, by 'snubs and double-crosses'.[22] Jordanian-Israel relations have never fully recovered from the actions taken during the Netanyahu administration that shattered the nascent trust between the two parties, including the opening of the Temple Mount tunnel, the construction of the Har Homa settlement, and the Mish'al incident (all discussed in Chapter Four).

Furthermore, the ascendancy of the Likud party and specific hard-liner elements within it, created a strain in the Jordanian-Israeli relationship that hindered the full implementation of the peace within a few short years of its signing. Increasingly harsh military approaches to the Palestinian problem without an associated political solution, the abandonment of the Oslo process, and the continued expansion of settlements have all made it more difficult for Jordan to carry the weight of the peace with Israel, while maintaining its relationships with other Arab states. Jordan, too, withdrew its ambassador from Israel following heightened violence between the Israeli military and Palestinians stemming from the controversial visit to the Temple Mount by Ariel Sharon, then Likud chairman[23]. Palestinian reaction to the visit has become known as the Al Aqsa *intifada*; the incident marks a turning point in Israeli-Palestinian relations, since it contributed to Likud victory in subsequent elections. Israel continues to maintain an ambassadorial presence in Amman, but its embassy staff is not accompanied by dependent children, out of security concerns.

A particular provocation to more extensive relations between Jordan and Israel, both at the societal and governmental level, is the so-called 'transfer option', which views Jordan as the solution to Israel's Palestinian problem. This idea, first articulated by Sharon in 1975, makes Jordan the *watan badil* or 'alternative homeland' for all Palestinians, including the ones from Israel's occupied territories. The further implication of this proposal is that once transferred Palestinians become a majority in Jordan, they will overthrow the Jordanian monarchy.[24] Recent voices in Israel, notably tourism minister Benny Elon's call for a vast internationally-financed plan to move the estimated 1.5 million Palestinians from the West Bank and Gaza Strip to Arab states,[25] reawakened Jordanian concerns on this matter. Though most Israelis are quick to dismiss this option as the rhetoric of a fringe group that will never achieve political dominance, the very nature of Israeli democracy, where small parties can exercise enormous influence if the survival of the ruling coalition is at stake, contributes to Jordanian unease. The long-term survival of this idea in Israeli politics lends credence to Jordanian perceptions that support for the 'Jordan as Palestine' option extends beyond the 'fringe element' that has made it an important part of its political platform.

The Palestinian Issue and the Failure of the Peace Process

The Jordanian-Israeli peace was concluded amidst the euphoria of the Oslo Accords, at a time when many in the region believed that a resolution to decades of conflict lay just over the horizon. The peace treaty's infancy has been marked by the failure of this process and worsening relationships between the Arab states and Israeli governments, especially those under Likud leadership. This has forced Jordan to walk an increasingly difficult line, attempting to balance its peace with Israel, still a major strategic imperative, with the reinforcement of ties with other Arab countries, while simultaneously maintaining domestic stability during a period of substantial economic reform.

In Jordan, the phrase 'because of the situation' is often heard in discussions of Jordanian-Israeli relations. Increases in tourism are not possible, increased economic growth by opening Jordanian-Palestinian trade is not possible, long-planned joint projects are not possible, all 'because of the situation'. In short, Jordanian expectations regarding the peace cannot be met because of the current phase of the Israeli-Palestinian conflict and the attitudes and realities associated with it. The phrase takes into account the restrictions resulting from the security aspects of the second *intifada* and Israeli response as well as the possibilities at the governmental and societal level amid growing criticism of Israel's Palestinian policy. As in Egypt, many Jordanians place the failure of the Israeli-Palestinian peace process squarely on Israel's policies, and its failure is inexorably linked to the limitations on the Israeli-Jordanian peace.

While it would be a mistake to believe that the Jordanian government and societal relations are always in concert with the goals of the Palestinians, the Jordanian-Israeli relationship is intimately responsive to the state of Israeli-Palestinian affairs. Though Jordan's strategic interests consistently dominate decision making over specific Palestinian-related concerns at the governmental level, the Palestinian situation creates enormous pressure at the societal level, which the government cannot afford to ignore. With a majority of its population made up of Palestinians (though many hold Jordanian citizenship), most Jordanians have family connections to the occupied territories, and Israeli policy in the territories has a direct effect on their families and friends.[26] Jordanians speak of a growing sense of frustration at the inability to alleviate the suffering within the territories. Like most of the Arab world, Jordanians, even those without Palestinian heritage, are sensitive to what is viewed as the collective of punishment of the Palestinians. Conversely, Jordan fears a potential mass exodus of Palestinians from the West Bank, a situation that increases its commitment to security relations with Israel.

For this reason, Jordan's peace agreement with Israel severely strained its relationship to the Palestinians and the Palestinian leadership. The issue of Jerusalem and sections of the treaty that acknowledged the kingdom's 'special role' in caring for Muslim holy shrines in East Jerusalem were of crucial concern. Palestinian fears, that this acknowledgement would undercut Palestinian claims to sovereignty over the same sites, were bolstered by the treaty provision giving the historic Jordanian role a 'high priority' in permanent status negotiations. Though King Hussein reportedly assured Yasser Arafat (then chairman of the Palestine Liberation Organization) that Jordan would relinquish custody when Palestinians obtained sovereignty over Jerusalem, the Palestinians considered the situation unsettled.[27] Indeed, Yasser Arafat did not attend the signing ceremony at Wadi Araba. A rapprochement of sorts happened in 1998, when King Hussein assured him that Jordan would not compete with the PLO as the sole legitimate representative of the Palestinians.[28] Even today, the Jordanian-Palestinian relationship remains deeply conflicted, with a lack of trust on both sides. Still, Jordan remains the key regional actor focused on the Israeli-Palestinian peace process, partly because it cannot afford to ignore it, according to Haddad:

When the situation between Palestine and Israel becomes too heated, the heat is transferred to the interior of Jordan and the government is caught between two fires. On the one hand, the government must show solidarity with Palestinian demands for self-determination, and rhetorically support Palestinian rights and the *intifada*. On the other hand, and at the same time, government support for the Palestinian cause must not overfuel the Jordanian Palestinians ardor and protests to such a degree that the government cannot keep control and order.[29]

A New King in Jordan

Following the death of King Hussein after 46 years of rule, his son, Abdullah bin Hussein, ascended to the throne in 1999. King Abdullah has taken a pragmatic approach to Jordan's foreign relations, forging relationships with Arab and Western states. The Jordanian government summed up this approach in a national publicity campaign with the slogan 'Jordan First'.

> The King's priorities are very clear: a stable internal situation, national unity, socioeconomic development, the battle against poverty and unemployment, peace and national security. However, in the absence of peace, none of the other goals can be achieved.[30]

King Abdullah has sought to expand Jordan's international role through hosting major events, such as the World Economic Forum. He is also a frequent visitor of Western capitals and participant in meetings such as the G-8 summit.

King Abdullah has sought to balance the Jordan-Israeli relationship with closer ties to Arab governments and cooperation at the official level has faced the strains of increased regional conflict. Satloff notes that Abdullah has maintained security and military connections to Israel, while also restoring ties to Kuwait and Saudi Arabia that were strained during the first Gulf War. A key result of this strategy was the normalization of Jordan's relationship with Israel and the Arab world.[31]

On King Abdullah's approach to the peace treaty, Nevo argues that there is a key distinction between the two monarchs:

> But, while Hussein always referred to the *peace* with Israel, Abdullah has reiterated his commitment to the *peace treaty*. That is, he feels bound more by the legal aspects of the treaty than by the conciliatory spirit and the general atmosphere of peace.[32]

King Abdullah has not emphasized the Jordanian-Israeli relationship, which was already deeply frayed when he assumed power. Indeed, his first visit to Israel, some 14 months after he took the throne, and following the election of Labour candidate Ehud Barak as Prime Minister, was a decidedly low-key affair. His brief four-hour visit to Eilat, by boat from Aqaba, included a meeting with the Prime Minister, though no joint press conference. Abdullah's statements during the meeting emphasized his hope for a breakthrough in the peace process between Israel and the Palestinians, Syrians and Lebanese.[33] Abdullah had previously met with Barak on a number of occasions, but delayed a trip to Israel because of regional tensions. Abdullah's meetings with Prime Minister Sharon have been few, and always followed by statements emphasizing the need for movement on the peace process.

A recent radio program on English language Jordan Radio, in celebration of Abdullah's first five years of rule, highlighted the priorities for his reign, which included expansion of educational opportunities, economic progress and pushing for a resolution of the Israeli-Palestinian conflict. In the two-hour program, peace with Israel was not mentioned once. Publicly, at least, the peace with Israel is a sensitive issue for Jordan and the monarchy, though cooperation with Israel in key areas still remains.

The Asymmetry of the Jordanian-Israeli Relationship

There is an inherent asymmetry in the Jordanian-Israeli relationship, based on differences in both political and economic power. This asymmetry, and the dependencies created by it, also influences the bilateral relationship.

Although Jordan and Israel's populations are of roughly comparable sizes—5.4 million and 6.7 million, respectively—their economies are vastly different. Jordan's gross domestic product of $9.3 billion in 2002 is dwarfed by Israel's $103 billion for the same year. This ten-fold gap is also reflected in the national trade statistics, with Israel exporting $25.8 billion in goods in 2002 as compared to Jordan's $2.2 billion. For this reason, potential increases in joint economic cooperation, even small ones by Israeli standards, would have a much larger proportional impact in Jordan.

Though Jordan has forged a closer relationship with the United States in recent years, Israel enjoys a much larger amount of foreign aid (approximately $3 billion in military and economic grants per year[34]) and easy access to the political leadership. Therefore, Israel is able to exert greater leverage in the tripartite relationship (Jordan-Israel-USA), sometimes to the frustration of Jordanian expectations. In its dealings with Israel, Jordan must be wary not to impinge upon its critical relationship with the United States.

Jordanian-Israeli relations are greatly influenced by a complex array of factors, ranging from the demands of specific domestic constituencies to key third party relationships. In the last decade, the idealism with which the treaty was written has confronted the realities of implementation and a deteriorating regional situation. As Israel and Jordan approach the ten-year anniversary of their treaty, it may be too early to declare the peace 'cold', but many areas have clearly failed to meet expectations. In the following chapters, analysis of the relations between the states identifies key areas of success as well as disappointment. The assessments in this volume focus primarily on Jordanian attitudes and perceptions of the Jordanian-Israeli relationship. This is an intentional result of my residency in Jordan, greater familiarity with Jordanian society, and a recognition that little research has been done from this viewpoint. The volume concludes with an attempt to draw lessons from the Jordanian-Israeli experience, with the hope of informing future peacemaking efforts in the region.

2

THE ROAD TO PEACE BETWEEN JORDAN AND ISRAEL

The historic meeting at Wadi Araba was the outcome of a number of interrelated events that finally enabled Jordan to make open peace with its neighbour Israel. King Hussein, a pragmatist and key defender of Jordan's security, had long recognized the need to have open channels of dialogue with his militarily more powerful neighbour. This approach, which he justified to critics by arguing that 'engagement is not endorsement',[1] ultimately laid the groundwork for the peace with Israel. Though this dialogue had existed for thirty years, it was not enough to bring peace by itself. In the early 1990s, several key factors fell in line, finally leading to a Jordanian-Israeli agreement.

Critically, the post Gulf War period gave rise to the Madrid Peace process, which led—indirectly—to the Oslo Accords between Israel and the Palestinians. In the aftermath of the Gulf War King Hussein also made a decisive realignment of Jordan's strategic relationships, moving his country closer to the United States. His earlier relinquishment of administrative control over the West Bank had removed a further obstacle to a formal agreement between Israel and Jordan. Finally, the personal commitment of both the late King Hussein and Prime Minister Yitzhak Rabin to establish formal peace between their countries cannot be overstated: working together, they played a key role in moving their peoples towards peace.[2] Collectively, these factors created the necessary preconditions.

The Role of Secret Relations

The 1991 Madrid Peace Conference ultimately allowed the covert Jordanian-Israeli relationship to move out into the public, yet it was based on understandings developed over decades of discussion. Nearly thirty years lay between the first contact between Jordan's King Hussein and Israeli

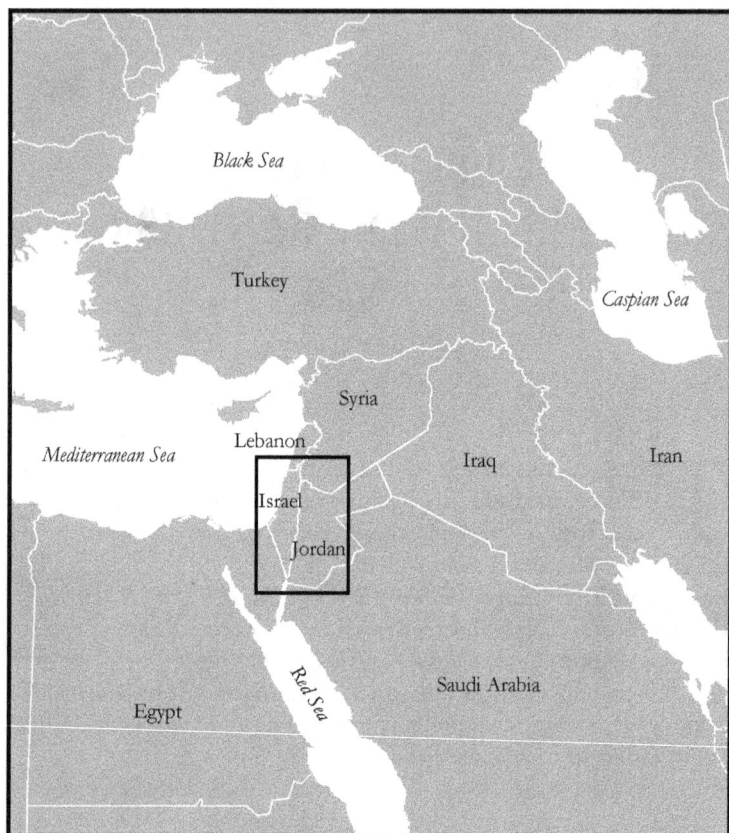

Map 2.1 *The Middle East Region.*

leaders, which took place in London on 24 September 1964, and the public signing of the Common Agenda between Jordan and Israel in September 1993. The London meeting was the first of many secret rendezvous held in safe houses, distant countries and, reportedly, one of King Hussein's palaces. Such meetings, according to Zak, 'logged over seven hundred hours of conversation' and led to thirty-nine—mostly secret—agreements between Jordan and Israel.[3]

In his outstanding review of the secret negotiations, Zak demonstrates the direct link between these previous agreements, noting, for example, a water-sharing agreement for the Jordan River (1964) and two border demarcation accords in the Araba region (1970, 1975). These latter accords, in which 75 km of land southeast of the Dead Sea (A Safi and A Fifi sectors) was given to Jordan, and the Israeli border was modified to allow construction of the Jordanian highway to Aqaba along a preferred route, were key precursors to the peace treaty. Indeed, the treaty includes an arrangement—identified as 'special regimes'—allowing Israelis to cultivate two areas inside Jordanian territory for a renewable 25-year period. This highly unusual situation, in which Israeli law applies to Israelis living in the area and Jordanian criminal law is not applied in cases involving only Israelis, is an indication of the attitude of compromise during the creation of the peace treaty.[4]

Jordanian-Israeli relations in the 25 years prior to the peace treaty were largely pragmatic, rather than hostile. Lukacs demonstrates the status quo prior to the treaty:

> After 1967 Jordanian-Israeli relations were predicated on a mutual understanding whereby the formal state of war was maintained while, concomitantly, the two countries continued an ongoing dialog on issues of mutual concern ranging from water sharing to the return of missing persons. Given the myriad formal diplomatic breakthroughs between Israel and her neighbours, many of these past examples of functional cooperation seem trivial at best, but in the 1967–88 period they were meaningful, and, most importantly, Israelis and Jordanians regarded them as genuinely significant and beneficial.[5]

From the Jordanian perspective, a certain level of pragmatism was needed in dealing with a, especially in military terms, stronger neighbour. In the 1967 June (Six Day) War, in which Jordan lost control of the West Bank and suffered a devastating defeat, King Hussein had chosen to side with his Arab allies, namely Egypt and Syria, rather than remain out of the war. As Salibi explains, Jordan's role in the Arab world meant that 'in a showdown with Israel, Jordan could take only the Arab side, no matter what the cost'.[6] And indeed the cost was high: Jordan not only lost control of the West Bank, which comprised approximately half of its territory, but control over Arab parts of Jerusalem as well.

In the 1973 War, however, Jordan opted for a different path, and did not participate in Egypt and Syria's attempts to regain territory lost in the Six Day War. Ever mindful of Jordan's position in the Arab world, the Kingdom did send a brigade to Syria, a move Henry Kissinger described as 'the least provocative'. It followed a 48-hour delay on any action at his request, and came as the battle for the Golan Heights had nearly ended.[7] More than any other Arab state, Jordan had much to lose through participation in broader 'Pan-Arab' military conflict with Israel.

In fact, even during times of conflict and outright war, proximity forced Jordan and Israel to develop joint relations and understandings in a number of areas. From the Israeli perspective according to Lukacs, the 'open bridges policy', in effect from 1948–1994, was the 'centrepiece' of the Jordanian-Israeli relationship based on functional cooperation. Under this policy, Palestinians were able to pass from the West Bank into Jordan, though the West Bank borders remained controlled by Israel. It also enabled Jordan to continue administering the West Bank, including running its education system and paying civil servants, while controlling the movement of Palestinians into the country. For Israel, the policy provided a 'pressure release valve' in the West Bank by enabling Jordan to exercise socio-political influence on the Palestinians, while developing mutual interest between Israel, Jordan and the Palestinians through trade activities. Arguably, the policy gave Israel a period of nearly twenty years of calm (1967–1988) in the West Bank, and probably delayed the Palestinian uprising, or *intifada*, which finally occurred in 1987.[8]

Though the second *intifada* (2000) has led to major changes in this policy (discussed in Chapter Three), it remains an important means by which Jordan controls the influx of Palestinians. Over 100,000 Palestinians without Jordanian citizenship still remain in Jordan on a green card status, which allows them to work. For its part, Israel, having signed a peace treaty with Jordan, viewed the post-1994 changes in the 'open bridges policy' as a Jordanian domestic issue.

Letting Go of the West Bank

Despite a high level of secret and pragmatic collaboration between Jordan and Israel, peace would not have been possible as long as Jordan continued to administer the West Bank. During the 1967 War, the Israeli army quickly occupied the West Bank. In the aftermath, Palestinian inhabitants of the West Bank remained Jordanian citizens, with Jordanian passports under Israeli occupation. Jordan continued to support the territory's institutional infrastructure by paying salaries and pensions for civil servants and Jordanian currency remained in use.[9] The West Bank was represented in the Jordanian parliament and its education system run by Jordan. More importantly, after the 1967 June War, Jordan continued to negotiate with Israel for return of the West Bank under the terms of UN Resolution 242, which called for Israel to withdraw from all territories occupied during the war.

Since 1967, Jordanian administrative control and claims to the West Bank met growing resistance from the Palestine Liberation Organization (PLO) and the rising tide of Palestinian nationalism that envisioned a separate state outside Jordanian (or Israeli) control. Established in 1964, this organization was to serve as the only 'legitimate representative of the Palestinian nation', and its goal was the liberation of Palestinian 'occupied territory' seized by the Jews to create the state of Israel in 1948. King Hussein's support for the creation of the PLO was conditional on its agreement to cooperate with Jordan, as he sought to maintain Jordan's role as interlocutor for the Palestinians with Israel.

Though the headquarters of the PLO were set up in Amman, disagreement over the activities of the PLO's military wing, the Palestine Liberation Army and another Palestinian organization called Fateh, illustrated the contradiction between Jordanian security needs and Palestinian armed conflict with Israel. For a time, Jordan was able to assert control over the PLO and Fateh, but in the aftermath of the 1967 War, the PLO established deeper footholds in Jordan, especially in the kingdom's refugee camps.

Unable to effectively set up military units in the West Bank because of Israeli military control, the PLO began to use Jordan as a base to develop its military capacities and stage attacks on Israel. They organized formal military units under its control, while Palestinian irregulars (*fedayeen*) in Jordan's refugee camps wore PLO uniforms. These events seriously challenged King Hussein's control over his own country, and potentially endangered Jordanian sovereignty by pushing it towards conflict with Israel. Guerrillas operated unauthorized roadblocks in the capital, while the Popular Front for the Liberation of Palestine tried to organize workers and peasants in the north of the country into soviets, and Fateh spoke of converting Amman into the Palestinian Hanoi, a base from which to attack Israeli Saigon.[10] Prince Ali, then an intelligence staff officer, reportedly told King Hussein, 'The PLO was more in control of Amman than we were; Amman was their city, not ours.'[11]

Events escalated inside Jordan throughout 1968 and 1969, culminating in the hijacking of five airplanes by the Popular Front for the Liberation of Palestine, forcing them to land in Jordan and precipitating a showdown between King Hussein and the Palestinian factions for control of the kingdom in September 1970. On the brink of full-scale civil war, known as 'Black September', the monarchy called out the military, Palestinian groups declared parts of northern Jordan a 'liberated Palestinian area', and the fighting that followed included tanks, artillery and airpower. Recently released British documents reveal that King Hussein made an extraordinary appeal to Israel for air strikes against Syrian troops and tanks that were aiding Palestinian *fedayeen*.[12] Though Israel did not undertake these air strikes, they did reinforce the Israeli military presence on the Syrian border as a warning to Syria at the request of the United States. After Black September, Jordan expelled all PLO from the country and shut down its offices. Conflict between Palestinian militants and Jordan did not end there: in November 1971, the Prime Minister of Jordan, Wasfi Tell, was gunned down in Cairo by assailants seeking revenge for his role in uprooting Palestinian guerrillas from Jordan the previous September.[13]

Through the 1970s and 1980s, Palestinian nationalist claims to the West Bank increased. According to Salibi, the Hashemite ruling family held opposing opinions over the best position to take vis-à-vis the West Bank:

> Some, like the King, maintained that Jordan should not relinquish her moral and material obligations towards the West Bank Palestinians for as long as the status of the occupied territories remained unresolved. Others opposed this view, urging that Jordanians should settle the East Bank and abandon all responsibilities for the West Bank and its population.[14]

By 1988, efforts to resolve political conflict with the PLO, and achieve a solution that combined Palestinian nationalist goals and a Jordanian role in the territory, had clearly failed. Moreover, the situation in the West Bank, embroiled in the first Palestinian *intifada*, was causing growing tension between Jordan's Palestinian population and the Hashemite-led government.

Within this context, the Hashemite monarchy disengaged from the West Bank and formally renounced its claim to this territory on 31 July 1988. It is important to note however, that King Hussein, as the head of the Hashemite dynasty and direct descendant of the Prophet Muhammad, did not renounce his special status as guardian over the Muslim shrines in East Jerusalem. In doing so, he sought to maintain a role for Jordan in future peace negotiations between the Palestinians and Israel. The renunciation of Jordanian control over the West Bank, however, eliminated a major obstacle to peace between Jordan and Israel.

A New Regional Landscape: The Impact of Madrid

The Madrid and Oslo Peace Processes

Today, after over a decade of constant Middle East 'peacemaking' activities that support a veritable cottage industry of track-two meetings and official meetings, it may be hard to remember the process of negotiations (such as they were) prior to the Madrid Peace conference. Before the Gulf War, Middle East peacemaking largely amounted to the discussions about the possibility of holding talks between the parties. US Secretary of State James Baker undertook intensive shuttle diplomacy in the eight months following the Gulf War, during a time, when the parties to the negotiations would not meet directly with each other. Israelis, who were willing to meet with representatives of the Palestine Liberation Organization, had to violate the Law of Association, forbidding contact with the PLO, and risk imprisonment.[15] Moreover, the Arab states had long had a policy against individual negotiation with Israel, which King Hussein directly challenged, declaring that 'the taboos must disappear', while at the same time calling for resolution of the Arab-Israeli conflict within a 'global framework'.[16] For King Hussein, the Madrid Conference was important not only because it offered the potential for resolution of the Palestinian issue, it also created a large enough umbrella to legitimize Jordan's willingness to meet openly with Israelis.

Research by Zak suggests that the Jordanian-Israeli peace was very long in the making. He reports that King Hussein was ready to sign a peace treaty with Israel shortly after the June 1967 War, but he was constrained by the position of the other Arab states, declaring 'I must go along with the Arab world.'[17] Furthermore, a separate peace with Israel, outside the framework of a comprehensive solution to the Arab-Israeli conflict, remained a serious redline for King Hussein. Egypt had crossed this line in 1978, by signing the Camp David Accords, which set into motion the negotiation processes leading to Egyptian-Israeli peace, and suffered nearly a decade of isolation from other Arab states as a result. Moreover, King Hussein was critical of Egypt's peace with Israel, which he viewed as incomplete.[18]

With the Madrid Peace Conference, and the first open negotiations between Israel and its neighbours since the Camp David agreement, Jordan was able to move forward. The significance of the Madrid Conference in launching an extraordinary process should not be underestimated, as described by Amro:

> There was no precedent in the Middle East for peacemaking on that scale, no effective channel of communications, and no established mechanisms for negotiation. The peace process has forever altered the political landscape of the Middle East. So thorough has this transformation been that, notwithstanding many problems, we are now within view of our ultimate goal. We stand poised on the verge of that accomplishment, long sought but always thought unattainable: a comprehensive, just, peace. And now we find ourselves contemplating together the shape of our common future.[19]

While the Israelis and Palestinians pursued a secret track, outside the Madrid framework, Israel and Jordan engaged in several rounds of bilateral negotiations. The seventh round of talks, in October 1992, led to a breakthrough and an agreement on a set of issues for discussion within the context of an overall treaty. Significantly, the Israelis and Jordanians kept the content of their discussions secret, even from the United States, which had played a key role in bringing the parties together, for fear that the details would be leaked before the timing was right.

Yet the timing of any Jordanian-Israeli agreement remained dependent on movement on the Israeli-Palestinian track. The Washington-led track floundered, and indeed remained deadlocked. The highly secret Oslo track, initiated by the Norwegian government, made significant progress, surprising the United States with an agreement, the Declaration of Principles on Interim Self-Government between Israel and the Palestine Liberation Organization, also known as the Oslo Accords. On 13 September 1993, Israeli Prime Minister Yitzhak Rabin and PLO Chairman Yasser Arafat, under the auspices of a smiling President Clinton, exchanged a historic handshake on the White House lawn. Barely twenty-four hours after the Declaration of Principles was signed, Jordan and Israel also signed a 'common agenda' for peace that had been completed for nearly a year. The Common Agenda officially ended the state of belligerence between Jordan and Israel and set an agenda of topics to be resolved in order to reach a peace treaty.

As Satloff notes, the timing of the Common Agenda was hardly coincidental; the Oslo Agreement had indeed 'changed everything', allowing Jordan to move its peacemaking with Israel out of the shadows and into the public spotlight.[20] With mutual recognition between Israel and the Palestinian Liberation Organization, it was possible for King Hussein to argue that a solution to the Palestinian issue was at hand. The Oslo Accords provided, in the words of Nevo, 'a broad enough fig leaf' for Jordan in its relationship with other Arab states.[21] Even then, King Hussein was careful to place his peace efforts with Israel within a broader context: the primary goal in the Common Agenda is 'the achievement of just, lasting and comprehensive peace between the Arab States, the Palestinians and Israel as per the Madrid invitation'.[22]

Rebuilding the Jordanian-US Relationship

Political decision-making in Jordan, especially at the strategic level and in the foreign policy arena, is controlled by the monarch and the governmental institutions linked to the monarchy.[23] These include the Royal Court, the Cabinet and the Parliament as well, for although the lower house is elected, the upper house—the Senate—is appointed by the King. Therefore, foreign policy decisions, though sometimes responsive to public opinion, are primarily the domain of the monarch and his close advisors. Historically, the monarchy has placed the stability of the regime at the forefront of its foreign and domestic agenda. Within the tumultuous politics of the region, King

Hussein himself had acquired a strong reputation as a survivor, leading his country through numerous regional wars and internal strife.

In the aftermath of the Gulf War, a number of factors led King Hussein to conclude that an alliance with the United States was necessary, and that a formal, open peace with Israel was the means to achieve this goal. During the Gulf War, King Hussein had seriously strained his historically close relationship with the United States. Following Iraq's invasion of Kuwait, Jordan attempted to occupy a somewhat 'neutral' position by refusing to join the US-led coalition against Iraq. Unlike the 2003 Iraq War, many other Arab countries, including Egypt, Saudi Arabia and Syria, had openly joined the coalition while others discreetly lent their territory to coalition forces.

Though Jordan did not join the coalition, it also did not commit its armed forces to fight alongside Iraq, its traditional ally. This position allowed Jordan to quell internal domestic concerns, as much of the population favoured Jordanian participation on Iraq's side. It must be remembered that the goals of military intervention in the Gulf War, from the outset, were decidedly more limited than the 2003 Iraq War. The overthrow of the Saddam Hussein regime was not expected, which meant that Jordan very likely would need to continue to deal with Saddam Hussein at the end of military action. Iraq was a key economic partner and the major source of oil imports into Jordan. Indeed, the Hussein regime survived another twelve years after the 1991 Gulf War, during which it continued to have a strong economic relationship with Jordan.

The US and its allies, however, did not appreciate the nuances of the Jordanian position on the Gulf War. Jordan was quickly perceived as pro-Iraq and often described as Iraq's closest ally. Economic aid from the United States, as well as Kuwait, Saudi Arabia and other Arab countries, was quickly cancelled. Regional trade with other Arab states dramatically declined. Hundreds of thousands of Jordanians and Palestinians were expelled from Kuwait and Saudi Arabia, losing jobs that were critical sources of remittance income that had fuelled Jordan's impressive economic growth in the 1980s.

The economic impact of Jordan's attempt to straddle a neutral line during the Gulf War was profound. The US immediately canceled $35 million in economic aid and $20 million in military aid to punish King Hussein for what the US perceived as support for Saddam Hussein. Aqaba, Jordan's only port, was blocked to stop any potential trade with Iraq, which also strangled overall Jordanian exports. In addition, the Gulf States stopped transfers amounting to $1.6 billion; 200,000 Jordanian workers and their families returned home from the Gulf, with $150–300 million lost in remittances from Kuwait alone. Unemployment reached 25–30 per cent, while personal income plunged between 13–14 per cent. The state, with $8.4 billion in external debt, struggled to cope.[24]

By the end of the Gulf War, Jordan, which had historically prospered by deftly working alliances, found itself isolated both within the region and internationally. This isolation was short-lived, within a year its efforts in bringing Israel and the Palestinians to the Madrid peace conference had restored warm US-Jordanian relations.

The US actions in the Gulf War, taking on Iraq to protect Kuwait (as well as other US interests), probably made King Hussein's decision to make peace with Israel easier, as he could expect that Jordan, as well as Israel, would be protected by the United States in the event of hostilities. Moreover, considerable economic incentive was offered as encouragement. Clinton's promise to write off $700 million in debt, and press for further debt relief by other Western lenders was a key factor in the king's decision-making.[25] Unfortunately, the economic rewards of the peace were not as great as expected: though Britain made a minor reduction in Jordan's debt, the kingdom still owed $5.5 billion in 1995, most of it to Britain, Germany, France and Japan.[26]

In the 2003 Iraq War, Jordan maintained a stance in alliance with the United States, despite strong public sentiment in Jordan against the war. Hundreds of US troops were stationed inside Jordan, manning Patriot missile batteries in case Saddam Hussein launched Scud missiles at Israel or Jordan. US Special Forces also crossed into Iraq from Jordan, and it appears that Jordanian airspace was used by US bombers to strike targets inside Iraq. At the same time, King Abdullah II was under intense pressure by opposition groups to condemn the US policy of regime change in Iraq.[27]

Jordan's position has already reaped dividends; recent increases in funding from the United States Agency for International Development raised US economic aid to $348.5 million for fiscal year 2004, a substantial increase over the $7 million allocated in 1996, two years after the peace with Israel.[28]

The Death of Rabin and a New King

The main architects and supporters of the Jordanian-Israeli peace agreement, Prime Minister Yitzhak Rabin and King Hussein, are both dead. The process of 'building the peace' passed on to new leadership. In Israel, Rabin's willingness to make peace ultimately cost him his life. King Hussein never had the same close, personal relationship with subsequent Israeli leaders, including Shimon Peres, as he had with Rabin. Though Hussein initially was less troubled by Binyamin Netanyahu's election as Prime Minister than leaders of many Arab states, this attitude changed following a series of events that dramatically challenged Jordanian-Israeli post-treaty relations. By as early as 1996, these events, examined in detail in Chapter Four, had ended the short honeymoon phase of Jordanian-Israeli relations.

The death of King Hussein and the succession of his son King Abdullah II to the throne also marked a new phase in Jordanian-Israeli relations. From the outset, King Abdullah's reign was marked by pragmatism, with an emphasis on meeting the challenges of advancing Jordan's domestic development and international stature. The King's priorities, 'a stable internal situation, national unity, socio-economic development, the battle against poverty and unemployment, peace and national security' are all dependent on continued peaceful relations with Israel.[29] Though supportive of Jordan's relations with Israel, King Abdullah has also reaffirmed Jordan's ties to other Arab states, renewing connections to countries such as Syria, Libya, Sudan and Iran. Abdullah's policy, captured in the national campaign 'Jordan First', has placed Jordan's interests front and centre, while reaffirming its identity as both an Arab and Islamic state and a strong advocate for the Palestinians.

> 'Jordan First' reiterates that a strong, honourable and invincible Jordan
> is a source of power and capability to the Arab Nation and a lever
> for the enhancement of the steadfastness of our kin and brethren in
> Palestine, relying in that on an uninterrupted legacy of adherence to
> national interests.[30]

In its implementation, the 'Jordan First' program has meant an intensive investment in education and technology infrastructure, reform of the economy and increasing governmental accountability. At the same time, King Abdullah remains a strong regional voice for just and comprehensive peace, occasionally challenging US politics in the region, but maintaining a close strategic alliance with the United States.

The Benefits of Peace: The Jordanian Expectation

Economics and the expectation of economic benefit played a central role in the marketing of the Jordan-Israeli peace to the Jordanian public. While the monarchy sought the strategic gains of a new relationship with the US, the public was more wary of making peace with Israel without the promise of clear and tangible benefits. This was particularly true for the large Palestinian population and opposition parties made up of both Islamist groups and left-wing parties. Though the Israeli Knesset approved the peace treaty by a vote of 105 to 3, the ratification of the treaty in the Jordanian Chamber of Deputies was by a much closer vote of 55 to 23.[31] Still, for most Jordanians the peace treaty came as a surprise, negotiated by the monarchy and presented to the people.

The potential for economic growth, in an economy hard-hit by the 1991 Gulf War, was the government's major means of building public support for the agreement. In July 1994, just months prior to the signing of the agreement, the University of Jordan's Centre for Strategic Studies found that 82 per cent of respondents believed that the Jordanian economy would benefit from peace with Israel. Hesitation remained, however, as many respondents also feared potential Israeli domination of the regional economy.[32]

While the economic relationship between Jordan and Israel is the focus of Chapter Six, it is important to understand that, while there was support for the peace treaty within the Jordanian population, there existed also a clear expectation of a tangible peace dividend to follow shortly after the treaty and of significant movement towards resolving the Israeli-Palestinian conflict. The monarchy, too, badly needed rapid results to justify its break with other Arab states and its decision to make peace with Israel before the Palestinian issue was settled. A significant gap in perception between the palace, with its emphasis on the strategic and macro-economic gains of the peace with Israel, and the people's expectation of an impact at the micro-level existed, when the peace treaty with Israel was signed.

The following chapters examine the main areas of bilateral relations covered in the peace treaty, illustrating that the road to comprehensive neighbourly relations faces perhaps greater obstacles than the road to the formal written agreement.

3
THE JORDANIAN-ISRAELI SECURITY RELATIONSHIP

Cooperation on security issues is perhaps the most essential element of the past and present bilateral Jordanian-Israeli relationship. Unlike other areas of their relations, security cooperation has been able to withstand increased political tension more easily. This is in part due to a shared vision between the Jordanian and Israeli leadership regarding Jordan's role. A key aspect of this role, according to Alpher, is its function as 'a regional buffer, sharing Israel's fear of Palestinian nationalism and potential irredentism, and ready to join in finding ways to contain it'.[1] This represents a liability and strength, as well as an integral part of its relationship with Israel.

This chapter examines the security aspects of the treaty, their implementation and limitations. It closes with a brief analysis of the effect of current external events, both international and regional, on the bilateral security relationship.

Common Strategic Interests

Even prior to the peace treaty, there was little concern on the Israeli side that Jordan itself would attack Israel,[2] nor was Israel likely to attack Jordan, but the treaty paved the way for closer and more public collaboration on a set of shared security objectives. Despite the remote possibility of open warfare in the 1990s, the treaty alleviated deep-seated Jordanian concerns regarding the inviolability of its territory. These concerns are rooted in the memory of past Israeli infiltration into Jordan. The largest event of that manner was the dispatch of Israeli forces during a 1968 raid in the Jordan valley to attack a village utilized by the Palestinian *fedayeen* faction, Fateh. In this battle, the Battle of Karamah, Jordanian forces fought alongside the *fedayeen* to drive out the Israeli military and destroyed several of their tanks.[3] Though the Hashemite leadership itself would be at war with the *fedayeen* a few short years later, the preservation of territorial integrity against a more powerful enemy helped drive this temporary alliance with Palestinian *fedayeen*, even to the extent that King Hussein at the time declared 'We shall all be *fedayeen*.'[4]

In the years prior to the peace treaty, Israeli forces crossed into Jordan many times without the consent of King Hussein: in one serious incident even exploding a Jordanian police station while searching for Palestinian *fedayeen*. On a more strategic level, Israeli desire to control the Jordan Valley gave rise to concerns within the monarchy and armed forces that Israel would seek to occupy the Western Mountains in Jordan, near the cities of Ajloun, Salt and Madaba. Finally, ideology also played a role in Jordanian territorial concerns, especially the Zionist call for a Greater Israel, entailing its expansion to the eastern side of the Jordan River.

Despite these concerns, Israel and Jordan forged a successful foundation for the present security relationship during the pre-treaty period, when the pursuit of common goals often meant that Jordan and Israel took actions that benefited the other, even if they were not in direct alliance. The strategic relations between the two countries date back to the early part of the twentieth century and are well documented.[5] Israel's relationship with Jordan also addressed one of Israel's main security concerns, the potential revival of an 'Eastern Front' to include Syria, Jordan and, potentially, Iraq.[6]

Cooperation in the security sector is pragmatic and reflects similar concerns, mainly the continuity of both states and their ruling regimes against internal and external destabilizing forces. Historically, Israel and Jordan have pursued individual security policies that benefited the other party, even during periods of hostility. A notable incident in 1964 demonstrates this state of affairs: a team from the armed Palestinian faction known as Assifa (The Storm) had set explosives in Israel. The charges failed to detonate, but the team ran into a Jordanian patrol, which shot and killed its leader Ahmad Musa.[7] By 1970, cooperation between Israel and Jordan had become more explicit, and Israel lent support to the Hashemite monarchy during the Palestinian revolution of Black September. To prevent Syria from sending additional tanks and military aid to assist the Palestinian *fedayeen*, Israel reinforced its border with Syria; though the move assisted the Jordanian monarch, it strained Jordan's relationship with the Arab world. Not only did Libya and Kuwait suspend financial aid to Jordan, but 'rumour spread like wildfire that Israel's action was part of a concerted plan against the Palestinian resistance which King Hussein and Israeli Prime Minister, Golda Meir, had worked out at secret meeting in Wadi Araba.'[8] This unspoken alliance between Israeli and Jordanian strategic interests was quite evident at times, such as when Shimon Peres claimed in his autobiography that, while negotiating the Oslo Accords, 'we were motivated not only by our own direct and obvious security interests but also those of Jordan.'[9]

In the post-peace period, Jordan and Israel also share security concerns related to recent regional events. New levels of violence in the Israeli-Palestinian conflict since the start of the Al Aqsa *intifada* (2000), the absence of a political peace process, the de-legitimization of the Palestinian Authority by Israel and the United States, and widespread perception that the Palestinian Authority is corrupt, have further destabilized the West Bank and Gaza, posing a threat to both Israel and Jordan. The growing influence of militant Islamist forces following the 11 September 2001 attacks and the United States' response has rattled both governments. Suicide bombings in Israel and attacks on US interests in Jordan, including the assassination of US diplomat Lawrence Foley, reinforce the mutual security relationship. Events in nearby countries, such as large-scale bombings in Saudi Arabia and Turkey, further raise fears of possible spillover into Jordan and Israel. Though the removal of Saddam Hussein reduced a significant security threat from the Israeli perspective, it has plunged the region into a period of instability, where outcomes are not yet known. Both Jordan and Israel have a mutual interest in a stable Iraq that retains its territorial integrity. The rising violence against both civilians and soldiers in US-occupied Iraq, some of it linked to the Jordanian Abu Musab Zarqawi, raises growing concern that Jordan cannot avoid getting drawn into the conflict.

Despite these shared concerns, Jordanian and Israeli approaches to security issues are typically not coordinated at the political level; indeed, deep differences exist, especially over how to handle the Israeli-Palestinian conflict. The assassination of Sheikh Ahmed Yassin, the Hamas spiritual leader, by Israeli rocket fire in the Gaza Strip in April 2004 highlights the political liability of cooperation with Israel for Jordan. The Israeli killing of Sheikh Yassin happened only three days after a meeting between King Abdullah and Prime Minister Sharon; the timing of the assassination thus implied Jordanian complicity, at most, or at least acquiescence in this operation that touched off fury in the region.[10]

While the king was quoted as being 'embarrassed' by the assassination and strong condemnations were issued by the Prime Minister's office, opposition leaders called for the government to sever all diplomatic ties with Israel and cease all normalization efforts,[11] a reaction that closely mirrored the public's mood. Thousands of Jordanians took to the streets in the capital and other major cities to protest the assassination, with the most severe demonstrations at the Palestinian refugee camp in Wihdat (eastern Amman). In the demonstrations, a member of parliament was assaulted and the Jordanian flag burned alongside those of the United States and Israel,[12] posing serious challenges to symbols of the state and Hashemite legitimacy. Incidents such as these reinforce the Jordanian conviction, held by many at both the official and societal level, that Israel does not balance the needs of its key strategic partner in the region against its own security and political aspirations. Today, this sentiment may be the greatest challenge to further peace-building, in security as well as other fields of cooperation.

Building a Security Relationship

The close familiarity between Jordanian and Israeli military officers was apparent at the Wadi Araba signing ceremony in 1994. Many of the officers had met secretly in the past, and appeared relaxed in each other's company. Greeting his Israeli colleague with a hug, one Jordanian sergeant declared: 'How nice to see you here after 12 years, finally we can meet under the sun.'[13]

It is fair to say that a substantial level of trust on security issues between both security apparatuses—defined here to include military as well as intelligence agencies in both countries—existed prior to the signing of the treaty. Of course, the history of secret meetings, mentioned previously, contributed to this trust, as key members of the security services were involved in these undertakings. Over the years, a series of mutual assurances between Jordan and Israel fortified the security relationship, including Israel's agreement to act against the Palestine Liberation Organization if it threatened Hashemite rule in Jordan, and Jordan's assurance, that it would not allow its territory to be utilized to attack Israel. More recently, Israel agreed not to use missiles to retaliate against Iraqi missile attacks in the 1991 Gulf War. This was a significant concession on Israel's part, as by that time Jordan and Iraq had a history of past close cooperation. Jordan had even granted Iraq permission to overfly its territory to perform intelligence sorties on Israel.[14] The United States, of course, played a role in Israel's adoption of this position, mainly because they feared that Israeli retaliation for Iraqi Scud missiles could escalate into a full-scale Israeli-Jordanian war. To encourage the Israeli position, the US provided Patriot anti-aircraft missile batteries and a special grant to partially cover the costs of Israeli war damages.[15]

Despite such agreements on larger strategic issues, the number of individuals aware of or involved in the secret meetings and negotiations was very limited, especially on the Jordanian side. While it would be correct to say that security individuals were involved in these pre-treaty relationships, true security collaboration at the institutional level did not begin until the Madrid Peace Process. At Madrid, Jordanian-Israeli bilateral security cooperation talks were initiated under the third-party umbrella of the United States. In these meetings, a small group of security officials participated on both sides, a first step in extending the circle of security professionals involved in the bilateral relationship. Though the talks were not formally part of the negotiations of the Jordanian-Israeli peace agreement taking place at the same time, they were clearly related to this process, both in terms of discussing the substantive issues in the treaty, as well as beginning to build institutional links between the security forces. Finally, direct bilateral talks between Israel and Jordan, without the involvement of a third party, began in 1992 in preparation for the peace treaty.

Prior to the treaty, the two countries also collaborated on more common problems, as efforts to resolve these frequently contained a security dimension. While the need to eradicate flies and mosquitoes may not seem a security issue, insects fail to respect state borders, and efforts to combat a particularly severe black fly infestation required the joint military forces of Israel and Jordan. Agricultural activities in both countries contribute to the insect problem, as they breed in the organic fertilizers used by Jordanian farmers and agricultural waste stored in Israel. In the Red Sea region, the main Israeli tourist city of Eilat was especially affected.[16] The development of a coordinated cross-border eradication plan was another opportunity to create collaborative structures across security services.

Joint actions, such as black fly eradication and police operations to combat drug smuggling, were key trust building experiences, allowing the establishment of relationships between military and security leaders, and laying the foundation for wider cooperation after the peace treaty. Much, if not most, of these pre-treaty collaborative efforts happened well out of the public eye. They also explain the warm relations, indeed much warmer than those of many of the politicians present, between military personnel at the Wadi Araba signing.

Security Parameters of the Peace Treaty

The Jordanian-Israeli peace agreement fundamentally addresses three major aspects of the bilateral security relationship: demarcation and subsequent control of their shared international border, the nature of relations between the two parties, and the potential influence of third parties, either through alliances or utilization of either party's territory, to commit acts of aggression or terrorism. As the Jordanian-Israeli security agreement, signed on 9 February 1995 remains secret, detailed knowledge of the bilateral security relationship is still unavailable. Yet, the examination of current practices and key incidents reveals much about the nature of this relationship.

Borders

The determination of the international boundary between Jordan and Israel proceeded rapidly following the signing of the peace treaty. It required, however, a certain amount of flexibility by the two parties concerning the transfer or right of usage of specific pieces of land. For Israel, the treaty stipulated the return of two areas under Israeli control to Jordan. The Israel Defence Force (IDF) completed its withdrawal from the first sector, located in the Al Ghamr area, on 30 January 1995. This territory encompassed a 170-km tract running from the Red Sea Aqaba/Eilat border through Wadi al-Araba.[17] The second area in Baqura or Naharayim near Irbid in the north of Jordan was evacuated by IDF troops by 10 February 1995.

Though formal sovereignty over these territories was transferred from Israel to Jordan, unique 'special regimes' were put in place to allow continued Israeli utilization of the land. In Annexes to the treaty, Israeli 'land users' in the Kibbutz Tsofar were granted the right to use approximately 1200 *dunums* of land in the Wadi Araba for an automatically renewable period of 25 years, provided the agreement of both parties. The handover was subdued, given concerns raised in the Israeli parliament about its legality, since the Israeli government had not yet ratified the Jordan-Israel peace treaty, some three months after the signing at Wadi Araba.[18] As a result, Israeli military officials did not participate in a formal ceremony, but offered a quick handshake before leaving the area. The Jordanian government, in an effort to demonstrate tangible benefits from the peace, flew journalists to the scene to view the erection of new Jordanian fences marking the border and the raising of a four-meter-high Jordanian flag on the newly reclaimed land.[19]

In the Baqura/Naharayim area, Israelis were given the right to 'own' land in the area for an automatically renewable 25-year period, again with the agreement of both parties. Under these arrangements, the government of Jordan does not receive any payment for usage of its territory. In both pieces of territory, Jordanian law is in effect, with the exception of criminal incidents that involve only Israeli citizens, in which case Jordanian criminal law does not apply (see Annex I[B] and I[C]).

The process of demarcating the countries' 220 km shared land border with concrete pillars began in mid-1995, while the maritime border in the Gulf of Aqaba was determined in October 1995. Of considerable importance, both symbolically and economically, was the opening of the Sheikh Hussein crossing between Israel and Jordan. Located northern Jordan, this crossing has since played a vital economic and political role in the Jordanian-Israeli relationship. Built with Japanese funding, it is one of only two land crossing-points between Jordan and Israel, the other being the Wadi Araba crossing (Eilat–Aqaba), which is significant for tourist traffic.

Officially opened in August 1999, the Sheikh Hussein Bridge is a main artery for Jordanian trade into Israel and through the Israeli port of Haifa to other parts of the world. Though there are problems with the regulations of this trade, discussed in more detail in Chapter Six, the bridge supports a considerable level of economic activity. It also plays a major role as a neutral and convenient site for meetings of Israeli and Jordan officials, and as a station for the coordination of security processes. Israelis wishing to enter Jordan can get an immediate visa at Sheikh Hussein (as well as Queen Alia Airport), while those entering through the King Hussein/Allenby Bridge in the West Bank must apply through the Jordanian Ministry of the Interior in advance.

Following a tradition long established under the 'open bridges' policy, Jordanian and Israeli officials collaborate on the control of Israel's border crossings with Jordan, as well as the crossing between the West Bank and Jordan at the King Hussein/Allenby Bridge. The control of Jordanian borders is crucial to a combined operation against Palestinian extremists and terrorists. In the event of a serious Israeli clampdown, all crossing points into Jordan are closed.[20] Border control is so critical to Jordan that King Hussein's endorsement of the Oslo Declaration of Principles was conditional on the fact that the bridges to Jordan would not be handed over to the Palestinians, lest they flood the country.[21]

After the second *intifada*, Jordanian concern regarding a potential flood of refugees to Jordan increased. To prevent such an event, Jordan introduced new restrictions on Palestinian entry into the country, and is not accepting any more Palestinian refugees. Under the new guidelines, Palestinians may enter Jordan for treatment in hospitals, or to travel abroad via the Amman airport, given a valid visa and ticket. Palestinian students accepted to Jordanian universities can also enter. For a Palestinian to visit relatives in Jordan, that relative must inform the Ministry of the Interior and guarantee the visitor's return to the West Bank. Visas for Palestinians from Gaza are even more complicated to obtain, and must be requested through the Jordanian consulate in Gaza. This current system differs substantially from the pre-*intifada* procedures, when Palestinians could receive a 'yellow card' allowing entry for one month, with extensions available through the Ministry of the Interior.

Jordan is also concerned about the influence of Palestinian militant groups, posing a threat to its internal stability and the Jordanian-Israeli relationship: the Jordanian decision to remove Jordanians of Palestinian origin from border patrols following the *intifada* was the consequence. Any increase in the size of the Palestinian population, already a potential majority in the country, is of serious concern to the monarchy. Additionally, the movements of Palestinians in Jordan are monitored by the state. Jordan's concerns are not entirely unfounded. In December 2001, a Palestinian group, believed to be acting from inside Jordan, ambushed an Israeli patrol: one soldier was killed and several wounded. A Jordanian military officer, on a visit to Israel, used an Israeli base to oversee his troops' search for the gunmen.[22] Recent attempts to use Jordanian territory as a base to fire rockets into Israel or at settlements in the West Bank have also been thwarted.

A set of detailed protocols and procedures enhances the joint control of border crossing and regulates routine security functions between Jordanian and Israeli officials. Joint security committees and border committees meet regularly, despite tension at the political level. Even during the first year of the *intifada*, Israeli Minister of Defence Binyamin Ben-Eliezer secretly visited Jordan to coordinate joint actions against Palestinian militants. Further, Jordanian and Israeli liaison officers hold joint responsibility for resolving border and security problems. At a functional level, these officers maintain direct communications through both landline and cellular phone systems.

The set of protocols and communications also serves to avert potential security crises. In the event of a serious Israeli military operation in the occupied territories, for example, all crossing points into Jordan are closed.[23] This came into effect during an incident in November 2003, when a Jordanian gunman open fired on a group of Ecuadorians as they crossed from Jordan to Israel. One woman was killed and four wounded at the border crossing that also marked the place where Jordan and Israel signed their peace treaty in 1994. The local Jordanian authorities launched an investigation into the incident, and the Jordanian governor held meetings in Israel with the Israeli Minister of Tourism on their progress.[24]

Bilateral Relationship

According to security experts in Jordan and Israel, the bilateral security relationship has flourished at the implementation level as a result of the policy to build parallel structures in both countries. Emphasis on effective communication and the creation of an atmosphere of mutual respect and professionalism has further assisted their relationship.

At the political level, the bilateral security relationship is more responsive to the overall political relations between Israel and Jordan than the pragmatic daily security relationship. In the first few years after the treaty, high-level reciprocal meetings between the Jordanian and Israeli political and intelligence leadership took place. In March 1996, Israeli Foreign Minister and former IDF Chief of Staff Ehud Barak met with Crown Prince Hassan and intelligence officials from both countries in Amman. The Jordanians reciprocated with a visit by Chief of Staff Gen. Abdul-Hafez Marei-Kaabneh, the first commander of an Arab army to visit Israel officially, when he met with Prime Minister Shimon Peres and IDF Chief of Staff Lt. Gen. Ammon Shahak.[25] Further meetings of this type, as well as other events, followed, including a joint air show with a peace banner, highlighting Jordanian and Israeli cooperation to the public.

Cooperation also took place on various substantive issues, including joint police action on drug trafficking and smuggling, intelligence exchange and other forms of cooperation.[26]

Within the armed forces, joint naval exercises were conducted in 1997.[27] Coordination at the divisional and brigade level takes place between Jordan and Israel and maps with joint points of reference are utilized,[28] though much of the cooperation is kept intentionally quiet. The peace agreement has also allowed Israel to reduce the number of Israel Defence Force troops stationed along the border, replacing them with reservists. Furthermore, Israel authorized sales of light arms and ammunition by an Israeli firm to Jordan.[29] Agreements have been reached to expedite the passage of search and rescue teams across the border, and to bring personnel, vehicles, communication, and search and rescue equipment. Potential rescuers also work from a coordinated set of maps, to reduce confusion.

Intelligence cooperation between Israel and Jordan, though often focused on tracking extremists, has yielded some unusual activities. As both countries share a deep suspicion of Syria, they reportedly collaborated in an effort to gain information on the state of Syrian president Hafez al-Assad's health. During his visit to Jordan following King Hussein's death, the Mossad and Jordanian secret service secretly collected a urine sample from the ill leader, which was analysed in Tel Aviv. Based on the urinalysis, a medical file was prepared to assess his likely lifespan and to plan foreign policy decisions accordingly.[30]

Third Party Threats

Both Jordan and Israel share a major concern that Jordanian territory might be utilized by radical groups in the region to stage attacks, including missile attacks, on Israel. For this reason, security cooperation is often very close, including the existence of a Mossad office in Amman to share information on extremist groups operating in the region. After the second Palestinian *intifada* in 2000,[31] cooperation on this front, especially the control of Palestinian extremists, increased; it is, however, still kept quiet within Jordan. Its foundations were included in the final preparations for the peace treaty.[32]

Despite tensions caused by the deteriorating Israeli-Palestinian relations, both Jordan and Israel perceived major security threats posed by Iraq, and worked collaboratively to address them. In content, however, their threat perceptions were quite different. Israel, often the target of Saddam Hussein's rhetoric, feared that Iraqi rockets would again hit Tel Aviv, as they had during the first Gulf War. Jordan's concerns focused on the permeability of the Iraqi-Jordanian border, which made it an easy crossing for smugglers, carrying everything from merchandise to weapons. Though the fall of Saddam Hussein's regime has perhaps lessened Israeli fears vis-à-vis Iraq, concerns are now mounting over the vulnerability of Jordan—and the Hashemite monarchy—to instability originating in Iraq.

The Jordanian-Iraqi border stretches 185 kilometres, with one official crossing point. Previously, a ditch ran along the border to discourage illegal crossing. The sanctions regime imposed on Iraq throughout the 1990s, however, encouraged illegal immigration, mainly for employment, and high Iraqi exit fees discouraged crossing the border in a legal manner. In addition to smuggling, especially of livestock and weapons, the Iraq-Jordanian border became a known route for militant infiltration into Jordan and through Jordan to other places. As the sanctions regime collapsed in Iraq in the late 1990s, attempts to permeate the border increased significantly.

The shared concerns led to close Israeli-Jordanian cooperation in the construction of the early warning system (EWS) along the Jordanian-Iraqi border. Jordan envisioned its development as the first step in a new regional security system. The EWS would improve Jordan's ability to detect hostile elements attempting to enter Jordan's territory for purposes of terrorism, arms or drug smuggling, or illegal trade of goods. It also would offer advanced warning of any threats on its border and better ability to detect aircraft and missiles. Israel's goals in developing the EWS reflect traditional Israeli concerns regarding the fear of a combined Arab attack through Jordan. The system would allow Israel to overcome the limited range of its radar, and provide an early warning about concentrations of ground forces and missiles close to Jordan's territory. In addition, Israel shared Jordanian concerns regarding infiltration by hostile third parties.

Despite Jordan's and Israel's shared strategic vision, and the role the EWS would play in it, political constraints in Jordan necessitated certain restrictions. Most importantly, visible sections, especially those close to the border, would have to be operated by Jordanian personnel. While non-visible elements could include European Union and United States personnel in technical support roles, Israel would not be involved in operating systems on Jordanian territory.

The early warning system, which went into operation prior to the Iraq War in 2003, fulfils the following functions: timely detection, tracking and reporting of concentration and movement of ground forces and air defence elements in the areas that border Jordan, deployment and status of preparedness of surface-to-surface missile launchers, deployment of air assets to airfields, traffic of aircraft and helicopter, monitoring of Jordanian borders with Iraq, Syria, Saudi Arabia and Israel for the prevention of infiltration of persons and vehicles, and monitoring environmental risks in the border areas.

Limitations of Security Cooperation

As the EWS experience illustrates, there are limitations to the security relationship. Some of them are external, imposed by Jordan's continued need to balance its relationship with Israel with its ties to other Arab states. Other limitations stem from tensions at the political level, limiting the ability—or desire—to deal with security issues at the strategic level either bilaterally or within a regional framework.

A major red line, at least maintained publicly, is not to allow Israeli soldiers to cross into Jordan and thereby compromise Jordanian territorial integrity. Officials on both sides take great pains to illustrate this commitment. In December 2001, gunmen in Jordan opened fire at Israeli forces, causing the largest military operation on the Israeli-Jordanian border since the treaty, involving helicopters and Israeli reinforcements. Both governments issued statements saying that all Israeli military operations were exclusively on Israeli territory, though this appeared to conflict with statements made by the local Israeli army commander at the scene.[33]

Indeed, Israel would like to have seen deeper cooperation with Jordan on issues involving the use of each other's territory. Its small size gives Israel limited options for key military training activities, such as line of fire exercises and air navigation training: Jordan's vast deserts could have provided attractive training sites. In exchange, Israel could have offered training on high-tech equipment or the use of simulators to Jordanian armed forces.

A further red line to the Jordanian-Israeli relationship, dictated by Arab states, is that it cannot be utilized by Israel to form new regional alliances, such as one with Turkey. With bilateral relationships with both Israel and Turkey, Jordan would be a natural addition to the Turkey-Israel military alliance. The Jordanian government, while not openly engaging in a tripartite alliance, has refrained from commenting on reports that its officials have met on the issue and participated in strategic dialogues.[34] Though Jordan participated as an observer in a Turkish-Israeli-United States military manoeuvre,[35] it insists that it is 'not promoting pacts' or forming new regional alliances.[36]

Peace with Jordan has failed to integrate Israel into wider regional security structures as anticipated in the treaty. The treaty called for the creation of a Conference on Security and Cooperation in the Middle East (CSCME), modelled after the European Union Conference on Security and Cooperation in Europe (CSCSE), as well as the creation of a Multilateral Working Group on Arms Control and Regional Security. Quite simply, other Arab governments have refused to engage in a regional strategic dialogue with Israel; Egypt, specifically, dashed attempts to create the CSCME. Some of the failure to create regional security structures can be blamed on the rising tension caused by renewed levels of conflict between Israel and the Palestinians, which, for example, led to the suspension of the Middle East and North Africa economic summits. However, even Egypt maintains a security dialogue with Israel to this day, despite its vacant ambassadorial post in Tel Aviv. While certainly the state of Israel's relations with key Arab states (notably Lebanon and Syria) will mitigate against the creation of any regional strategic conference in the near future, other states engaged in a security dialogue with Israel prefer to keep this fact out of the public spotlight.

Even more revealing is the lack of a bilateral strategic dialogue between Jordan and Israel at the political level. A number of factors reduce their desire for dialogue, including the Israeli concern that it could limit its policy options. Furthermore, the Palestinian factor limits the range of policies Jordan is able to consider, given its position in the Arab world. As a result, the depth of the security relationship has changed little in the last ten years, nor is there any regular assessment of the relationship, its changing goals, or the volatile external context within which it exists. The closest Jordan and Israel have come to in terms of a strategic dialogue may be the activities of retired generals to maintain a joint forum through the non-governmental sector, discussed in Chapter Eight.

As in many areas of the bilateral relationship, the nature of Israeli bureaucracy hinders joint security activities with Jordan. In one case, Jordan wished to purchase weapons from Israel but encountered two problems: its own inability to pay for the weapons and bureaucratic hurdles inside the Israeli military. The financial problem was solved by the provision of US funds to Jordan, with the support of Israel. Then, on the Israeli side, approval was needed from a special committee to authorize the sale of weapons. After much delay and the intercession of key military officials involved in the Israeli-Jordanian relationship, it was discovered that Jordan was on a list of countries to which Israel would not sell weapons. The list predated the peace treaty and had never been updated to reflect the new relationship between the parties.

The assurance of mutual security and the removal of threat from each other is a major and significant outcome of the peace treaty for both Jordan and Israel. In this regard, the treaty has achieved perhaps its most central goal, the one upon which all other cooperation is dependent. This is no small feat, given the history between the two parties, and the potential in the region for parties to get drawn into conflicts they themselves did not initiate.

In the Jordanian-Israeli case, the security relationship has been based largely on mutual trust between the countries' political leaderships, rather than a detailed agreement in the peace treaty covering military issues. Though King Abdullah's relationship to Israeli leaders has been more distant than that of his father, security cooperation remains. Both parties appear satisfied with the security of their shared border and joint attempts to combat terrorism. However, the escalating Israeli-Palestinian conflict and the utilization of techniques such as targeted assassinations by the Israeli military have placed the Jordanian political leadership in the difficult position of reacting to unilateral Israeli actions. The building of the separation fence/wall and the Gaza separation plan, which have significant security ramifications on the bilateral relationship, are further examples of issues, where Jordan has little or no input. Such actions retard deeper security collaboration that would benefit both parties. According to one retired Israeli general, the Israeli government must be aware of the necessity of consulting with Jordan, 'even when we don't need them', since there is value even in symbolic consultation.

While confidence between the security forces is a major reason for the stable relationship between Israel and Jordan, security concerns (which are distinct from security guarantees) continue to frustrate cooperation in other areas. Observers liken security in Israel to a 'black box', where no one is quite sure what the regulations or security requirements may be for a given activity, yet where 'security' is given as a reason for stopping activities normally associated with peaceful relations, such as the flow of goods or people between two countries. The forthcoming chapters illustrate the tension between Israeli security needs, which emphasize issues such as fighting militancy, and the political will to facilitate other key areas of the treaty, like economics and trade. Even Jordanian security officials, though generally respectful of Israeli's security needs and repulsed by suicide bombings, suspect that security concerns are utilized to protect Israeli economic interests or to score political points, rather than addressing real security needs.

4

A RELATIONSHIP CHALLENGED: THE TUNNEL, NAHARAYIM AND MISH'AL

Though the security relationship can be considered the bedrock of Jordanian-Israeli relations, moments of political crisis have seriously strained even this dimension of their affairs. Moreover, key security incidents have taken place against the backdrop of a worsening political climate, both within the region, as well as in the bilateral relationship, amplifying their effect on the development of peaceful relations. The security incidents discussed in this chapter also marked the end of the 'honeymoon period' of the Jordanian-Israeli peace, and cast a pall over the relationship that has not lifted.

Though Sharon's visit to the Temple Mount/Harem al-Sharif and the Al Aqsa *intifada* in September 2000 are often used as benchmarks for the deterioration of the situation in the region, the Jordanian-Israeli peace had begun to falter years before the *intifada*. The incidents delineated in this chapter, which all happened in 1996 and 1997, had already undermined the potential for a truly 'warm' peace based on mutual trust at the societal level. The fact that these incidents did not escalate beyond disparaging comments in local newspapers and diplomatic reproach, which could have led to an abrogation of the treaty, is a result of the manner in which they were resolved, involving concessions made by both parties.

The Temple Mount Tunnel

In late September 1996, the Israeli government decided to open the Hasmonean (Western Wall) Tunnel in the old city of Jerusalem without first consulting Jordan. Though facilitating tourism was the stated objective of the opening, the move clearly had strong political overtones, both in terms of Israeli domestic policy and Israel's relations with the Palestinians and Jordanians. The recently elected Likud-led government of Prime Minister Binyamin Netanyahu directly challenged Jordan's special role over Jerusalem's Muslim holy places, contained in Article 10 of the peace treaty:

> In this regard, in accordance with the Washington Declaration, Israel respects the present special role of the Hashemite Kingdom of Jordan in Muslim holy shrines in Jerusalem. When negotiations on the permanent status will take place, Israel will accord a high priority to the Jordanian historic role in these shrines.[1]

Moreover, both the Palestinians and the Jordanians interpreted the opening of the tunnel as a violation of agreements made between Israel and the Palestinians in 1993 and 1995.

The Hasmonean tunnel runs along the Western Wall, the last remaining portion of King Herod's temple, which is the main religious site for Jews. The Western Wall, however, is adjacent to the plaza on which stands the al-Aqsa Mosque, one of Islam's holiest shrines. The opening of the tunnel, even to only allow tourist access, could be interpreted as an attempt to extend Israeli control over portions of the holy sites. Put more plainly, it could be seen as a unilateral Israeli move to change the 'facts on the ground' in Jerusalem, which both Palestinians and Israelis claim as their capital, in advance of final negotiations under the Oslo framework.

The move touched off violence on the ground and diplomatic furore, following a commercial strike and Palestinian demonstrations. Nearly 70 people were killed and more than 1,500 injured, mostly Palestinians. Jordan registered its reaction to the tunnel opening in the strongest possible terms, delivered in writing to the Israeli ambassador in Jordan, accusing Israel of violating the October 1994 peace treaty.[2] Within Jordanian civil society, and especially opposition groups, the opening prompted a declaration calling for resistance to all forms of normalization with the Zionist enemy. Thirty-eight groups, including political parties, professional associations and non-governmental organizations, signed it.[3] This collective protest helped to broaden and deepen the anti-normalization movement in Jordan (Chapter Nine). Public outrage in Jordan also constrained the government's ability to confront this movement, while trying to maintain the difficult domestic balancing act between having relations with Israel and supporting key Arab issues, especially the Palestinian cause.

The tunnel opening immediately caused a diplomatic rupture between Jordan and Israel at the highest level, but Jordan's efforts to balance its important relationship with Israel with its ties to Arab neighbours were evident. King Hussein refused to see Israeli Prime Minister Netanyahu or his ministers, but Israeli President Weizman, who holds no political power, was invited to visit Jordan in a 'ceremonial role'. At the same time, King Hussein drew new emphasis on his relationship with the Palestinians and his support for the Palestinian cause. Shortly after the Israeli opening of the tunnel, King Hussein invited Palestinian President Yasser Arafat to Amman, promising to support the Palestinians in their negotiations with Israel. Though the king did travel to Washington to meet with the Israeli leadership under the auspices of the United States, his visit was made in consultation with Arafat and Egyptian President Hosni Mubarak.

Israel tried to downplay the disagreement over the tunnel opening, and reaffirmed its commitment to the peace process in a statement issued by the Israeli embassy in Amman, arguing that the opening did not violate its interim agreement with the Palestinians.[4] There are at least two explanations for Netanyahu's actions: the first argues that he did not foresee the problems that the opening of the tunnel would create with Jordan; the second maintains that it was a deliberate attempt to assert sovereignty over East Jerusalem.[5] Regardless of which explanation is accurate, the incident had a palpable effect on Jordanian-Israeli relations.

Incidents such as the tunnel opening were a clear indication that the Oslo process was faltering; agreements were not being implemented and the peace process was in jeopardy. In reality, the tunnel incident was about much more than the opening of an archaeological site.[6] It also marked a significant change in the Jordanian relationship to Jerusalem, despite the contents of its treaty with Israel. Following the tunnel opening, Netanyahu agreed to renovations to Solomon's Stables, proposed by the Palestinian religious authorities (*waqf*), despite the Hashemite Kingdom's 'special role'. Shortly thereafter, Jordan transferred numerous properties in Jerusalem to the Palestinian Authority and ceased to pay the salaries of *waqf* employees, reducing its institutional role in Jerusalem. King Hussein's personal relationship to holy sites in the city was reinforced by a gift of 2,000 square metres of new carpet to the Al Aqsa mosque.[7]

Despite the obvious anger at Israel, the monarchy's reaction was to some extent symbolic, a necessary move for this guardian of Islamic holy places, and contacts between Jordanian and Israeli ministers continued. Jordan's desire to resolve the situation within the context of the bilateral relationship was made clear, when the former Jordanian ambassador to Israel, Marwan Muasher, travelled to Jerusalem to meet with the then Israeli Foreign Minister, David Levy. In a meeting described as 'fruitful and constructive', the two officials committed to strengthening their countries' bilateral relations and made plans for Levy to visit Jordan.[8]

At least at the rhetorical level, Israel also restated its commitment to the Israeli-Jordanian relationship. Netanyahu declared Jordan a very important country for Israel and described Jordanian concerns as 'a passing cloud, and I believe we can have brighter days ahead'.[9] More importantly, Israel highlighted the significance of Jordan's role in the Israeli-Palestinian peace process with the signing of the second redeployment of Israeli troops from Hebron in January 1997.

The Naharayim Incident

It is impossible to ignore the symbolism of the killings on Naharayim, the 'Island of Peace', returned to Jordanian sovereignty under the 1994 peace treaty. Here, on 13 March 1997, Ahmed Mousa Dakamseh, a Jordanian soldier, opened fire on a group of Israeli schoolgirls visiting the site—killing seven. He was overpowered by other Jordanian soldiers and disarmed. His family claimed that the assailant was mentally deranged, though he later stood trial, and was eventually sentenced by a military court to life imprisonment with hard labour; a disappointment to many Israelis who sought the death penalty.

The single act that best symbolized King Hussein's commitment to the peace, if not that of the Jordanian population as a whole, was his visit to the families of the murdered schoolgirls. Interrupting a trip to Spain and postponing a visit the United States, King Hussein personally visited their homes, where he kneeled—*kneeled*—before their bereaved families, an image that was broadcast around the world. In one home, the king stated:

> I feel I have lost a child, and I feel that if there is anything in life, it is to ensure that all the children enjoy peace and security. I hope you consider me a brother and a member of the family.[10]

King Hussein's visit clearly moved much of the Israeli public, leading even the right-leaning *Jerusalem Post* to state: 'That the king made the visit, and that the Israelis accepted him so readily, shows that the peace between Israelis and the Jordanian leadership has sunk deep roots.'[11]

It was clear to Israeli and Jordanian observers that the King's actions were meant not only to console the bereaved families, but also to try to reinvigorate the faltering Israeli-Palestinian peace process. Crucially, he not only drew attention to the grieving of families caught within conflict, but also reestablished phone contact between Prime Minister Netanyahu and President Arafat, a critical move forward.[12] The viewpoint that the tragedy could be used to move political processes forward was echoed by the generally pro-government *Jordan Times*, which called for the king's gesture to be seized upon as a means to salvage the peace process. However, scepticism was also evident; commentaries in both Israeli and Jordanian newspapers expressed concern that others in the region would not follow Hussein's example. A *Jordan Times* editorial reflected some of the cynicism felt in Jordan: 'It is true that no matter how powerful King Hussein's message is, it will be difficult for it to sink in, unless and until the Israeli government is willing and ready to reciprocate its overtures for peace.'[13]

Undoubtedly, King Hussein knew that the sight of an Arab monarch kneeling before Israelis would not improve his relationship with other Arab states, and that many of his own citizens would be angered by it. He could expect that many Arabs shared the opinion expressed by Palestinian Preventive Security Service chief Col. Jabril Rajoub, who stated that 'This massacre of seven school girls by a Jordanian soldier is definitely a mistake, but not a reason for King Hussein to come afterwards to kneel down in Israel.'[14]

Surprisingly, Israel hinted at King Hussein's culpability in the attack, when Foreign Minister David Levy linked the killings to statements by the king, who had accused Netanyahu of being 'bent on destroying the peace efforts'. Such statements, according to Levy, 'created a psychological atmosphere that could lead to such tragic acts'.[15] Jordan's Prime Minister Kabariti bitterly attacked Prime Minister Netanyahu for these accusations, a move that contributed to his ouster a short time later.[16] Still, within Jordanian public opinion, such comments by the Israelis were seen as opportunistic, if not worse.[17] Reaction in Jordan was undoubtedly influenced by the realization that the killings by one of their citizens reinforced Netanyahu's arguments regarding the security threats to Israel from the Arab world in general. The killings, therefore, strengthened Netanyahu's stance against returning more West Bank territory to the Palestinians.[18]

Within some sections of Jordanian society, the Naharayim killings contributed to anti-normalization sentiments and mounting anger at Israel over the failing peace process and the treatment of Palestinians. The Jordanian assailant claimed that the girls mocking him, taking pictures and laughing while he prayed had prompted his actions. The sentiments expressed by his lawyer that 'It appears the soldier's motives were patriotic, and he acted out of a rage on the spur of the moment,'[19] were likely shared by many people in Jordan, where great sensitivity to perceived acts of aggression or arrogance by Israelis exists.

In the soldier's defence, his lawyers tried to tie his actions to the general sense of Arab frustration over the suffering of Arabs at the hands of Israel. As the case drew broad attention, some Jordanian peace opponents lauded the defendant as a 'hero,' and competed among themselves to defend him in the court proceedings. The Jordanian Bar Association, a leading anti-peace group, tried to lead a group of 200 supporters to visit the accused soldier's family, but was prevented by police.

The continued tension between Jordan and Israel erupted two months later to mar the memorial ceremony for the seven Israeli schoolgirls killed at Naharayim. The envisioned full-day event included the dedication of a hill of flowers to the girls and the planting of trees, with a meeting between Crown Prince Hassan and Prime Minister Netanyahu planned for the evening.[20] The event was abruptly cancelled on the morning it was to be held. Diplomatic finger-pointing ensued over responsibility for the cancellation, and Jordan's ambassador claimed that the ceremony was cancelled at Israel's initiative, and that Jordan had never said that Crown Prince Hassan would attend the ceremony, as reported by Israel.[21]

As the Israeli-Jordanian relationship is complex and multi-faceted, the memorial ceremony and the families of the murdered girls were likely the victims of another diplomatic crisis emerging between Israel and Jordan, this one over water allocations, provided for in the 1994 treaty (the focus of Chapter Five). At the same time, King Hussein cancelled a planned trip to Haifa to accept an honorary doctorate.

Just prior to the Naharayim killings, the Israeli-Palestinian and Israeli-Jordanian relationships faced another crisis, resulting from the Israeli decision to construct a new Jewish neighbourhood at Har Homa in Arab East Jerusalem. This led to the breaking-off of negotiations within the Oslo framework. Israeli-Jordanian relations were dealt another blow, when Israel announced plans to build additional settlements in the East Jerusalem neighbourhood of Ras el-Amud. Jordan condemned the settlements, which it claimed to be violating the peace process.[22]

By the summer of 1997, Jordan and Israel had experienced discord on a variety of levels and on a number of issues that had put great strain on their relationship. The faltering Israeli-Palestinian peace process was at the root of much of this conflict, illustrating the vulnerability of their relations to external events. King Hussein's personal involvement and Israel's recognition that the deaths were the result of actions by a single individual, rather than an organized group, kept the Naharayim incident from severely testing the treaty. Here again, the security relationship played a fundamental role. Following criticism by Israel regarding delays in evacuating the wounded children from Naharayim because of Jordanian security regulations, Israeli and Jordanian military officials met to establish new protocols for emergency situations. Though Jordan disputed the Israeli claims, new guidelines were established to allow Israeli military ambulances and commanders to enter the Jordanian enclave in a future emergency and a joint drill was carried out to train Jordanian and Israeli soldiers on the new procedures.[23] Jordan also removed Jordanians of Palestinian heritage from border patrols.

The Mish'al Assassination Attempt

This event may mark the lowest point in Israeli-Jordanian relations, one that—from the Jordanian point of view—illustrated Israel's ability to totally discount the peace treaty when it suited them. Moreover, it displayed an amazing disregard for the internal dimensions of Jordanian state–society relations, where the peace with Israel was becoming an increasingly difficult issue for the monarchy to promote. At a very personal level, it must have seemed a provocative rebuke for King Hussein, coming so soon after his extraordinary act of humility towards the families of the killed schoolgirls in the Naharayim incident.

Barely six months after the peace island shooting, two Israeli Mossad agents attempted to assassinate Khalid Mish'al, the political head of the Islamic Resistance Movement (Hamas). Mish'al, a Jordanian citizen, was living in Jordan at the time. In September 1997, during a dispute with two Canadians on the street, he was struck with an object that left him nauseous and with breathing difficulties. The 'Canadians' were eventually revealed to be agents of the Israeli Mossad, who had tried to poison Mish'al. At Hussein's insistence, Israel provided the antidote that saved Mish'al's life. In return for the release of the two Israeli agents posing as Canadians, Israel further agreed to release Hamas spiritual leader Sheikh Ahmed Yassin and seventy other Jordanian and Palestinian prisoners held in Israeli jails.

The Mish'al incident was a serious embarrassment for Israel, undermining the reputation of its much lauded intelligence agency, straining its relationship with Canada and prompting much criticism from the international community. It also crossed a serious red line in the Israeli-Jordanian relationship, as it was a flagrant violation of Jordan's sovereignty. For years, the parties had been careful to maintain the (possible) fiction that Israeli military forces never crossed into Jordan, even in hot pursuit of criminals. This was important, not only to dissuade domestic Jordanian concerns, but for Jordan's appearance to the greater Arab world overall. Yet here, in the Mish'al case, the Israeli Mossad was acting openly in Jordan, against one of the countries' own citizens.

Further, the incident came at a point when King Hussein was expending enormous effort to prod forward the flagging Israeli-Palestinian peace process. A successful assassination would have prompted considerable rage among the Palestinian population (both in Jordan, and in the West Bank and Gaza); in all likelihood, demonstrations would have lead to clashes with Israeli forces and further set back the peace process. Additionally, Hussein saw Mish'al as an integral part of his effort to get the process back on track. This perception of Mish'al's role in the peace process was evident in Hussein's comment: 'When I contacted US President Bill Clinton I told him that the whole peace process hinged on the life of this Jordanian man. I made it clear that if he dies, everything ends.'[24]

Only days before the assassination attempt on Mish'al, King Hussein had relayed a message from Hamas regarding the possibility of a 10-year moratorium on violence.[25]

Though Israel claimed the message did not arrive until 24 hours after the assassination attempt, it still took no subsequent action, a move that, according to Israeli analyst Moshe Zak, constituted a missed opportunity for both countries. Zak argues that, had Israel responded to the offer even after the assassination attempt, 'it is possible that the whole disaster wouldn't have turned into an international scandal, and the two sides would have preferred to discuss mediation between Israel and a Palestinian organization rather than getting mixed up in a scandal.'[26] The assassination attempt was also a personal slap in the face to Hussein, who recently had surprised many observers by declaring a change of heart in his relationship with Netanyahu, referring to him as a 'peace partner', and stating his willingness to work with him.[27] These declarations were apparently designed to create a new partnership towards the peace process.

The Mish'al incident provoked a strong reaction from the Jordanian monarchy and government. Jordanian intelligence services severed all contact with the Mossad, expelled its agents from Jordan, and ended all forms of security cooperation three days after the attempt (though Israeli accounts of this period differ on this point, denying a suspension of security cooperation). Cooperation between the armed forces continued, as did cooperation in key areas of the 1994 peace treaty.[28] Moreover, Jordan extracted the promise that Israel would not carry out any more such operations in Jordan.[29]

After months of hesitation, which angered Jordanian officials, Israel finally agreed to the resignation of Mossad chief Danny Yatom to repair the damage to its relationship with Jordan. The resignation was a condition laid down by King Hussein before security cooperation between the countries could be renewed.[30] An Israeli commission, whose findings were released as the Ciechanover report, found Yatom responsible for the attempt, but did not call for his resignation, and Yatom had initially refused to step down.

Six months after the incident, high-level meetings between King Hussein and Sharon in Amman attempted to move beyond the issue and reinvigorate the bilateral relationship. Particular emphasis was placed on achieving progress in the area of water resources, which had caused discord the previous year, disrupting the Naharayim memorial plans. This time, Israel indeed undertook a variety of measures to repair its relationship with Jordan. In addition to a visit by Infrastructure Minister Sharon, meetings were scheduled with Israeli Industry and Trade Minister Natan Sharansky to address trade related problems. Prime Minister Netanyahu received Crown Prince

Hassan, his first meeting with a member of the Jordanian royal family since the Mish'al incident. Hassan's visit included discussions on restoring security cooperation and means to move forward on the Israeli-Palestinian peace process, specifically the second redeployment of Israeli troops.[31]

These attempts to diplomatically patch up the affair were hindered by statements from Ariel Sharon, less than a week later. Sharon said that Israel intended to 'finish the job' of assassinating Mish'al, though not on Jordanian territory. This put Jordanian government officials in a difficult situation, which was solved—at least technically—by a letter of clarification from Sharon, stating his respect for Jordanian sovereignty and that Israel did not intend to attack any Jordanian citizen; though it was not clear if such attacks would be considered outside Jordanian territory.[32] A further interview with Defence Minister Mordekhay failed to clarify Sharon's statements, with Mordekhay saying only that he 'would like to respect the Jordanian state and the Jordanian people'.[33] His statements were in direct contradiction with promises made by Netanyahu and other members of the Israeli government in the days after the attack, which sought to regain its understanding with Jordan.[34]

The findings of the official Israeli inquiry into the Mish'al affair did little to mitigate Jordan's outrage over violation of its sovereignty. The report stated that the decision to carry out the attack was based on the principle that 'no place in the world should be allowed to serve as a safe harbour for those who plan to carry out murders and acts of terror in Israel.' Moreover, statements by Prime Minister Netanyahu after the release of the report reaffirmed Israel's commitment to this policy, despite promises made in Amman that such an attack would not be repeated.[35]

In contrast to the diplomatic wrangling, there was at least one private Israeli initiative attempting to restore Israeli-Jordanian relations. Weeks after the assassination attempt, an Israeli television host took his crew to Jordan and flew an Israeli plane over the capital, displaying a large banner in Arabic stating 'sorry' and the name of his show. The helicopter belonging to King Hussein, who had helped to arrange the flight, escorted the plane.[36]

Though the diplomatic crisis prompted by the Mish'al incident was eventually resolved, it contributed to growing animosity towards the peace treaty among the Jordanian population and undermined the Jordanian government's attempts to promote normalization at the societal level. Even the pro-government *Jordan Times* reported that the attack, and subsequent Israeli investigation into the incident, 'weakened Jordanian efforts to boost normalization with Israel and reaffirmed popular perceptions that the Jewish state remains an enemy that could never be trusted'.[37] The attack on Mish'al fuelled the anti-normalization movement: one of its key members, the Arab Lawyers Union, filed suit in the International Court of Justice in The Hague against Ariel Sharon for his threats to assassinate Mish'al. Their decision to file charges came in response to Sharon's statements in March 1998 that, despite the failed attempt, Israel still intended to kill Mish'al.[38]

The fact that Jordan and Israel survived these series of tests to their bilateral relationship has been cited as evidence of the strength and resilience of the peace treaty and their relations. Zak, writing shortly after the Mish'al incident, argues: 'The storm that rocked the countries on both sides of the Jordan over the last 10 days did not change the course of the river, and did not even challenge the peace treaty between Jordan and Israel.'[39] He points to the restraint exercised by King Hussein in criticizing Israel and especially Prime Minister Netanyahu publicly, and to the continuation of bilateral meetings. Zak's assessment in this area might have been premature, for shortly after his analysis the diplomatic crisis did spill into the media arena with sharp public exchanges.

Beyond this issue, there is much to support Zak's analysis, in which both parties sought to resolve the conflict in recognition of essential ties between them. Indeed, the back channels at the highest level, which created the groundwork for the treaty long before 1994, alleviated the crisis and maintained the functional relationship between the two parties. Commenting on the Mish'al affair, Bligh notes that reversion to these old secret channels is a familiar pattern of political behaviour, designed to ensure continued joint strategic cooperation.[40]

Indeed, the centrality of the security relationship, within a whirlwind of political discord, remains evident. Again, Zak notes the negotiations conducted at a high level for the release of the Israeli hit team as evidence of the continued strength of these channels. A further reminder that security is the bedrock of the Jordanian-Israeli relationship is the continued operation of joint training missions between the Royal Jordanian Special Operations Command, part of the Royal Jordanian Special Forces under command of then Prince Abdullah, and their Israeli counterparts. These forces cooperate on a key area of the peace treaty, counter insurgency and anti-terror. Though their cooperation continued two months after Mish'al, where once the cooperation with Israelis was openly discussed, now all details remain classified.[41]

While, in the medium term, cooperation on essential security issues was not harmed by this series of crises, the Jordanian-Israeli peace treaty is about more than basic security. Though it is possible to argue that these events did not seriously endanger the treaty, their contribution to the failure to 'grow the peace' must also be recognized. A closer examination identifies patterns of behaviour, especially on the part of Israel, that frustrate Jordanians at the official and societal level, and lead to their conclusion that the peace with

Jordan is not a priority for Israel. Two aspects of Israeli behaviour stand out in the Jordanian perception: a failure to match words with deeds and an inability or unwillingness to recognize internal dimensions of the Jordanian political scene and its responsiveness to Israeli actions vis-à-vis the Palestinians.

In the tunnel incident, for example, Israel's failure to inform Jordan of the opening, despite the presence of Netanyahu's advisor, Dore Gold, in Amman the day before the opening, was dismissed (at least publicly) by Netanyahu in an interview that appeared both in the Arabic daily *Al-Hayat* and the English language *Jordan Times* with a simple, 'we did not anticipate that the opening of the tunnel would be used to agitate the mass demonstrations that followed'.[42] While Israeli security assessments prior to the opening did not anticipate the violence, from the Jordanian viewpoint, this was not the main issue. That a key ally would take unilateral action that could not only disrupt a failing peace process, but also touch on a major aspect of the Jordan-Israel peace treaty without prior notification, showed an Israeli ability to dismiss or overlook the bilateral relationship. This pattern of unilateral action towards the Palestinians, with disregard to the potential impact on Jordan, continues to this day with the assassination of Hamas spiritual leader Sheikh Ahmed Yassin only days after a meeting between King Abdullah and Prime Minister Sharon.

Numerous statements by Jordanian government officials—and even the king—in the period from 1996 to 1998 point to a growing crisis of confidence between Jordan and Israel, from which they have not fully emerged. Comments by Jordanian Prime Minister Karim Kabariti in late 1996, referring to Prime Minister Netanyahu, 'you hear from him one thing and on the ground you see something else',[43] highlight the Jordanian belief that Israel's commitment to the peace is sometimes largely rhetorical. Even prior to the damaging Mish'al incident, political analyst Rami Khouri noted the growing expression of Jordanian distrust:

> The numerous statements critical of Israel in recent weeks by King Hussein, Crown Prince Hassan and Prime Minister Karim Kabariti are noteworthy both for their strong, almost apocalyptic political tone and for their powerful cultural dimension, i.e. that Jordan and its leadership, which have been embraced by Israel as a true friend and an example of how Arab-Israeli peace and bilateral relations should develop, should reproach, warn and even scold the Israeli leadership in public, is a sign of the magnitude of Jordanian anger and concern.[44]

The Mish'al incident served only to increase the level of distrust openly expressed in Jordan towards the Israeli leadership. A Jordanian official, commenting on Mish'al, offered an opinion likely held by many in the country: 'How could Jordan cooperate with a state that stabbed it in the back on its own land?'[45] Even King Hussein, who had exercised such restrain and dubbed Netanyahu a 'peace partner', declared on Jordanian television that his trust in Netanyahu 'had all but evaporated', and drew a distinction between Netanyahu and the Israeli people, most of whom he believed were still committed to peace.[46] The belief that the Israeli leadership does not follow through on its promises was echoed in the pro-government *Jordan Times* editorial:

> And relations with Jordan, which Netanyahu was able to strain to the limit in September by the attempt on Khalid Mish'al's life, are still to be restored to their normal level, not because of unwillingness among the Jordanian leadership, but because Netanyahu had not been genuine in respecting his pledges and promises.[47]

In many ways, Israel seemed unwilling or unable to recognize the relationship between progress in the peace process with the Palestinians, which first allowed the covert Israel-Jordanian relationship to blossom into a formal treaty, and the post-peace Israeli-Jordanian bilateral relationship. By early 1998, even King Hussein was publicly mentioning the need for Israel to honour the Oslo Accords, the Hebron Accords and the second redeployment.[48]

Israeli actions towards the Palestinians were often frustrating and confusing for Jordanian officials, as they forced Jordan to at least publicly align itself closer with other Arab states, than might have been the case otherwise. Such actions, putting a chill on Israeli-Jordanian relations, were often viewed in Jordan as not in Israeli self-interest and led to negative conclusions regarding the centrality of the Jordanian relationship to Israel, and the level of understanding or sensitivity towards the Jordanian position. A further example of this lack of sensitivity was the subsequent appointment of Yatom in August 1999 to oversee the Jordan relations file within the Israeli government, and to serve on the joint Jordanian-Israeli committee for implementation of the peace agreement. The political opposition in Jordan used it to further support their anti-Israel stance.[49] The monarchy, however, did not protest the appointment, again demonstrating both the supremacy of cooperation on key issues, as well as the gap between perceptions held by the Jordanian monarchy and top officials and other members of the government and public.

Though the actions in 1996–1998 did not permanently fracture the peace treaty, they dimmed the prospects of a truly 'warm peace' at the societal level and added momentum to the anti-normalization movement in Jordan. Brand recounts the series of incidents, the tunnel opening, the

Har Homa construction, and the Mish'al assassination attempt, arguing that the actions infuriated the population: 'It seemed there was no end to Israeli outrages (even on Jordanian soil in the context of "peace"), just as it seemed that there were no limits to what the regime was willing to put up with to maintain the relationship.'[50] The incidents fuelled widely held Arab fears of Netanyahu, and provided a strong platform from which to launch attacks against normalization between Jordan and Israel. The continued deterioration of the Israeli-Palestinian peace process, an enormously sensitive domestic issue in Jordan, prompted one of King Hussein's strongest negative comments on the peace treaty, warning that he would 'review the Jordanian-Israeli treaty if the accords signed with the Palestinians are not respected'.[51] Barely out of its honeymoon phase, the immature Jordan-Israeli peace found itself severely challenged by these events and unable to build a strong and extensive foundation.

5
'THE FRUITS OF PEACE': SHARING WATER RESOURCES

Clichés attesting to the central importance of water in the Middle East abound. The peace treaty between Jordan and Israel includes what amounts to a highly detailed water sharing agreement between the two parties. The annex on water-related matters is by far the longest and most detailed, exceeding even the main treaty sections on borders and security. The water agreement resulted in an immediate net increase in water supply for Jordan, along with a commitment to jointly seek additional future supplies through desalination processes.

Despite the high level of detail in the water agreement, it failed to address potential water shortages under conditions of regional drought, as occurred 1999. Initial Israeli plans to cut delivery of water to Jordan despite its treaty commitments, led to an official warning from Jordan that the integrity of the treaty in its entirety was in doubt, and exacerbated Jordanian public opinion, which had already grown increasingly negative about Jordan's peace with Israel. Still, the resolution of the water problem, at least in the short term, again showed the resilience of the treaty. However, main aspects of water resource development, as outlined in the treaty, remain unimplemented. As a result, a strong potential for future conflict over water remains.

Water in the Jordan Valley

Despite the small size of the Jordan Valley and its riparian system, its water resources are extremely complex, partly because four countries share them: Lebanon, Syria, Jordan and Israel. Furthermore, allocation of water resources will play a critical role in any potential Israeli-Palestinian peace agreement, a situation that complicates current utilization of water resources. The Jordan basin, its water usage, its future development, and its relationship to conflict and conflict resolution have been the subject of

Map 5.1 *Israel and the Jordan River Basin.*

extensive study.[1] Though I will discuss the general parameters of the water resource situation in the Jordan basin, my emphasis will be on the shared use of water by Jordan and Israel following the 1994 treaty.

The Jordan River basin is made up of two main sources of surface water, the Jordan River and the Yarmouk River, as well numerous streams such as the Zarqa (Map 5.1). The Jordan River flows north to south and is fed by three springs originating in Syria and Israel. The Yarmouk River, which forms the border between Jordan and Syria, converges with the Jordan River inside Jordanian territory, and then flows into the Dead Sea.

There have been numerous attempts to develop plans for sharing the water resources among the riparian states, especially after the creation of the state of Israel. Two plans bear mentioning, because of their role in the historical Jordanian-Israeli relationship over water. Following the formation of the state of Israel, and the creation of 800,000 Palestinian refugees, Jordan and UNRWA agreed to divert part of the Yarmouk River for irrigation of the East Ghor area of the Jordan Valley, so that refugees could be resettled along the banks of the river. The United States were involved in this plan, known as the Bunger Plan, which called for building a dam on the Yarmouk River at the Jordanian-Syrian border and a second dam near the Israeli-Jordanian demarcation line. Israel protested this unilateral Jordanian move and periodically closed the gates that controlled the downstream flow of the Jordan River at the tip of Lake Kinneret. As a result, the Jordan River water became too saline for irrigation, threatening all crops in the Jordan valley. Israel also pressured the US, which covered nearly half the costs, to withdraw its financial support for the project.[2]

Controversy continued, when Israel announced the second phase of the All-Israel water plan in 1953, which would bring water to the Negev desert, diverting it from the upper Jordan River in the demilitarized zone with Syria. This unilateral move by Israel led to Syrian protests at the United Nations Security Council; Israel refused a request by the United National Truce Supervision Organization to halt construction, and shooting took place between Israeli and Syrian troops. Concerned that the situation would spark renewed regional conflict, the US announced its suspension of foreign aid to Israel until it acceded to the United Nations request.

These incidents underlined the need for a regional water plan. The United States became deeply involved in its development, trying to forestall unilateral efforts that could ignite conflict. The proposal, known as the Main (after the Charles T. Main, Inc. engineering firm) or 'Unified' plan, was completed in 1953. In an attempt to seek an agreement by all parties, Eric Johnston was appointed special ambassador by President Eisenhower; over the next two years, he undertook the most extensive water negotiations in the region. They were based on the proposed division of water shown in Table 5.1.[3]

Johnston's proposal met little enthusiasm in Israel or the Arab states. Haddadin summarized the Arab response:

> ...first, they viewed Johnston's mission as yet another manifestation of American pro-Israel policy, second, they viewed America's intention not as a humanitarian gesture to improve socio-economic

Table 5.1 Johnston Plan allocations (MCM per year).

	Syria	Lebanon	Jordan	Israel
(A)*				
Jordan River	42	35	100	375
Yarmouk River	90	–	377	25
Total	132	35	477	400
(B)†				
Jordan River	42	35	100	375
Yarmouk River	90	–	377	25
Southern tributaries	–	–	243	–
Total	132	35	720	400

* Source: Salameh, E. and H. Bannayan, *Water Resources of Jordan—Present Status and Future Potentials* (Amman, 1993), p. 15.
† Source: Kliot, N., *Water Resources and Conflict in the Middle East* (London, 1994), pp. 196–97.

conditions throughout the Jordan River basin, but rather as an attempt to promote Arab cooperation with Israel and seduce Arabs into recognizing the Jewish state; third, they feared that America's intention was to resettle Palestinian refugees in the Jordan Valley in lieu of implementing United Nations Resolution 194 of 11 December 1949, which called for their repatriation and compensation.[4]

Israel, too, considered the plan gravely flawed and not in the best interests of its national security, as it would interfere with existing plans for water development projects, especially those utilizing Jordan River water. Johnston's extensive round of negotiations from 1953 to 1955 produced numerous plans and counter plans; the highly modified final version became the basis for an informal agreement between Israel and Jordan in 1955.[5] It remained a starting point for discussions at the Madrid peace conference, and served as a negotiating baseline for the Jordanian delegation in the peace talks.[6]

In the decades following the Johnston negotiations, halted by the outbreak of the Suez Canal War in 1956, Israel and Jordan both constructed extensive water distribution networks. In 1956, Israel began construction of the National Water Carrier, the largest water project in Israel; completed in 1964, the carrier transports Jordan River water from a point at Lake

Kinneret in the north through a system of canals and pipelines to drier areas along the coastal south. The East Ghor canal, now known as the King Abdullah canal, is the backbone of Jordan's water management system. Opened in 1961, the 70 km-long canal brings water from the Yarmouk to the Zarqa Rivers to the Ghor valley, which greatly increased agricultural output in this predominately Palestinian area of Jordan. The canal was damaged four times by Israeli shelling after the 1967 War, but has been rebuilt and extended under USAID financing.[7] Now 110 km long, the King Abdullah canal and a system of dams also collect water from side streams flowing into the Jordan River from the east.

Water Issues in Jordan and Israel

As the countries along the Jordan River basin have experienced rapid population growth since the Second World War, the water resources have become increasingly stretched. By the mid 1990s, total population of the region amounted to 29.5 million (Lebanon 3.7 million, Syria 14.7 million, Jordan 4.1 million, West Bank 1.5 million and Israel 5.5 million), an increase of seven times the population in the 1920s, and nearly double the population in the early 1970s.[8] The universal pressure to stretch limited resources increases the need for water agreements among the riparian states.

In recent decades, Jordan has witnessed a rapid increase in its rate of water consumption in both agricultural and domestic sectors. In agriculture, irrigation usage in the 1960s was estimated at 250 MCM per year; by the early 1990s this figure had risen to 650 MCM. In the residential sector, the increase in demand was even more rapid. As Jordan underwent urbanization and population growth, the numbers grew from 40 MCM in the 1970s to 180 MCM in the 1990s.[9] A USAID Jordan estimate projected an annual water demand of 1.2 billion cubic meters (BCM) by 2000, far above the 750 MCM available on a sustainable basis.[10]

Jordan's lack of water resources is the primary constraint on further development of the agricultural sector, which employed 5 per cent of its labour force in 2001. Agriculture remains the largest user of water at about 75 per cent of the total; household consumption accounts for 22 per cent and industrial usage, though still quite low at 3 per cent, is growing.[11] At the same time, agriculture contributes only 4.5 per cent to GDP (2000).[12] The rising level of household water consumption is an issue for concern. If Jordan reaches an urban consumption level similar to Israel's, that is approximately 100 MCM per capita instead of 44 MCM, this would have an enormous impact on total water consumption.[13] As such per capita increases are associated with increased economic growth, it may be some time before Jordanian levels rise that high.

Israel has a total annual amount of renewable water of 1,550–1,650 MCM, supplied by the Jordan River and a series of aquifers. Its usage has also increased in recent decades. In 1965, total annual water usage was 1,329 MCM. Agriculture accounted for the largest share (80.9 per cent), followed by domestic usage (15.0 per cent) and industry (4.1 per cent). By the mid-1980s, demand had risen to over 2,000 MCM a year, 1,300 of which was utilized for agriculture. Domestic water consumption has increased steadily, from 200 MCM in the 1960s to 550 MCM in the mid-1990s. Agriculture utilizes 60 per cent of all water in Israel, but produces only 2 per cent of gross domestic product.[14] The close bond between agriculture and Zionist ideology results in a strong governmental commitment, including water subsidies to farmers. The volume of water used in irrigation, however, has declined by approximately one-third since the 1980s, and modest amounts of reclaimed water are now also used for irrigation. Still, Israel's water demand is expected to be 2,090 MCM by the year 2000, against total renewable resources of approximately 1,650 MCM.[15]

Water Provisions in the Treaty

Water gets extensive coverage in the treaty, first in Article 6, which states the goal of 'a comprehensive and lasting settlement of all the water problems between them', and in Annex II, which details water allocation from the Yarmouk and Jordan rivers during different seasons, storage and quality of such water, development of future water resources and the operation of a Joint Water Committee.

The Jordanian government heavily promoted the water agreement as a major 'fruit of peace'. According to Elmusa 'The importance of restoring Jordan's water claims was often stressed in the daily press during the negotiations, and even before the terms of the treaty were made public, Jordanian officials were quick to emphasize what they said were the significant water gains that Jordan realized in the negotiations.'[16] Beaumont, on the other hand, finds the terms of the peace treaty 'particularly favourable' for Israel. He notes that the allocations to Israel exceed those under the Johnston Plan by approximately 56 per cent (625 MCM per year, instead of 400 MCM). Jordan's situation is much less favourable, when measured against Johnston Plan guidelines: Jordan receives between 165–282 MCM from the Yarmouk River, depending on the actual yearly flow, though any deficiency is largely resulting from heavy withdrawals by Syria in excess of the Johnston Plan provisions. Further, the treaty guarantees Jordan only 30 MCM per year from the Jordan River, 10 MCM of which have to come from desalination processes. The total is far below the 477 MCM allocated to Jordan in the Johnston Plan.[17]

The treaty specifically allows Israel to pump 12 MCM from the Yarmouk River during the summer period (15 May–15 October), while Jordan gets the rest of the flow. Similarly, in the winter period, Israel pumps 13 MCM and Jordan is entitled to the rest—with a key provision. In the agreement, Jordan allows Israel to pump an additional 20 MCM from the Yarmouk River in winter, in exchange for the transfer of 20 MCM from the Jordan River to Jordan during the summer period. This transfer comprises Jordan's summer period allocation, and Jordan is responsible for the operation and maintenance of the transfer system. During the winter period, Jordan is entitled to store a minimum average of 20 MCM of the floods in the Jordan River south of its confluence with the Yarmouk for later transfer. In addition, 10 MCM of water from saline springs near the Jordan River were to be desalinated for use by Jordan. Until the desalination facilities were operational, Israel agreed to provide 10 MCM of Jordan River water during the summer period. Finally, Israel was to cooperate with Jordan to supply an additional 50 MCM/year of water at drinkable standard. A plan to locate and deliver this water was to be developed by the Joint Water Committee, composed of three members from each country.

In all, the treaty offered generally modest, though important, water gains for Jordan. As Beaumont and Elmusa both note, the treaty generally provides guaranteed amounts of water for Israel, while Jordan's allocations are quite variable, as in case of the Yarmouk River, whose flow has decreased significantly in recent years, due to upstream usage by Syria. As for the Jordan River, Jordan's guaranteed net gain is only 30 MCM per year, including the 10 MCM from desalination.[18] Furthermore, Israel is allowed to maintain its current uses of the Jordan River, with Jordan entitled to a quantity equivalent to Israel's, provided that it will not harm the quantity and quality of Israeli uses. Though the development of future water resources is meant to increase Jordan's available water resources, nothing has happened in this area so far.

The 1997 and 1999 Droughts

Jordan and Israel have faced two significant crises over water allocations in the period since the peace treaty. The first, in 1997, was intertwined with political skirmishing around the opening of the Hasmonean Tunnel, Har Homa, and the Naharayim killings discussed in Chapter Four. The second, in 1999, resulted from drought conditions across the region and may foreshadow conflict Jordan and Israel will face, as water usage increases more quickly than water resource development. The 1999 incident also highlights the connection between water and the ability of Jordan to survive in the eyes of the Jordanian leadership, as well as its role in selling the peace treaty to the Jordanian population.

The 1997 'Mini-Crisis'

Though accounts vary between Jordanian and Israeli sources over the origin of the so-called water 'mini-crisis' in 1997, the root of the problem lay in differing interpretations of the peace treaty. By the start of the summer period in early May 1997, Israel had provided only 50 MCM of the total annual 150 MCM owed to Jordan (from all sources) under the peace treaty. Though both parties agreed on the total, there was disagreement over the source of the remaining 100 MCM. While Jordan considered the water 'missing' and not linked to any future dam construction,[19] Israel responded that 'the Jordanians would get it (the 100 MCM) from new resources to be created by building dams on the River Jordan and desalination'.[20]

At this time, neither country had succeeded in attracting international financing for the construction of two dams inside Jordan or the construction of desalination plants, despite the treaty's requirement that a plan be prepared within one year of the its implementation. The Jordanian position was that Israel's commitment to supply the 100 MCM of water did not depend on the dam or desalination funding, while Israel contended that the water was to be provided by dam construction and desalination. Comments by Jordan's ambassador to Israel, Omar Rifai, summed up the Jordanian frustration: 'The water issue is not new.... We have been talking of the water problem for a year and half, and we are still at the same point.... There are 100 million cubic meters of water still missing.'[21]

The disagreement surfaced at a meeting between Infrastructure Minister Ariel Sharon and Munther Hadadin, head of the Jordanian delegation on water and the environment, and immediately became entangled with the memorial ceremony for the girls killed at Naharayim.[22] It also coincided with growing Jordanian disillusionment over Israel's role in the peace process, the backdrop of continued violence in Hebron, and the failed mission by US special envoy Dennis Ross to alleviate this violence.[23]

Again, in a demonstration of the role of back channels and high-level interaction in the ongoing Jordanian-Israeli relationship, secret meetings between Prime Minister Netanyahu and King Hussein resolved the water dispute. An agreement was reached and approved by the Israeli cabinet, in which Israel agreed to provide Jordan with additional water over the next three years.[24] The agreement called for an immediate transfer of 30 MCM of fresh water from Israel, in addition to the required 50 MCM, and the development of projects to provide an additional 50 MCM in the future.[25]

Shortly thereafter, joint plans to build a dam inside Jordan, as agreed to under the peace treaty, became a new source of conflict. In August 1997, Israeli officials announced that the Hammah dam would be built on a disputed border territory claimed by Syria, rather than at a site on the Yarmouk River undisputed by either Israel or Jordan.[26] Though former Israeli Prime Minister Yitzhak Rabin, the main architect of the peace, had directed to build the dam in undisputed territory, Prime Minister Netanyahu had changed the site to a demilitarized zone just below the Golan Heights in an attempt to preclude potential return of the territory to Syria in an eventual peace agreement.[27] Jordanian officials, hotly denying the proposed location on Syrian-claimed territory, accused Israel of trying to harm their relationship with Syria.[28]

The 1999 Drought

This water crisis was much more severe and garnered much stronger reaction from the Jordanian government than the 1997 'mini-crisis'; moreover, its impact on the population was considerable. As a result of lower than expected rainfall in the winter of 1998–1999, only 2 per cent of the seasonal average for December and January, Jordan was already granting aid packages to hard-hit farmers by early 1999. It declared a 'state of drought' and provided loans for livestock farmers to purchase feed.[29] By March, Jordan had developed an emergency water plan, seizing control of private wells and limiting domestic water supplies going into the summer months. Seventy per cent of the farmers in the Jordan Valley did not bother to plant seeds this summer growing season,[30] a disaster for households highly dependent on agricultural production. The amount of water pumped to agricultural areas was reduced by 10–50 per cent, depending on the region.[31]

Indeed, the whole region, including Israel and Jordan, was in the midst of the worst drought in over 50 years; the winter rains had produced only 40 per cent of normal.[32] Israel cut its water supplies to farmers by a quarter, and an official drought was expected to be declared by April.

Israeli government statements that it may cut its water supply to Jordan to meet its own domestic needs, caused a deep crisis with Jordan, the first under the leadership of its new king, Abdullah bin Hussein. Though the lower house of Jordan's parliament rejected a motion to revoke the country's peace treaty with Israel over the water issue, the introduction of this motion by Bedouin leaders, who were typically pro-government, highlights the severity of the situation as a test of the treaty.[33]

Jordanian statements at the time strongly hint at the connection between the water agreement and other portions of the peace treaty. Unnamed senior sources stated: 'Given that there are many agreements signed between the two sides, and since it is Israel, which has begun to renege on them, this makes us ready to respond in an appropriate manner,' though the exact nature of response was left vague.[34] Potential Jordanian retaliatory moves were given greater credence following statements by King Abdullah that 'if Israel wants to put pressure on Jordan on the water issue, than there are issues that Jordan can use to put pressure on Israel',[35] who at the same time mentioned Jordan's improving relations with Syria and other Arab countries.

Throughout the crisis, Israel maintained that the decision to cut water supplies to Jordan was only one option under consideration, and that the situation was under discussion through bilateral channels, expressing confidence that it would be resolved.[36] By the end of April, Israel agreed to provide Jordan with its full share of water this summer, as well as the increase promised by Netanyahu in 1997, following rejection of the proposal to cut supplies by 40 per cent.[37] Israel also gave Jordan approval to accelerate construction of the Adasiya Dam.[38] This decision was apparently based on the calculation that to risk abrogation of the treaty and its security dimension was secondary to the water issue.[39]

Despite the delivery of its full water share from Israel,[40] Jordan faced severe consequences from the drought. The United Nations provided Jordan with 15,000 tons of wheat and pulses in emergency food aid, in addition to 200,000 tons of aid from the United States.[41] In Amman, residents received water in their homes only one day a week. The effects of the drought, and news of Israel's intention to withhold water, contributed to an increasingly negative public view of Israel.

Israel's initial position on the water allocations effectively moved Jordan closer to Syria, an important development under the new reign of King Abdullah II, who adopted a policy of closer relations to the Arab world. Syria committed to supply Jordan with an additional 8 MCM of water during the summer of 1999 to combat drought conditions.[42] At the same time, the two countries signed a series of agreements on agricultural and trade issues. In 2002, Syria again increased its fresh water deliveries to Jordan beyond the 33,000 cubic meters per day provided in the 1999 agreement.[43]

In the midst of the water crisis, Jordan and Syria agreed that the damming of the Yarmouk River, a project idea that had lain idle for 40 years, should move forward.[44] Though scheduled for implementation in the 1980s, Syrian President Hafez Al-Assad, who disapproved of King Hussein's peace with Israel, had halted the construction of the Al-Wehda dam. The sudden turn-about in Jordanian-Syrian relations was initiated, when President Assad, who had surprised many observers by attending the funeral of King Hussein in February, immediately supplied drinking water to the kingdom, at Jordan's request, during its crisis with Israel.[45] The Al-Wehda dam project would produce over 100 MCM of water per year for Jordan and electric power for Syrian consumption[46].

Construction on the Al-Wehda dam began in February 2004, financed with funds from the Arab Economic and Social Fund, the Islamic Development Bank and the Abu Dhabi Development Fund. As a result, the

Jordanian-Syrian relationship will play a more central role in future water resource development.

Joint Projects: The Dead Sea–Red Sea Canal

The conflicts over water allocations in 1997 and 1999 were exacerbated by the fact that Jordan and Israel have not moved forward on major water projects called for in the treaty or in subsequent discussions of the Joint Water Committee. Many of these projects were of key importance to Jordan's economy; failing to implement them constitutes a lost opportunity to show the Jordanian public a tangible dividend of the peace, and contributes to feelings that—beyond security—the peace is not a priority for Israel.

Under the 1994 treaty, Jordan and Israel were to produce desalinated water in the Jordan Valley, using brackish water supplied by Israel. The plant was expected to cost $150 million, towards which Israel would supply $50 million.[47] To date, the plant still has not been constructed, nor does it look likely to be built any time soon, despite a provision in the treaty that states: 'Saline springs currently diverted to the Jordan River are earmarked for desalination within four years.'[48]

Nor has there been much movement on the Dead Sea–Red Sea canal project, anticipated to produce 851 MCM of water per year: 580 MCM for Jordan, 150 MCM for Palestine and 50–70 MCM for Israel, plus hydroelectric power.[49] This 299-kilometre canal would also promote tourism in the Jordan Valley by saving the Dead Sea. Due to the constant diversion for irrigation from the Jordan River, the amount of water eventually reaching the Dead Sea is not sufficient to maintain its water levels. Forty years ago, its surface was 392 metres (1,286 feet) below sea level—today it is at 412 metres.[50] Currently, the water level is dropping at three feet per year and, without a plan to replenish its waters, the sea could 'disappear' within 50 years. A canal and pipeline, linking the Dead Sea to the Red Sea at Aqaba, was projected at an anticipated cost of $5 billion. Despite the completion of a feasibility study, the lack of progress in the Israeli-Arab conflict forestalled any progress, even before the onset of the Al Aqsa intifada put the project on hold. Israeli Foreign Minister Shimon Peres had promoted the project in 2001; referring to the canal as a 'peace conduit', he declared: 'While we are going to live politically separated; a Jordanian Kingdom, an Israeli state and a Palestinian state; economically we have to cooperate on the Dead Sea, the Red Sea, and the Jordan River.'[51] In September 2002, Israel and Jordan announced they would indeed move forward with the project, and that it would take two to three years to create a detailed plan, pending on the positive outcome of a nine-month study by the Israeli Geological Institute, assessing the ecological impact.[52] Though a joint Jordanian, Israeli and Palestinian plan was formally presented at the World Economic Forum in May 2003, funds for a final feasibility study were still lacking by June 2004.[53]

The project drew criticism from other Arab states: Egypt, Syria and Lebanon protested that the project would violate Arab League resolutions against normalization with Israel. The Palestinians further criticized its potential impact on the borders of a future Palestinian state.[54] The Egyptian government even threatened to rescind discounts given to Jordanian ships passing through the Suez Canal (10–15 per cent), if the country moved forward with the project.[55] Regardless of Arab opposition, Jordan faces a critical water need, as well as the economic benefit of tourism to the Dead Sea, and is keen to move forward quickly.

Though the treaty did provide a modest increase in water resources to Jordan, drought and bilateral wrangling over the delivery of this water have largely countered a positive assessment of this aspect of the treaty in the eyes of the Jordanian public. While the diplomatic skirmishing in 1997 and 1999 over water allocations may indeed be a normal part of state-to-state relations, it placed a serious strain on the newly formed relationships and the immature peace. Israel's initial refusal to deliver the water Jordan believed it was owed was viewed by many in Jordan as an attempt to backtrack on the treaty. Unfortunately, the timing of the water scarcity and droughts coincided with the overall collapse of the Israeli-Palestinian peace process. This made it possible, in Jordanian eyes, to see a connection between the two issues, especially since a number of elements were common to both the water delivery incident and the Israeli-Palestinian peace process. The water issue was caused by a differing 'interpretation' of the treaty, with Israel determining to meet its obligation to Jordan through the creation of future water sources. Such differences in interpretation were already a major factor in the deteriorating peace process; when they became the focus of the water issue, they heightened the annoyance of a Jordanian public already sensitive to any perceived attempt by Israel to renege on its commitments. Indeed, statements made in the Jordanian parliament at the time echo the language of the Israeli-Palestinian conflict:

> The House of Representatives condemns Israel's position and its attitude towards Jordan's right to its water, which is a legitimate national right, and not a favour or grant given by Israel whenever it wants. This is also a violation that amounts to weaselling out of the peace agreement and that casts doubts on the sincerity of Israeli intentions towards the peace process.[56]

And some people drew even more explicit connections between the water issue and the Israeli-Palestinian conflict:

> Independent Member of Parliament Salama Al-Hiyari, who represents the hardest hit area of the Jordan Valley, says the water Jordan gets from Israel does not compensate for the 2 million Palestinian refugees who fled to Jordan because of Israel's independence in 1948, and its occupation of the Jordan held West Bank in 1967.[57]

Though the Israeli compromise resolved the water crisis and kept the treaty intact, at least from their perspective, neither party has taken measures to prevent future conflict. Future water scarcity remains a likely future flashpoint between Jordan and Israel.

6

ECONOMIC COOPERATION AND TRADE: LITTLE KNOWN TANGIBLE RESULTS

The peace treaty places great emphasis on the role of economic relations in creating peace, declaring economic development and prosperity the 'pillars of peace, security and harmonious relations between states, peoples and individual human beings…'.[1] Indeed, economic relations, though moulded and regulated at the macro-level between governments, clearly impact on individuals and families at the micro-level. The realization of the economic benefits of peace with Israel was a major motivator in Jordan's decision to sign a treaty. Furthermore, the expectation of tangible economic benefits for the people of Jordan was the government's main means of selling the treaty to an often-unenthusiastic public. The anticipated post-peace foreign investments and other economic opportunities were expected to 'kill the spectre of unemployment and poverty in Jordan'.[2]

In many ways, economic benefits have been some of the most tangible results of the peace treaty. Jordan has greatly reduced its external debt and trade between the two countries has grown. The joint production of goods in the Qualified Industrial Zones (QIZ) is a concrete manifestation of the peace, creating both revenue and much needed jobs. Jordan's Free Trade Agreement with the United States will have the most significant long term economic impact on the country's economy; ironically, despite its origins in the Jordanian-Israeli peace, the FTA may eventually diminish current Jordanian-Israeli economic cooperation.

And yet, disappointments within the Jordanian-Israeli economic relations persist, especially on behalf of Jordan. The goal of this chapter is to take stock, not only of the positive achievements, but also of areas where outcomes have been less than expected. In assessing the economic relations between the two states, it is necessary to keep the overall regional economic climate in mind, which has worsened considerably in the last five years. With the onset of the Al Aqsa *intifada*, heightened Israeli military activity in the West Bank and the Gaza Strip, the impact of the 11 September 2001 attacks in the United States and the 2003 US-led war in Iraq, economic relations have suffered several severe external shocks.

The external environment, however, is only partially responsible for the failure to realize the full potential of Jordanian-Israeli economic cooperation. Technical bilateral issues, such as transportation procedures, security measures and administrative barriers, have taken a great toll on the relationship. The anti-normalization movement in Jordan also suppresses more extensive Jordanian participation and widespread public recognition of the existing cooperative efforts' economic benefits.

Jordanian Expected Economic Benefits

Future economic benefit figured prominently in Jordan's decision to move forward towards peace with Israel. First, the Jordanian government expected to receive immediate economic relief and future foreign investment from the United States and other governments that supported the peace treaty. Secondly, direct economic relations with Israel were expected to produce new trade opportunities, including in the West Bank, and a growth in tourism. Given the political sensitivity to making peace with Israel among the Jordanian population, most of whom are Palestinian, economic benefits were placed front and centre in the marketing of the peace to Jordanians.

Among the earliest disappointments was the failure of donor countries, such as Germany, France and Japan, to follow the US lead and forgive Jordan's debt. Though Britain made a minor reduction in Jordan's debt, the kingdom still owed $5.5 billion in 1995, most of it to Britain, Germany, France and Japan.[3] President Bill Clinton agreed to cancel $702 million of Jordan's debt to the United States, nearly three-quarters of what the kingdom owes the USA, over a three-year period.[4]

The United States provided additional economic benefit to Jordan as a result of the peace. Economic aid to Jordan through the US Agency for International Development and other programs increased, as did military aid. In fiscal year 1996, Jordan was granted a $182.7 million aid package; though it was the third largest in the Middle East, the value was tiny compared to the billions received by Israel and Egypt each year.[5] Jordan has continued to receive larger amounts of US foreign aid, totalling $384.5 million in fiscal year 2004,[6] in part for its support for the United States in the Iraq War, and its role as a voice of moderation in a region that the US government perceives as increasingly overtaken by extremism.

Jordan reaped further economic and security benefits in December 1996, when it received $100 million of US military equipment under the defence security assistance program. Items supplied included tanks, personnel carriers, and a C-130 transport plane. The month before, the country had been granted the status of a non-North Atlantic Treaty Organisation (NATO) ally, allowing it to receive advanced US military equipment and technology.[7] The peace agreement moved Jordan closer to the United States in many ways; most significantly, it paved the way for a free trade agreement between both countries, described in more detail later in this chapter.

General Jordanian perceptions of the bilateral economic benefits of the peace treaty range from satisfaction, especially in the official press, to harsh criticism. Over the last ten years, a general lowering of expectations of both the Israeli and Jordanian governments and business communities has taken place. Unlike the first few years after the treaty, there is little mention today of the future economic benefits from peace.

Jordanian assessments made shortly after the peace treaty reflected a slow start and perhaps an unrealistic expectation as to how quickly relations could move forward and benefits be realized. Barely two months after the peace treaty, disappointment with the economic benefits was already pulling down the Jordanian stock market. At the year's end, the market showed its first year-to-year fall, down 9.4 per cent from 1993. Israel's refusal to open the Palestinian market was blamed for this drop.[8] Indeed, access to the Palestinian market would remain, and still is today, a continuous source of friction. A year later, reports indicated that Jordanians were still looking for tangible benefits from the peace and a delivery on 'empty promises'. Despite some progress in the field of tourism, even the Israeli newspaper *Ma'ariv* noted the lack of real economic cooperation, stating: 'The first year of open relations between the sides has been wasted.' Other observers, however, argued that the peace was deepening creating a climate of trust that would draw additional entrepreneurs.[9]

Noted Jordanian political analyst Rami Khouri assessed the treaty at the two- and five-year marks. In 1996, he found slow but steady growth in areas such as transport, tourism, security and water, but a failure to move forward on the big 'showcase' projects promised in the treaty and associated agreements.[10] To this day, most of these 'showcase projects' remain unrealized, and their fundamental economic feasibility and the wisdom of including them in bilateral plans are questioned.

Five years after the peace, there was optimism about two key areas of cooperation: tourism and the QIZ. In 1995, in the midst of hopes for a permanent Middle East peace, the growth in tourism could be described as a 'boom' that generated new investments, jobs and foreign currency inflows. The first Qualified Industrial Zone, whose duty-free access to the US market had already led to several hundred millions of dollars of new investments and more than 3,000 jobs, operates in Irbid (Jordan). It comprised more than 80 companies and $500 million of exports in 1998, and plans were made to double its capacity in the following two years, with three more QIZ projected to open in 2000.[11]

By October 2000, the situation in the region had changed dramatically; the optimism of 1999 was dashed, as the Al Aqsa *intifada* and Israeli military operations in the Palestinian territories affected the Israeli-Jordanian relationship. A year-end report in the *Jordan Times* noted: 'The sixth anniversary of the peace treaty went unnoticed in October as businessmen and officials lamented peace that was once heralded as a cure for the country's economic woes.'[12] Four years later, general economic relations seem to have moved little beyond where they stood in 1999, with the notable exception of the QIZ. Worse, the tourism boom has ended, and many in the tourism industry find themselves in a more difficult economic situation than before the peace (see Chapter Seven).

The Impact of the Regional Situation

Economics and politics often cannot be separated; economic relations between Jordan and Israel have always been responsive to changes in the overall relations between the two countries and the deterioration of the regional peace process. In the aftermath of the Naharayim incident, for example, Jordanian officials accused Israel of downsizing trade activity between the two countries and adopting negative policies towards Jordanian products, including excessive security checks and delays.[13] Indeed, security-related issues remain a point of tension within the economic relationship, particularly when suspected to fulfil political instead of real security goals. In another incident in early 1997, Jordanian officials boycotted a ceremony for a new air link with Israel out of displeasure over the deteriorating peace process and Israel's role in it. Though not directly calling for abrogation of the peace treaty, one official stated: 'Jordan is committed to all its agreements with Israel, but is not going out of its way to show any warmth as long as the Israelis are not forthcoming in their dealing with other Arabs.'[14] Formal ties further deteriorated following the onset of the Al Aqsa *intifada*. By October 2003, when the Jordanian Minister for the Economy, Dr. Mohammad Abu-Hammour, attended an economic conference at the Sheikh Hussein border crossing, it had been three years since a member of the Jordanian government had set foot on Israeli territory.[15]

At the regional level, the Middle East and North Africa (MENA) summits, a tangible result of the peace process in which Jordan had been the key facilitator, ceased amid rising political tension. Established in the euphoric period following the Declaration of Principles between Israel and the Palestinians, the first MENA summit was held in Casablanca (1994), followed by Amman (1995) and Cairo (1996). Although Libya, Lebanon and Syria boycotted each of these meetings because of Israeli presence, the summits had sought to address regional economic issues and to strengthen peaceful relations between Israel and the Arab states. By late 1996, however, the stalled peace process had taken its toll; cooperative projects agreed upon in the previous meetings had not moved forward and regional projects were not on the agenda for the Cairo meeting.[16]

The last MENA meeting in 1997 became a flashpoint for worsening Israeli-Arab relations. Few Arab states agreed to attend; numerous countries, including Morocco, Algeria, Egypt, the United Arab Emirates and Bahrain, boycotted the conference. The attending countries lowered their level of representation; instead of the foreign ministers, who had attended in the past, representatives now included undersecretaries from the trade and industry ministry (Oman) and finance ministry (Kuwait). For protocol reasons, the Israeli Foreign Ministry subsequently had to lower the level of their delegation, where earlier Prime Ministers Rabin and Peres had attended.[17] Yet, amid the tension of the Doha meeting, Jordan and Israel quietly signed an agreement on the sidelines to establish a joint industrial zone with United States support.[18] Though Jordan and Israel would have signed the agreement anyway, the time and location of the signing were a gift to the US hosts of the MENA conference.

Jordan's move was considered controversial, not only because of the state of the peace process, but because Israel was blocking trade between Jordan and the Palestinian Authority at the time. Reactions, however, were mixed; while one Jordanian expert cited Israeli plans 'to penetrate our markets and economically dominate the region', another lauded the agreement's potential to give Jordanian products unlimited access to the US market.[19]

Attempts to reinvigorate regional economic cooperation within broader frameworks, such as the World Economic Forum held at the Dead Sea in June 2003 and 2004, have not yet produced extensive results and are compounded by investor concerns regarding stability in the region. Though plans for a Middle East/North Africa common market, a regional development bank and a tourism board exist, Arab leadership warns that cooperation with Israel 'would only be possible with resumption of the peace process'.[20] Given that real movement on the peace process at present seems unlikely, and that relations with most Arab states will remain chilly at best, the Israeli minister of Trade and Labour called for 'a distinction to be made between political altercations and business related cooperation when it comes to Israel, Jordan and the Palestinian Authority'.[21] So far, however, this has not happened.

Looking towards a reconfigured regional economy in the aftermath of the Iraq War, King Abdullah has proposed to set up an economic zone that would include Israel, Jordan, the Palestinians and the new Iraq.[22] According to a report in *Al-Arab Al-Yawm*, Jordanian businessmen have rejected offers from American companies to cooperate with their Israeli counterparts to get contracts in Iraq, which has been opened to Israeli companies possessing the advanced technology considered necessary by senior US officials to contribute to reconstruction and investment in this country.[23] Indeed, despite Jordanian support for the Iraq War, which caused considerable internal discord, Jordanian firms report difficulties in obtaining contracts to supply goods and services to the Iraq reconstruction effort. At present, it is not yet clear how regime change in Iraq will impact on Jordanian-Israeli economic ties.

Jordan and Israel: Economic Profiles

Economic relations between Jordan and Israel must be understood within the context of their vastly differing economic circumstances. The Israeli economy dwarfs that of Jordan. Though the population difference between the two countries is not that significant, with Israel at 6.1 million people (2002) and Jordan at 5.4 million (2003), Israel's gross domestic product has a purchasing power equivalent of $ 117.4 billion dollars (2002), while Jordan's is only $22.63 billion.[24] The two economies are at different stages of development and have different needs. With a per capita GNI of $1,760 (2002), Jordan is striving to rise above its lower middle-income classification, while Israel, a high-income country, has a per capita GNI of $16,020.[25] This disparity contributes to concerns that Israel benefits more from the peace and can exert more control over the bilateral economic relations. Moreover, Israel has far greater economic opportunities than Jordan and is much less dependent on the potential economic benefits of peace.

Israel has realized significant economic opportunity in the period since the peace treaty, which almost ended the—officially still existing—Arab boycott of Israeli products, clearing the way for potentially large increases in regional trade. Israeli trade with the European Union, Turkey and Asia also increased; Asian trade grew from $3.0 billion in 1990 to $8.2 billion in 1999. Foreign direct investment reached $5.3 billion in 2000, compared to an average of $400 million during 1985–1995, and is significantly higher than investment levels in Jordan, which averaged around $350 million per year between 1997–2001.[26] Though Israel's overall economic performance cannot be attributed to the peace treaty alone, it has supplied expanded opportunities.

While economic difficulties motivated Jordan to make peace with Israel, Jordan today is in a much-improved macro-economic position, with economic growth averaging almost 6 per cent in real terms throughout the

1990s.[27] Though the Iraq War lowered GDP growth to 3.2 per cent in 2003, a growth rate of 5.5 per cent was anticipated in 2004. Moreover, Jordan's debt, which once stood at over 200 per cent of GDP in the late 1980s, is now $9.8 billion or 92.4 per cent of GDP and projected to decline to 80 per cent by 2007. The inflation rate has also remained steady at 3 to 3.5 per cent.[28]

Jordan's economic recovery is the result of a major reform program launched in response to poor growth in the mid–late 1990s, when growth ranged between 1–2 per cent a year. Though Jordan began to work closely with the International Monetary Fund prior to King Abdullah's ascension in 1999, the pace of reform has accelerated under his leadership. Abdullah declared the economy his top priority, instituted a privatization program in 2000 and a five-year reform plan in 2001.[29] In the short term, however, the population has had to bear much economic 'belt-tightening'. As the state has reduced its foreign aid dependency, the government's ability to direct resources to constituencies that provide the population's traditional base of support has also declined, leading to dissatisfaction.[30] Income inequality is great, with half of the country's one million-strong workforce earning $1,200 in per capita income and nearly 30 per cent earning only $800.[31] These factors reinforce the government's need to demonstrate significant economic gains from its relationship with Israel.

Despite economic change in Jordan, this economic asymmetry will continue to be a part of the bilateral relationship and affect each country's perception of the other. Generally, Israel tends to view the QIZ and especially the FTA as benefits Israel brought to Jordan, a by-product of their close relationship with the United States. Israeli economists and academics speak of what the Jordanian economy would have looked like without the peace, while Jordanians tend to focus on the anticipated economic benefits that did not materialize. While undoubtedly the QIZ and FTA would not have happened without Israel, this fact evokes a complex reaction even from Jordan's strongest peace supporters: appreciative of the benefits, but uncomfortable with the feeling and reality of dependency on Israel that they produced. This feeling is compounded by frustration that Israelis seem to feel that the QIZ and the FTA are sufficient economic outcomes of the peace treaty and have not moved forward on other areas of bilateral economic relationship. At the same time, Jordanians also fear a 'takeover' of Jordan's economy by Israel and are resistant to further cooperation.

Treaty Provisions

The Jordanian-Israeli peace treaty refers to economic development and prosperity as 'pillars of peace' and affirms their 'mutual desire to promote economic cooperation between them, as well as within the framework of wider regional economic cooperation'.[32] To this end, Jordan and Israel sought to remove barriers to normal economic relations and to promote economic cooperation, including trade, the establishment of a free-trade area, investment, banking, and industrial relations.[33] A separate article was devoted specifically to the development of tourism (Article 17), joint development of Aqaba and Eilat (Article 23) and the integrated development of the Jordan Rift Valley area (Article 20).

The development of infrastructure has played a key role in facilitating the bilateral economic relationship. Of major importance are transportation corridors between Jordan and Israel:

> ...following the 1994 Israeli-Jordanian peace agreement, one of the first infrastructure projects between the two countries was rebuilding the King Hussein Bridge located in the Jordan Valley south of the Sea of Galilee. The Israelis destroyed the bridge on the eve of the 1948 war in order to block the advance of the Arab Legion into Israel. Nowadays, as in the pre-1948 period, this bridge serves as the main transportation link between Israel and Jordan.[34]

Today, the Sheikh Hussein crossing is crucial to the export of products from the QIZ through Haifa port to overseas markets, especially the United States. Trade volume with a value of nearly $1.2 billion is expected to pass through the bridge in 2004, with 100–120 trucks crossing daily.[35]

In accordance with the treaty, Jordan also removed legal barriers to economic relations with Israel. In 1995, the Jordanian parliament cancelled Law 66 (1953) that outlawed trade with Israel and the Unified Boycott Law (1958), under which Jordan participated in the general Arab boycott of Israel. The parliament also adopted new legislation, which opened the Jordanian economy to foreign ownership, ending the discrimination against non-Arab investors, facilitating foreign investment, and allowing repatriation of capital by Israelis and other foreigners.[36]

The treaty also called for a number of 'mega-projects' to facilitate Jordanian-Israeli cooperation and to showcase the benefits of peace to Jordanians and Israelis, as well as the international community. Many of these projects, such as the Jordan Gateway and 'peace airport', are not part of the treaty but were discussed at the same time and are linked to the promotion of the peace. There is now a growing recognition, especially among Israelis, that these projects might have been unrealistic:

> Israel initiated economic relations with Jordan on the wrong footing, when it presented overly ambitious and mostly unrealistic regional and bilateral projects. The problems started as early as the Casablanca

Conference, in which the Israelis were over-enthusiastic and not sufficiently sensitive to the concerns of their Arab interlocutors. While presentation of these projects was perfectly legitimate—because it illustrated the prospects that peace has to offer for regional prosperity, proposed a vision for the future and created a positive climate and setting for the peace process—the Israelis failed to explain to their Arab associates, and perhaps did not themselves understand, that long-term visions and concrete plans are not necessarily one and the same.[37]

Unfortunately, these projects were an integral part of the 'vision of peace' used to promote the treaty in Jordan; failure to realize these key projects contributes to beliefs that Israel does not abide by conditions of the peace.

Finally, the treaty provided for several projects focused on the development of tourism infrastructure, and designed to boost tourism and economic growth in the southern cities of Aqaba (Jordan) and Eilat (Israel). A cornerstone of the joint development plan was the creation of the 'Peace Airport' in Aqaba–Eilat. These projects are discussed in Chapter Seven.

Trade and Investment

Qualified Industrial Zones (QIZ)

Essentially, the QIZ are free trade areas that operate in specific locations in Jordan; most are located relatively close to the Jordanian-Israeli border. The goal of the QIZ program, established by the United States in 1996, is twofold: to promote cooperation between the business communities in Israel and Jordan, and to support Jordanian overall economic growth. Factories operating in a QIZ have the benefit of duty free export to the United States, and are not subject to quota restrictions for entering the US market.

Eleven QIZs are located in Jordan, though only seven are currently operating. Key QIZs include two in Irbid (Al-Hassan Industrial Estate and Jordan Cyber City), two in the Zarqa area (Al-Dulayl Industrial Park, El-Zai Readywear Manufacturing Company), three in Amman (Al-Tajamouat Industrial Estate, Al-Qastal Industrial Zone, Mushatta International Complex), and one each in Kerak (Kerak Industrial Estate) and Aqaba (Aqaba Industrial Estate). The Israel-Jordan Gateway QIZ is located on the northern border.

Under the QIZ guidelines, products must have at least 35 per cent of their appraised value added within the zone, with a minimum of 11.7 per cent coming from the Jordanian manufacturer, 8 per cent from the Israelis, and the remainder of 35 per cent can come from a Jordan QIZ, Israel, the

USA or the West Bank and Gaza. Jordanian and Israeli manufacturers must contribute at least 20 per cent of the total cost of production of goods.[38] Almost immediately, concern was raised in Jordan over the level of Israeli input, originally set at 11.7 per cent. Jordanian businessmen feared that such a high level, with its associated higher costs, would reduce competitiveness. By 1998, the Israeli component requirement was reduced to 8 per cent.[39]

Investment in the QIZ is dominated by the textile and apparel industries that take advantage of the free trade status with the USA. As 65 per cent of the production expenditure can come from anywhere in the world, international investors are heavily involved. In the Al-Hassan Industrial Estate, the first full-functioning QIZ, six of the 15 operating companies are wholly or partly Jordanian owned, two are Chinese, two are Pakistani, two are American, one is Indian, one is Taiwanese and one is Arab-Israeli. This ownership profile is similar to those in the other QIZ.[40]

Production in the QIZ has driven Jordan's large export growth and significantly bolstered its economy. Jordanian exports to the USA rose from $25 million in 1999, a year after the first QIZ became operational, to a projected $463 million in 2003. The United States is now Jordan's largest export market, accounting for 25 per cent of the kingdom's total exports in 2002. Textiles and apparel dominate exports from the QIZ, reaching JD 359 million (approximately $500 million) in 2002.[41] Production in the QIZ enabled Jordan to show impressive export growth even following regional economic downturn, posting a 25 per cent increase in exports in 2001, much of it to the United States,[42] and in 2003, exports to the US had more than doubled the 2002 level.[43]

Though the QIZ have generated employment, Jordanians are not filling many of these jobs. Contrary to the original assumption that a triangle of Jordanian, Israeli and US investors would form to take advantage of the benefits of QIZ conditions, it is actually Asian producers, mainly from Taiwan, Hong Kong and Pakistan, who are taking advantage of the duty free status. By 2001, the QIZ were producing $10–12 million per month in exports to the USA, with the workforce expected to reach 20,000 by the end of that year.[44] Asian employees are particularly commonplace in the QIZ-based garment industry, as they are considered to be more productive. The Jordanian government is now taking measures to reduce the numbers of Chinese, Indian, Sri Lankan, and Pakistani labourers in the zones' factories. Under the government initiative, Jordanians will be trained to decrease dependency on expatriate labour. In 2002, an estimated number of over 20,000 Jordanians were working in the QIZ.[45]

The QIZ have weathered the political and economic hardships in the region far better than most other areas of economic cooperation. Perhaps illustrating the pragmatism of businesspeople, the QIZ have continued to expand following the increased Israeli-Palestinian conflict in 2000, including an investment of $1.5 million by an Israeli textile company in three Jordanian factories operating in the Al-Hassan Qualified Industrial Zone. An Israeli embassy statement indicated that the volume of trade between Jordan and Israel increased to $75.5 million during 2000. Jordanian exports to Israel reached $37 million in 2000, an 80 per cent increase over 1999.[46]

Despite the economic benefit to both parties, Jordanian businesspeople operating in the QIZ have raised a number of concerns. Criticism that Jordanian companies largely play a subcontracting role to Israeli firms again reflects the economic asymmetry between Jordan and Israel. According to the head of the Israeli embassy's trade office in Amman, 30 Jordanian textile companies are cooperating to re-export finished goods to the US market. However, only three of these firms have entered joint ventures with Israelis: 'Most of these companies are subcontracting for Israeli firms. The design is Israeli, and the sewing takes place in Jordan before the goods return to Israel to be re-exported to the United States.'[47] As a result, the major share of the profits goes to the Israeli firm, instead of the Jordanian subcontractor. In part, this is also a result of Israeli firms having greater experience achieving contracts, while Jordanian companies must overcome newness in the market, as well as general perceptions about the risk of doing business with Arab firms.

The stated country of origin for goods from the QIZ has been an additional source of tension between Jordan and Israel, as items produced under subcontract to firms in the QIZ carry the label 'made in Israel', denying any recognition to Jordan. To some critics, this enables Israel to benefit disproportionately from the QIZ arrangement: 'They bring their own raw material to Jordan, somewhat exempted from customs fees, and manufacture in Jordan, using cheap labour compared to Israel. But the label, which says "Made in Israel," is misleading. We are helping Israel to promote its products at the cost of our own.'[48] Nonetheless, Jordan and Israel have sought a trade agreement with the European Union, which would allow the EU-Israel free trade agreement to apply to products produced in the QIZ; in May 2004, they signed a treaty in preparation for the future agreement.[49] The European Union, however, refused to enter the agreement, unless Israel ceased to label products manufactured by settlers in the occupied territories as 'made in Israel'. Israel's acquiescence to this demand in August 2004 cleared the way for a future Israel-Jordan-European Union trade agreement.[50]

Despite the economic success of the QIZ, few Jordanians realize the Israeli role in these economic zones. The reluctance of the Jordanian government to widely publicize this fact, and its relationship to the Jordan-Israeli peace, is a major source of frustration for Israel. Brochures produced on the QIZ fail to mention Israeli participation, nor is their role typically noted in press releases citing the economic success of the QIZ. Though Israelis acknowledge the influence of the anti-normalization movement in Jordan, and the need for businessmen who cooperate with Israelis to keep a low profile, the failure of the government to use the QIZ as a means to sell the peace is disappointing.

Though the anti-normalization movement is the focus of Chapter Nine, the experience of the Jordanian-Israeli Chamber of Commerce bears investigation here because of its relationship to fulfilling the goal of joint economic activity. Following a report on Israeli radio about the launch of a joint Jordanian-Israeli Chamber of Commerce, Jordanian business leaders responded that they knew nothing about this, and that it was 'designed to tarnish reputation of Jordanian private sector businesses', 'by disseminating such a report, Israel aims to sabotage ties between Jordanian private sector companies and the Arab states.' They refused to hold any meetings with the Israeli side.[51] Similarly, calls to halt all business ties with Israel by organizations, such as the Jordan Businessmen's Association, in response to Israeli military operations in the occupied territories, illustrate the persistent connection between attempts to fulfil the peace treaty and the worsening Israeli-Palestinian conflict.[52]

The Jordan Gateway Project

Straddling the Jordan River, the Jordan Gateway project was planned as a symbol of bilateral cooperation following the peace treaty. Located south of the Sheikh Hussein border crossing, the joint industrial zone, both a QIZ and a free trade zone, was to be built in three phases, accepting its first tenant in 1999. Total investment in the zone was anticipated at $200 million and would produce 15,000 jobs, mostly within Jordan to benefit from Jordan's low labour costs.[53] Modelled after *maquiladora* projects along the USA-Mexico border, the Jordan Gateway was to have joint Jordanian and Israeli administration, so that individuals entering the park on either side could move freely within the zone without a passport.

The Israel-Jordan Gateway project illustrates the frustrations faced by the business communities in both countries in their attempts to establish joint economic activity. Despite the agreement of the Jordanian government, the approval of the Israeli government in 1999, and the willingness of key Israeli and Jordanian investors to participate in the project, various components of the Israeli bureaucracy intervened to stall the project, as an analysis by Mishal (et al.) demonstrates.[54] Using the same tactics they had employed to frustrate construction of the Eilat-Aqaba airport (Chapter Seven), the Israeli Ministry of the Environment, along with other groups, intervened in the various committees, denying construction permits and threatening to take developers to court. The Israeli Ministry of the Environment was not alone in its opposition to the project. In August 2000, the following NGOs released a *Joint Statement from the Middle East Environmental Community*, condemning the Jordan Gateway Project and calling on the International Finance Corporation to deny a major loan: Friends of the Earth Middle East, Society for the Protection of Nature in Israel, Royal Society for the Conservation of Nature in Jordan, Palestinian Hydrology Group, Israel Union for Environmental Defence, Green Course, and the Jordan Society for Sustainable Development.[55]

Despite the opposition of some Jordanian NGOs, progress on the Jordanian side, with its more centralized governmental system, continued, while all work on the Israeli side has been suspended, even though the Israeli government officially approved the area of the project as a QIZ on 20 May 1999.[56] Once again, there was no overall coordinating body in Israel for issues related to the Israeli-Jordanian relationship that was able to overcome bureaucratic hurdles. Instead of helping to build a strong bilateral relationship, the Jordan Gateway project had the opposite effect: 'While the obstacles confronting the developers were to be expected, the fact that these are not regular domestic projects has international consequences. Thus, rather than encouraging cooperation, these projects have created new sources of tension.'[57] In July 2004, a petition was filed with the Tel Aviv District Court to liquidate Jordan Gateway Projects, Co., ten years after the company was formed to create a free trade zone and industrial park. The largest shareholder, FIBI Holdings (40 per cent of total), invested $15.8 million. The project ran into trouble even before it opened, and the company's collapse is blamed on political and security developments in the last decade. All planning, construction and marketing work on the project, which was to employ thousands of people, has ceased.[58]

The USA-Jordan Free Trade Agreement

Perhaps the most significant economic development for Jordan is the Free Trade Agreement (FTA) with the United States. Signed in December 2001, Jordan became only the fourth country to gain this status. Under the pact, US tariffs on Jordanian imports came down almost immediately, while Jordanian tariffs will be eliminated over ten years (by 2010) in four stages. The FTA applies to products that are goods originating in Jordan. This means they have undergone a 'substantial transformation' in the country, thus preventing the possibility of imports by Jordan from other countries. FTA defines 'goods originating' in Jordan as articles for which the sum of the cost or value of the materials produced in the kingdom plus direct costs of processing in Jordan 'is not less than 35 per cent minimum on the Jordanian value added'. Previously, Jordan had duty free access only through the Qualified Industrial Zones, which required an Israeli contribution to the value added.[59] Under the FTA, Jordanian products will have direct access to the USA.

It is not yet clear what impact the FTA will have on the comparative advantage of the QIZ, though it could undermine the need for Jordanian-Israeli cooperation in manufacturing. During the initial period of the FTA, when tariffs and quotas are being eliminated on specific items, manufacturers may find it advantageous to produce some items under QIZ regulations and others under the FTA. Even after full implementation of the FTA, some investors may find it difficult to achieve the full 35 per cent Jordanian value added and opt for the lower QIZ requirement. The QIZ face another risk: the phasing out of the Multilateral Fibre Agreement by 2005 might eliminate the US quotas that currently make QIZ production so attractive to Asian manufacturers. Though Jordan will still have the advantage of duty free access, it may find itself competing on price grounds with ultra-cheap producers such as China.[60]

A study by the Jordanian Ministry of Industry and Commerce, in cooperation with the Jordanian Qualified Zones (QIZ), found that Jordanian-Israeli projects in the QIZ will lose their economic feasibility in the long run. They related this conclusion to the fact that the ratio of Israeli manufacturing components in the products produced in the QIZ will increase from 8 to 11.7 per cent in 2004. Jordanian investors fear that the Israeli components will make the products (mostly garments) more expensive and risk loosing competitiveness.[61] This issue is of great concern to Israeli investors, who fear that Jordanians may view the QIZ is a temporary phenomenon to be replaced by the FTA, at which point the incentive for Israeli-Jordanian cooperation would be lost.

Bilateral Trade Issues

A number of issues impact on trade relations, both in QIZ-related trade and non-QIZ trade. Though Jordanian exports through Israel have increased dramatically, actual bilateral trade between Jordan and Israel, not including the flow of inputs into QIZ produced items, has developed very slowly. Shortly after the peace treaty, merchandise trade between the two countries was described as 'meagre', representing less than 1 per cent of each country's total trade bill. One analyst summed up the situation:

> While Israel can sell Jordan quite a lot of things, trade in the other direction is more problematic, with few Jordanian products capable of competing in Israel's larger market. The overall balance of trade between the two consistently favours Israel. Jordanians, on the other hand, blame strict Israeli requirements, in the name of quality control, for the modest trade figures.[62]

In ten years, merchandise trade has scarcely increased over 1999 levels, when it was described as a 'mere trickle'.[63] According to Hani Khalili of the Amman Chamber of Commerce, 'trade exchanges between neighbouring states normally run into hundreds of millions of dollars, but peace between the two sides has not matured yet and economic ties are faltering.'[64]

Exports to Israel remain a small portion of Jordan's total domestic exports, increasing from 2.3 per cent of total exports in 1998 to 5.6 per cent in 2002 (Table 6.1). Though Jordanian exports to Israel as a percentage of total jumped to 19.6 per cent in 2002, this was largely the result of a dramatic decrease in the share of trade with Iraq in the prelude to the Iraq War in 2003. The total value of Israel's trade with Jordan has increased considerably in the last decade, from $9 million in 1996 to $86.8 million in 2003, but as a percentage it only accounts for less than one percent (0.27 per cent) of total Israeli exports and imports (Table 6.2).

Trade growth has indeed proceeded slowly, with Jordanian and Israeli critics citing the following hindrances on growth: cumbersome border procedures and high tariffs, as well as quality control and health standards.[65] In an attempt to stimulate trade, beginning in 1995, Israel and Jordan signed a series of protocols, which have been extended numerous times,[66] most recently in May 2004; however, most agreements benefit production in the QIZ rather than merchandise trade.[67]

Hindrances to Economic Cooperation

Transportation Issues

Establishing a rapid and economically viable transportation system to facilitate trade between Jordan and Israel has been a difficult task. The initial transportation agreement took 15 months to negotiate, but Jordanian and Israeli businessmen still confront major transportation obstacles relating to the method and mode of delivery, and security and customs regulations. Of crucial concern are continued problems encountered by trucks passing through the Sheikh Hussein crossing. As Jordan is served by only one port, in the far southern city of Aqaba, most products manufactured in the QIZ are exported via Haifa port in Israel. Shipments leave from the Jordanian QIZ—generally in the northern section of the country—by truck, enter Israel at the Sheikh Hussein crossing and continue to Haifa. Israeli inputs in QIZ production also pass through this crossing. The Sheik Hussein crossing is a key economic artery, expected to handle trade valuing $1–$1.2 billion in 2004. A variety of problems currently limit the crossing's ability to efficiently handle this trade and to expand its capacity to meet very large anticipated future growth, estimated at $3–5 billion per year.

Table 6.1 Jordan: Domestic exports by major countries of destination (2001–2002, in thousands US dollar).*

Country	1998† Value	% of total	1999 Value	% of total	2000‡ Value	% of total	2001 Value	% of total	2002 Value	% of total	2003 Value	% of total
Total	1,475,856		1,482,867		1,524,425		1,907,434		2,195,695		2,362,588	
USA	7,896	0.5	13,144	0.9	63,255	4.1	232,090	12.2	429,327	19.6	664,154	28.1
Iraq	149,725	10.1	113,330	7.6	141,118	9.3	422,223	22.1	439,825	20.0	315,913	13.4
India	164,996	11.2	254,650	17.2	242,934	15.9	204,968	10.7	225,309	10.3	198,907	8.4
Saudi Arabia	146,293	9.9	140,502	9.5	129,829	8.5	134,776	7.1	148,574	6.8	154,279	6.5
Israel	34,207	2.3	52,839	3.6	77,962	5.1	102,755	5.4	122,870	5.6	96,635	4.1
U.A.E.	81,763	5.5	87,092	5.9	67,190	4.4	83,020	4.4	79,788	3.6	92,722	3.9
Syria	21,560	1.5	18,656	1.3	23,329	1.5	36,158	1.9	65,897	3.0	90,212	3.8
Lebanon	42,262	2.9	31,573	2.1	34,024	2.2	39,007	2.0	48,884	2.2	45,966	1.9
Other Arab countries	657,859	44.6	601,834	40.6	212,812	14.0	245,131	12.9	261,874	12.0	276,743	11.7
Other countries	169,295	11.5	169,247	11.3	531,972	34.9	407,306	21.4	373,347	17.0	427,057	18.1

* Converted from Jordanian Dinars at 1 USD=JD 0.709.
† Source: Personal Communication Yitzhak Gal.
‡ Source: Bank of Jordan, Monthly Statistical Bulletin, Table 38; http://uploads.batelco.jo/cbj/uploads/38.xls.

Table 6.2 Israeli trade with Jordan compared to total Israeli exports and imports (Israeli data, in millions US dollar).

		Israeli Exports				Israeli Imports		
	To Jordan	Total	% of total	% growth	From Jordan	Total	% of total	% growth
Year								
1996	9.0	20,511	0.04	NA	5.0	29,948	0.02	NA
1997	20.1	22,504	0.09	123.3	12.5	29,023	0.04	150.0
1998	25.3	23,305	0.11	25.9	17.1	27,469	0.06	36.8
1999	21.0	25,804	0.08	-17.0	20.4	31,086	0.07	19.3
2000	38.9	31,404	0.12	85.2	36.7	35,750	0.10	79.9
2001	52.4	29,081	0.18	34.7	42.0	33,303	0.13	14.4
2002	69.1	29,347	0.24	31.9	47.9	33,106	0.14	14.0
2003	86.8	31,577	0.27	25.6	44.5	34,213	0.13	-7.1

Source: Israel, Central Bureau of Statistics, Monthly Bulletin of Statistics, December 2003; http://www.cbs.gov.il/fr_trade/td1.xls and CBS, Selected Data series, compiled by Yitzhak Gal.

Due to security considerations, a back-to-back delivery method is in place. Under this arrangement, merchandise is transferred from trucks parked on one side of the border to trucks on the other side under the inspection of Israeli security guards.[68] Currently, 100–120 trucks pass through the crossing daily, a number expected to rise to 300–500 trucks per day. The back-to-back method of delivery, however, significantly increases both the costs to the manufacturer and the time for delivery. A truck arriving from the Jordanian side must clear customs and border control on the Jordanian side of the border and unload the cargo onto a waiting truck under Israeli security control. Though trucks can enter the Jordanian side of the crossing as early as 8 am, operational procedures by the Jordanians and Israeli security procedures mean that the first trucks do not enter the Israeli side of the crossing until midday; the last truck is accepted at 5 pm. Therefore, the crossing's capacity is fully utilized only a few hours a day, generally during midday and afternoon. As security procedures do not permit the overnight parking of trucks at the Israel side of the crossing, Jordan cannot begin to process trucks to be admitted to Israel early the next day near the closing hours. The opening and closing times of the Israeli and Jordanian sides of the border crossing are also not fully coordinated. These impediments, combined with the scheduling demands of the back-to-back system, requiring constant coordination between a specific truck arriving at one side and another truck to receive the load on the other side, cause severe congestion and delays for trucks coming through both sides of the border.[69]

The entry of Jordanian drivers into the Israeli side of the crossing is also problematic, involving both security and administrative issues. From the Israeli perspective, the entrance of Jordanian drivers poses a great security risk; it is often difficult for Jordanian shipping agents to get visas for their drivers, with some companies reporting waits of up to three years. Even with a visa, drivers must endure long waits in open waiting areas without access to food and beverages, while security checks are performed. The trucks themselves must also be inspected before entering the Israeli side of the crossing; Jordanian trucks often fail inspection based on Israeli safety standards, but Jordanian shippers say they cannot get a clear indication of what the standards are, as the list given to drivers of safety violations is not same in Hebrew and Arabic, all of which adds to the confusion.

These issues frustrate both Israeli and Jordanian manufacturers and encourage the view that security and safety concerns are being used to protect Israeli shipping companies, rather than to meet real security needs. Shippers and investors in both countries, in conjunction with the Israel-Jordan Chamber of Commerce, have worked together to devise potential solutions to these problems, such as: coordination of working hours between Israeli and Jordanian customs, working with Israeli security to create a list of approved Jordanian drivers, creating of a 'multiple-entry pass', and making arrangements for overnight stays on the Israeli side. Though there is much agreement among the users of the Sheikh Hussein crossing on what needs to be done, changes can only be made by the relevant authorities. The 'Crossings Committee', chaired by the heads of customs from both countries, was originally created to deal with such problems, but has not met in several years. In fact, according to Gal, '…all formal or informal forums between the relevant authorities on both sides, have been deactivated over recent years. Thus, there is no mechanism for joint working through the problems coordinating operations or development plans for the border crossing.'[70]

An Immovable Bureaucracy

Bureaucratic hurdles, especially on the Israeli side, frustrate attempts to ameliorate the bilateral economic relationship. Though the bureaucracy may not intentionally seek to quash economic relations between the two states, this is often the net result of the failure to overcome these obstacles. A colloquium, held in June 2003 under the auspices of the Peres Centre for Peace and the University Institute for Diplomacy and Regional Cooperation at Tel Aviv University, identified numerous obstacles and failures in Jordanian-Israeli bilateral relations. The Israeli bureaucracy, and a lack of political will to surmount its shortcomings, was identified as a major barrier to expanding bilateral cooperation:

A basic obstacle mentioned by many participants is the large number of Israeli agencies that deal with relations with Jordan. For example, the developers of the Jordan Gateway project had to go through 29 different planning committees. While in Aqaba, there is one central agency in charge (ASEZA), in Eilat five or six agencies operate. Moreover, the various Israeli agencies involved sometimes take conflicting positions. There is no single entity in Israel that is in charge of economic relations with Jordan and gives them high priority.[71]

All the following Israeli governmental bodies control some aspect of the crossing: the airport authority, customs, police, the ministries of agriculture, health, transportation, security and defence, two sections of the ministry of foreign affairs (Jordan and Middle East economy divisions), the anti-terror commission in the prime minister's office, and the Haifa port authority.

The problem of visas for Jordanian businessmen, most of them investors in QIZ enterprises, is a further illustration of bureaucratic obstruction. To obtain an Israeli visa, they need a letter of invitation and the processing time is one month. Typically, however, requests for visas are refused without explanation. The Israel-Jordan Chamber of Commerce, an Israel-based organization, has tried to get clarification from the Ministry of Foreign Affairs regarding their policy towards Jordanian business, but has had little success. As a result, Jordanian manufacturers cannot meet with their Israeli partners in Israel. Though not stated ambiguous security concerns are suspected as the reason for visa denials.

Access to the Palestinian Market

Another major source of frustration among Jordanian manufacturers and exporters is the inability to gain access to the West Bank market. Israel tightly controls trade between Jordan and the West Bank, often citing security concerns. Many in Jordan, as well as some former Israeli security officers and economists, suspect that the real goal is to keep this lucrative market closed for the advantage of Israeli businessmen. Chief among Jordanian complaints are the delays on the King Hussein/Allenby Bridge and the imposition of the back-to-back delivery method.[72] Jordanian businesspersons cite delays, financial losses and damaged goods as results of Israeli actions. The disparity between Israeli and Jordanian trade further reinforces Jordanian belief that the West Bank is a captured market. The kingdom's exports to the Palestinian market in 1998 stood at $23 million dollars, compared with Israel's $2 billion dollars.[73] By 1999, Israeli trade with the territories was estimated at $2.5–3 billion per year.[74]

Israel controls the Jordanian-Palestinian trade through the exercise of tariffs and security checks at the border. With the imposition of back-to-back delivery methods,[75] the costs of Jordanian products increase; one estimate found that $70 was added to the cost of a ton of Jordanian produce delivered to the West Bank, making it uncompetitive with Israeli products. As a result, Jordanian-Palestinian trade was lower at the end of the 1990s than it was in the 1980s. Jordanian economists estimate the potential for Jordanian-West Bank trade at $500 million a year; in 1997, Jordan exported only $7 million to the West Bank, a potential important source of trade for Jordan, as the Iraq War has almost eliminated trade with Iraq, its former main trading partner. Many Jordanians see economics, rather than security concerns, as the prime motivation for Israel to keep the West Bank as a captive market, arguing that:

> By maintaining control over borders, using security as a pretext and imposing tariff and non-tariff barriers, Israel has tightened its stranglehold on the fledgling Palestinian economy and retained its multi-billion dollar captive market by minimizing competition from other countries.[76]

Though Jordan signed trade accords with both Israel and the Palestine National Authority in 1996, its exporters argue that strict security measures, based on protectionist practices, and stringent standards and specifications keep Jordanian goods out of the West Bank.[77] Cement sales of 1.2 million tonnes to the Palestinian territories by the Israeli company Nesher in 1997, compared to Jordanian sales of 100,000 tonnes, are cited as one example of protectionist motives.[78]

Today, on the eve of its ten-year anniversary, the QIZ and the Free Trade Agreement constitute the most substantial economic outcome of the Jordan-Israel peace. Though numerous obstacles have dampened the full potential impact of the QIZs, their contribution to the Jordanian economy at the macro-level should not be underestimated. Other areas of the bilateral relationship, such as non-QIZ related trade, remain low-key. The mega-projects included in the peace treaty, designed to serve as a model for Israel-Arab cooperation in the new Middle East, still await realization. Finally, despite an initial flurry of activity, tourism has not flourished. Much of the economic potential of the Jordanian-Israeli relationship stays suspended in the face of heightened Israeli-Palestinian conflict and a bleak outlook for a political solution. In Jordan as in Israel, people across all socio-economic strata, from taxi cab drivers to ministers, speak of a lack of progress 'because of the situation'. This simple phrase captures much of the disappointment regarding not only the Jordanian-Israeli peace, but also the failure of the Israeli-Palestinian peace process that looked so hopeful in the early 1990s.

For the Jordanian public at large, there are few tangible gains from the peace. While debt relief and F-16s make significant contributions to Jordan's macro-economic position and geopolitical strength, they have done little to assuage micro-level economic hardship. Indeed the F-16s, which cost hundreds of millions of dollars, had limited social value and their benefits were truly appreciated by King Hussein and approximately sixteen other people. The QIZs are producing much-needed jobs, but Asian workers hold many of them, and the link between these jobs and the peace is little known. There is growing recognition, especially in Israel, that the economic goals of the peace were idealistic: 'Israel initiated economic relations with Jordan on the wrong footing when it presented overly ambitious and mostly unrealistic regional and bilateral projects.'[79] Though economic relations still may be one of the most active areas of the post-peace bilateral relationship, many in Jordan today would likely share the sentiments expressed in 1995:

> 'The King', said a reluctant admirer, 'used to tell us before the treaty that he would sit with (Israeli Premier Yitzhak) Rabin for the sake of this people's future. To the ordinary man, that meant that bright days were coming. Now he discovers that it meant nothing, that the economy continues to go to the dogs.'[80]

The outlook for future Jordanian-Israeli economic cooperation remains uncertain. The unresolved Israeli-Palestinian conflict will undoubtedly continue to negate potential tripartite Israeli-Jordanian-Palestinian cooperation, as well as negatively impact the regional economy overall. At this time, it is not yet clear how the occupation of Iraq will reconfigure the region and what effect it will have on Jordanian-Israeli economic relations. While some level of direct bilateral cooperation will continue, the volume may decrease as the FTA with the United States becomes fully implemented, although Haifa port will likely remain a key transportation artery. The level of direct bilateral economic activity could be stimulated, and the business communities in both countries seem eager for this to happen, however, considerable obstacles need to be overcome, especially within the Israeli bureaucracy.

7

TOURISM:
DASHED HOPES AMID
RISING TENSION

Jordan's tourism sector was expected to reap major benefits from the peace treaty and provide a significant increase in foreign currency earnings. Not only were Israeli visitors anticipated to arrive in large numbers, North American and European tourists, undertaking 'Holy Land' tours originating in Israel, would continue to Jordan. With varied tourist attractions, including the famed 'rose-red' Nabatean city of Petra, Christian religious sites such as Mt. Nebo and beaches along the Red Sea, Jordan saw the peace as a means to capitalize more fully on its extensive tourism resources. Besides cooperation in marketing and tourism packages, Jordan and Israel planned to jointly develop infrastructure between the Red Sea tourist towns of Aqaba and Eilat. The plans included a joint airport—the 'Peace Airport'—along the border, as well as a free trade area.

Tourism Growth in the Post-Peace Era

The tourism sector responded very quickly and ebulliently to the peace treaty. In 1995, Jordan's tourism revenue reached a record $723 million, representing 15 per cent of GDP; for the first time in the country's history, one million foreign tourists arrived. Expectations for continued growth were high, the private sector hoped to exceed 5 million arrivals by the year 2000, and the tourism sector was poised to be the largest foreign currency earner in Jordan's economy. Tourists from Israel came to Jordan in large numbers; from nearly zero visitors in 1994 to 100,079 arriving in the last ten months of 1995.[1] Though Israeli tourists represented only 9 per cent of arrivals, this number was expected to increase following the completion of a transportation accord between the two states. With complete mobility for tourists between Israel and Jordan, most of Jordan's tourism sites would be a mere two hours from Jerusalem. Israel, too, saw an increase in tourism following the peace, reaching a record of 2.2 million visitors in 1995 and posting $3 billion in revenue.[2]

Throughout the first year of the peace, Jordan and Israel laid the groundwork for the growth of their tourism sectors. Jordan's national airline, Royal Jordanian, and the Israeli national carrier El Al established joint ticketing arrangements that allowed passengers travelling on a package to arrive on one airline and leave on the other with a single ticket.[3] By 1996, the transportation agreement was fully implemented; Jordan's Royal Wings airline could land in Tel Aviv and Israel's El Al airline could land in Jordan. The rapid increase in Israeli tourists at first overwhelmed Jordan's nascent tourism infrastructure. When 52,000 Israelis came to Jordan in the first six months of 1995, Jordanian officials were forced to limit visas to 900 day to handle the influx. A year later, in June 1996, Petra received 20,000 visitors a day, compared to 8,000 the year before the peace treaty.[4] On the Jordanian side, tourist traffic was sluggish at first, with only 5,000 Jordanians visiting Israel in the fist eight months of peace. The first tourists from Jordan to Israel, a children's group, arrived only a month after the signing of the treaty. Their trip to an annual festival in Haifa was sponsored by a Jordanian businessman and made front-page news in the *Jerusalem Post*.[5] During the summer months, however, the number of tourists skyrocketed to approximately 30,000 crossing between June and October. By 1995, Jordanian tourists had expanded their itineraries to tour Tel Aviv beaches and cafes, in addition to visiting families in the West Bank and Galilee.[6]

After the Boom: Declining Tourism Expectations

As the Israeli-Palestinian peace process unravelled, the newfound tourism boom began to flounder. By 1998, Jordan's tourism sector, perhaps the most tangible positive result of the peace for the average citizen, was failing to show significant growth.[7] The total number of tourist arrivals in 1998 had increased by only 200,000 over the first year of the peace treaty; more problematic, however, was that Jordan had significantly expanded its tourism infrastructure in anticipation of far greater growth. Where 148 'classified' hotels existed in 1995, 211 were in place by 1998, and the number of hotel rooms had nearly doubled (Table 7.1).[8]

Through out the late 1990s, Jordan and Israel continued collaborative efforts to bolster the lagging tourism industry. Attempts included a joint tourism publicity campaign focused on the British market,[9] capitalization on millennium travel to the region,[10] increased border coordination to facilitate the flow of tourists, and continued promotion of tourism as a 'bridge for

Table 7.1 Jordan Hotels / Hotel Capacity, 1994–2002.

	1994	1995	1996	1997	1998	1999	2000	2001	2002
Number of Hotels	129	148	161	175	211	247	278	298	309
Number of Rooms	7,250	8,565	9,406	10,147	11,513	13,781	15,091	16,880	17,400
Number of Beds	13,692	16,093	17,756	19,074	21,941	26,295	29,002	32,001	32,658

Note: 'Classified' hotels only.
Source: Jordan Ministry of Tourism, Information and Statistics Department.

peace'.[11] These efforts were undermined by the deterioration of the Oslo process and growing conflict between Israel and the Palestinians; even a 'Global Summit on Peace through Tourism', organized by the International Institute for Peace through Tourism, and held 8–11 November 2000, fell victim to increased violence. The conference was supposed to discuss the role of inter-faith dialogue as a bridge betweens peoples and the ways in which conflict resolution management could contribute to a 'culture of peace'. Shortly before the conference, main dignitaries, including Nelson Mandela, who was kept away by the 'flu', cancelled. Even Shimon Peres did not attend, his absence was attributed to the 'unfortunate circumstances' surrounding the Palestinian-Israeli clashes in the Palestinian territories following Sharon's visit to the Temple Mount.[12]

On the eve of the *intifada*, tourism from Israel to Jordan did post an impressive gain, increasing 22 per cent in the first seven months of 2000, as compared a year earlier. A closer look, however, showed a shift in the type of visitors from Israel, with Israeli Arabs forming 90 per cent of the tourists visiting the kingdom.[13] Coming to Jordan primarily to see family, the increase in numbers of these tourists did little to help raise revenue in the tourism sector.

The second Palestinian *intifada* and the Israeli military response had an immediate negative effect on Jordan's tourism industry; revenues plummeted by 8.2 per cent in the first quarter of 2001 alone. This decline was followed by a severe shock to the global tourism industry after the 11 September attacks. The impact on Jordan's tourism sector was swift and severe. Tourist arrivals from North and South America plunged from 126,411 in 2000 to 74,568 in 2001. European arrivals dropped from 326,574 to 207,332 during the same time, and reached only 167,181 in 2002. Though increased arrivals from Arab countries (770,795 in 2000, 963,051 in 2001) helped to partially offset this decline, total tourism receipts dropped from JD 512.4 million (approximately $717.3 million) to JD 496.2 million (approximately

Table 7.2 Tourist Arrivals in Jordan, 1994–2002.

Tourist Arrivals	1994	1995	1996	1997	1998	1999	2000	2001	2002
Total	857,610	1,073,549	1,102,752	1,127,028	1,256,428	1,357,822	1,426,879	1,477,697	1,612,420
American countries	69,878	103,346	107,960	107,676	108,612	123,525	126,411	74,568	72,919
European countries	192,176	255,496	251,820	239,411	219,445	292,757	326,574	207,332	167,181
East Asia/ Pacific	30,960	45,767	46,806	47,877	33,933	51,603	59,990	41,955	73,861
Africa/non-Arab countries	779	2,300	2,313	2,338	2,750	2,811	6,372	4,516	5,467
Arab countries	553,050	566,561	572,657	604,101	772,427	761,598	770,795	963,051	1,131,287
Israel	10,767	100,079	121,196	125,625	119,261	125,528	136,737	186,275	161,705

Source: Jordan Ministry of Tourism, Information and Statistics Department.

$694.68 million) between 2000 and 2001.[14] It should be noted that the total number of tourists from Israel increased during this period, this growth, however, mainly reflects visits by Israeli Arabs (Table 7.2).

The 11 September 2001 attacks in the United States and heightened Israeli military offensive in Palestinian territories in March 2002 further affected tourism. Jordan saw a decrease of tourists from Europe and North America of 26 per cent and 41 per cent, respectively, in 2000–2001. The future of the sector clouded further, as potential investors grew wary of the region; even the much-anticipated privatization of the Royal Jordanian airline had to be postponed.[15] Between September 2000 and September 2001, 70,000 reservations and 40 charter flights were cancelled. The airline's profits in 2000 failed to exceed one million dollars, as compared with 28 million dollars in 1999. In 2001, it faced losses of over $17 million, but did manage to post a one million dollar profit in 2002.[16]

With large losses in the European and North American market, Jordan increased its efforts to draw tourists from the Middle East. The large increase in Arab tourists between 2001 and 2002 reflects the change in visitation patterns, and Jordan seems to be replacing Egypt as a regional destination. But gains in this area could not compensate for the overall decline. Tour operators estimated that business dropped by some 40 per cent in 2001, and many have gone out of business since.

Hotels in Petra, Jordan's major tourist site, have been operating at an unsustainable occupancy rate of 10 per cent. The government has taken numerous measures to try to stimulate tourism, including reducing sales taxes on hotel rooms, fees to enter archaeological sites and departure taxes. More than 70 hotels were constructed in the vicinity of Petra following the signing of the peace treaty to accommodate the influx of tourists expected to visit this UNESCO World Heritage Site. The hotel sector is saddled with JD 200 million in debt, placing its overall future development in doubt.[17]

The empty hotels and tourists sights are a strong visual reminder of the heady days of the early 1990s, when it seemed that the region as a whole was on the brink of a comprehensive peace. Jordan is now attempting to showcase itself as a 'safe place' in the region, by hosting such international meetings as the World Economic Forum, distancing itself from the violence of the Israeli-Palestinian conflict and no longer focusing on tourists from Israel.

The Jordanian perception of the relationship between Jordan's economic losses and Israel's actions against the Palestinian is made clear in public statements by officials:

'Jordan's tourism has been affected by Israel's continuing aggression against the Palestinian people and the deteriorated state of security in the Middle East', Biltaji (Jordanian Minister of Tourism) said, commenting on the kingdom's proximity to the fighting in neighbouring Israel and the occupied West Bank.[18]

This perception is shared at the societal level as well.

At the official level, tensions between Israel and Jordan over tourism were further worsened by Israel's appointment of Rehavam Ze'evi as tourism minister in March 2001. Ze'evi was a vocal advocate of 'population transfer' of 3.3 million Arabs from the occupied territories to other countries in the Middle East. Though described as voluntary 'population transfer', many Arab countries, including Jordan, viewed his proposal as ethnic cleansing. For Jordan, the issue is even more problematic, as potential scenarios for this transfer can be interpreted to include the forcible expulsion of Palestinians to Jordan, reviving the whole sensitive concept of the country as the alternate homeland for the Palestinians, the 'Jordan as Palestine' option. Even the normally diplomatic Jordanian Minister of Tourism, Aqel Biltaji, who has forged a close working relationship with the Israeli tourism sector, declared at an unofficial meeting: 'How can I stand with him on the same stage?'[19] In October 2001, Palestinian militants assassinated Ze'evi on the day his resignation from the cabinet was to take effect.

Critical Tourism Issues

Even during the height of the post-peace tourism boom, several hurdles affected the bilateral tourism relations. Technical issues, such as visas and transportation, restricted the realization of complete mobility for tourists between Israel and Jordan. Now formally at peace, neither society had much experience with the culture and customs of the other, nor did they share the same expectations regarding the outcomes of peace. As the political situation in the region worsened, the tensions caused by physical and psychological barriers increased. By 2004, the expectations of a large peace benefit for the tourism industry and the prospect of fostering warm relations at the societal level were dashed.

A continuous point of friction is the disparity in visa processes for Jordanians and Israelis wishing to travel to the other's country. This discrepancy was apparent from the early days of the peace, when Jordanian visitors experienced great difficulty getting visas to visit Israel, though Israelis could get visas to Jordan in less than 48 hours.[20] Plotkin found that hundreds of Jordanians waited in line to receive visas during the summer of 1996. Though initial delays might have been resulting from the lack of adequate administrative infrastructure at the Israeli embassy in Jordan, security considerations have complicated visa processing. Israeli security concerns include the identification of Jordanians of Palestinian origin, who might commit violence (especially after 2000) and, even during the more optimistic Oslo period, the exclusion of individuals seeking to remain in Israel illegally for work. Today, it may take months for a Jordanian to receive a visa, if it is granted at all. Israelis, however, can purchase a visa on site at the Sheikh Hussein crossing.

Israeli expectations regarding tourism from Jordan have also not been met. The small number of Jordanian tourists, even during the first years after the peace, was disappointing. Those Jordanians that do come to Israel predominantly visit family, a pattern that supports the Israeli view that Jordanians harbour deep sociological and psychological barriers against Israel.[21] Economic issues also dissuade Jordanian travel, as few Jordanians have the economic resources to travel for vacation purposes and Israel is an expensive destination. As Plotkin further notes, Jordan's travelling elite—and prosperous Arabs from other countries—prefer luxury vacations, which can be found more easily at a high class resort in London or Paris, than in Israel.[22]

In addition to the disappointing numbers of tourists from Israel, Jordanian tourism operators express dissatisfaction with Israeli visiting patterns. Many Israeli tourists visit Petra as a day trip from Eilat, not staying overnight in the hotels built in anticipation of the tourist boom. Even Israeli Prime Minister Binyamin Netanyahu, during a visit in 1996, did not stay at Petra, which led, according to one Jordanian analyst, to feelings among some Jordanians that King Hussein had 'oversold the peace process'.[23] When overall tourism to Jordan began to decline amid rising regional tensions in 1997, the number of Israeli tourists remained steady at 11 per cent, a significant factor in the country's tourism economy. But the number could not compensate the loss of Europeans and North Americans, who stayed four to seven nights on average.[24] Besides not staying overnight, Israelis often brought their own food, adhering to kosher dietary standards, giving the impression that Jordanian food 'was not good enough'.

By 2000, however, few Israelis were visiting Jordan for tourism, and Israeli Arabs made up 90 per cent of Israeli visitors. Jordan's embrace of Israeli Arab tourists also had obvious political overtones, especially within the domestic political scene:

They come here to perpetuate relationships with kinsfolk. To them, Jordan is the only ventilation hole from which they breathe Arab air. We also benefit from them economically. After all, they are our kinsfolk. As for non-Arab Israelis, we are at peace with them, but everyone is free to receive any one of them or not. Tourism forms bridges of economic growth for world countries… What we strive for is not peace through tourism. We want them (the Israelis) to understand us through tourism and to know that we are more generous, nobler, and more rational than they think….[25]

The growing perception of personal safety risks by Israelis also contributed to a drop in non-Arab Israeli tourism. From 1995–2000, no systematic violence against Israeli tourists to Jordan existed. The stabbing of a woman in 1997, when she resisted an attempt to steal her purse, leaving her lightly wounded, was seen as an isolated incident motivated by criminal intent.[26] Nor did a further incident later that year, when two Israeli embassy security guards were lightly wounded in an attack, prompt Israel to recommend cancellation of visits to Jordan by its citizens.[27] Political motivations seemed to be behind the shooting, as the assailants, who claimed membership in an unknown Islamic group, demanded that all Israeli tourists and embassy staff leave Jordan within a month. They further demanded the release of the Jordanian soldier serving a life sentence for the Naharayim shooting.[28]

As emotions raged in the region following the collapse of the peace process, the onset of the Al Aqsa *intifada*, and Israeli military operations, Israelis grew increasingly concerned about visiting Jordan. Following the killing of Israeli businessman Yitzhak Snir in Amman in 2001, the Israeli government warned its citizens not to travel to Arab countries, including Jordan.[29] Even a leading Israeli tour operator said that he personally would not travel to Jordan, which was perceived as more dangerous for Israelis than Egypt.[30] The Jordanian investigators' belief that Snir's murder was criminally motivated, instead of based on his national identity, did little to lessen the effect of his death. The Jordanian foreign minister assured in interviews to Israeli media that Jordan remained safe for Israelis. But even as he tried to reassure potential tourists, his comments, which noted the mounting pressure on the kingdom to 'cool its ties with Israel', illustrated the political tightrope Jordan walked between maintaining its relations with Israel and the broader Arab world.[31]

The Peace Airport

As in other areas of their post-peace relationship, Jordan and Israel planned a number of high-profile joint projects to reinforce their new bilateral relationship. To date, not a single one of these mega-projects has been realized; though increasing regional tensions have undoubtedly played a role, many projects had stalled even within the first two years of the peace. One of them, known as Peace City, was to be built jointly by Israeli and Jordanian entrepreneurs. The first stage of the project included 10,000 hotel rooms and an investment of $150 million. Over a ten-year period, the project cost was supposed to reach $1 billion and cover another 3,000 *dunums*.[32] Similarly, despite initial funding of $2 million from the United States, the 'Red Sea Binational Peace Park' has not been created. As cooperation on coastal reef protection in the Gulf of Aqaba was explicitly called for in an annex to the peace treaty, this project's goal was to save the reefs crucial to tourism in Eilat and Aqaba.[33]

A cornerstone project, heralding the Jordanian-Israeli peace, was to be the jointly operated 'Peace Airport' between Aqaba in Jordan and Eilat in Israel. The joint venture was designed to bring substantial benefits to both partners. The airport in the key tourist city of Eilat was already operating over capacity, forcing international flights to land at a military base to the north. Proximity to the city prevented expansion of the existing Eilat airport, and the under-utilized airport in Aqaba offered a cheaper option than the construction of a new one. Jordan hoped that the joint airport would increase tourism to Aqaba, which was much less developed than its sister city of Eilat. In addition, Jordan would gain revenue from more planes landing at Aqaba and job creation through tourism development.

Additionally, the airport was a central component of a joint regional development plan, including cooperation in transportation, which would eliminate duplication of resources and reduce costs for both countries. In advance of building the joint airport, Israel and Jordan agreed that planes carrying Israel-bound passengers could land at Aqaba and tourists could make the short trip to Eilat by bus. In November 1997, Israeli planes began using Aqaba airport for passengers to nearby Eilat.[34] The move was a trial phase, designed to build confidence between the parties in advance of construction of the new airport.[35]

In 2004, the Peace Airport remains yet another unrealized project between Israel and Jordan. An extensive analysis by Mishal (et. al) concluded that 'Israeli political-bureaucratic procedures, rather than lack of cooperation, are stalling the projects.'[36] A closer look at this issue, and its effect on the bilateral relationship, underscores the difficulty of achieving goals of the peace treaty that require active participation.

As Mishal notes, a three-stage plan was drawn up for creation of the airport. Following the pilot project, where some Israel-bound flights would land at Aqaba and their passengers bussed to Eilat, a new terminal was to be built adjacent to the Aqaba runway, though on the Israeli side of the border and managed by the Israelis. All Eilat flights, as well as those to Aqaba, would land at the Aqaba airport, but Israel-bound passengers would enter directly into Israel through the new terminal. In doing so, they would avoid paying Jordanian exit and entry fees. In the final stage, an additional runway was to be built in Jordan and a Jordanian-Israeli airport authority would jointly manage the airport.

The trial period brought several disappointments from the Jordanian perspective. Though it was only four months long, the first Israel-bound planes were not redirected to Aqaba until two months into the period. Moreover, Israel redirected at most three flights a week to Aqaba, a much lower figure than the anticipated 15–20 flights a week.

Attempts to implement phase two of the project succumbed to the contradictory nature of Israeli bureaucracy, which affected various bilateral projects. This normal, though maybe inefficient, functioning of the bureaucracy was perceived in Jordan as a lack of willingness on the Israeli side to implement the peace agreement, as there was little evidence of political will to overcome the obstacles. Though the government declared its intentions to proceed, the Ministry of Environment demanded completion of an environmental survey prior to construction, touching off rounds of bureaucratic scuffling.

Despite re-commitment by both governments to the project in 1999 and statements by Israel's Deputy Prime Minister and Transportation Minister Yitzhak Mordekhay, who said that '...I am sure we will do it and I will do all my best that it will be ensured again in the government and will be on the ground in a very short time',[37] today there is still little cooperation, and no authorization yet to build the second terminal.

The lack of progress has fed Jordanian suspicions that Israeli bureaucratic manoeuvring is a means to conceal the primary motivation for obstructing the project: Israeli concern that the Peace Airport in Aqaba would overshadow Eilat airport. Indeed, some domestic concerns weighed on Israel's participation in the second stage, including a fear that because of cost differentials between Aqaba and Eilat, especially in labour, investors would choose Aqaba over Eilat. Israeli firms that normally service Eilat-bound flights also stood to lose business in the second phase, as Jordanian firms would take over the servicing. Furthermore, Jordan would control the runway, raising Israeli fears that Jordan could 'hold it hostage', raise fees, or forbid landings if they chose. In this event, Israeli planes would have to divert to the military airport north of Eilat. From the Jordanian perspective, such concerns illustrate Israel's lack of faith in the treaty and their misgivings about the stability of their relationship with Jordan.

Several Jordanian concerns reflect apprehension regarding the potential benefits of the joint airport. Though an increase in tourists to Aqaba is anticipated, Israel might reap much of the rewards of development in the Aqaba-Eilat area, as Aqaba's tourist infrastructure is much less developed than that of Eilat. With Israel operating its own terminal in phase two, the Jordanian role would be limited to servicing the runway and airplanes. As a result of such misgivings, and the lack of will to overcome them, fears and apprehensions restrain a project of mutual economic benefit and of great symbolic importance to the peace.

Joint Development of Aqaba and Eilat

In addition, little progress has been made on the overall joint development of Aqaba and Eilat, despite the many potential benefits:

The joint development of Aqaba and Eilat not only embodies the cooperative attributes of the Jordanian-Israeli treaty, but presents significant economic potential for the parties and serves as a test-site for many aspects of normalization and bilateral relations, including transportation, tourism, agriculture and security.[38]

Plans called for the establishment of the an Aqaba-Eilat free-trade zone, the Peace Airport, transit facilities between the two cities, integration of the power grid and cooperation to protect the environment. International donors supported parts of this initiative including the Peace Park, funded by the United States Agency for International Development. The European Union focused on private sector collaboration, funding the TEAM (Taba-Eilat-Aqaba Macro) program. Jordan appointed Aqel Biltaji, the former Minister of Tourism who had extensive experience in working with Israel, as chief commissioner of the Aqaba Special Economic Zone Authority (ASEZA).

Despite the lack of progress on joint development of the area, Jordan has pushed forward forcefully with the development of the Aqaba Special Economic Zone launched in 2000.

The zone includes the largest container port in the Levant, an industrial zone with special financial exemptions, vast tourism projects including Tala Bay resort on the border with Saudi Arabia and Aqaba Lagoon, located on the border with Israel. Financial incentives designed to lure investors include no restrictions on foreign equity investments in tourism, industry or commercial sectors, no import tariffs for raw materials on manufacturing, and only a 5 per cent basic tax on business income.[39] Though some have criticized the slow pace of development, the zone's first industrial area, built at a cost of $22 million, was expected to be operational by October 2003.[40] By March 2004, 541 companies were registered by ASEZA, 276 of which had established new businesses after the zone's creation. The value of imports into Aqaba increased from JD 100 million ($140 million) in 2001 to JD 161 million ($225.4 million) in 2003.[41] By mid-year 2003, the value of total investments in the zone reached over two billion dollars.[42]

Although the Aqaba industrial estate has been granted QIZ status (see Chapter Six), the likelihood that Israeli firms will relocate from Eilat to take advantage of the free trade remains slim. Indeed, the development of Aqaba is raising concerns in Israel that it will be a more attractive destination to investors and tourists than Eilat. Aqaba offers many benefits and customs breaks not available in Eilat, has lower land prices and the labour cost differential is great, at an average of $100 a month in Aqaba compared to $1,200 a month in Eilat. The potential to undermine Eilat's tourism industry is also raising friction:

'The tourists we are expecting in the coming years will go to Aqaba rather than come to Eilat,' says Haim Ben-David, CPA, a specialist about the Eilat free trade zone. 'If Aqaba offers what Eilat does, they will prefer going there, because Aqaba has the same sun and sea. The competition will be improper and unfair. Aqaba's cheap construction costs, land and tax breaks will mean prices for hotel room prices that Eilat cannot compete against.'[43]

Far from the cooperative joint development of their shared Red Sea coast line, Jordan and Israel now compete with each other in the development of tourist and economic activity. Having missed the opportunity for a collaborative approach in the decade following the peace treaty, and each set on their own path to development, the prospect of extensive cooperation in the future seems unlikely.

The potential for economic growth through tourism development figured prominently in the public marketing of the Jordanian-Israeli peace treaty. Indeed, development of this sector offered the greatest potential for individuals in both countries to reap the benefit of the peace. Especially within Jordan, where the expansion of tourism could have created much-needed jobs and increased the income of those employed in the industry, the failure of expected benefits to materialize has dealt a severe blow to the perception of the peace with Israel.

Though the decline in tourism can be attributed to factors outside the Jordanian-Israeli bilateral relationship, such as the Israeli-Palestinian conflict and the Iraq War, Israel is held responsible by many Jordanians for the problems because of its increasingly aggressive military operations in the West Bank and Gaza. The tourism sector provides a further example of the effect of the Israeli-Palestinian conflict on the potential for normal relations between Jordan and Israel. Though extensive attempts by both parties to facilitate collaboration in the tourism field existed, the impact of regional conflict could not be overcome. Furthermore, the economic situation of the Jordanian tourism industry has been worsened due to heavy investment in expectation of growth. In the Red Sea region, logically an area for extensive regional development including Jordan, Israel and—potentially—Egypt, Jordan and Israel have become keen competitors.

8

BUILDING PEACE BETWEEN THE PEOPLE: THE EFFORTS OF NON-GOVERNMENTAL ORGANIZATIONS

As previously noted, the governments of Jordan and Israel hoped that the peace between them would be a 'warm' peace with a broad base of normalized relations. For such a warm peace to exist, however, contact would have to move beyond exchanges at the governmental level to include the population of both countries. The treaty explicitly calls for cultural and scientific exchange:

> The parties, wishing to remove biases developed through the period of conflict, recognize the desirability of cultural and scientific exchanges in all fields, and agree to establish normal cultural relations between them.[1]

Additional parts of the treaty refer to activities designed to promote a 'culture of peace' between Jordanians and Israelis. Also included in plans to 'foster mutual understanding and tolerance based on shared historic values', was a pledge to abstain from hostile propaganda and to prevent dissemination of such propaganda by groups and individuals in their respective countries. Artistic mediums were to play a role in bridging the cultural divides.

Nongovernmental organizations (NGOs) were expected to play a significant role in the development of joint projects at the societal level. However, ten years after the peace, projects involving both peoples are rare and there is little activity between Jordanian and Israeli NGOs. Ironically, the level of joint activity between Jordanian and Israeli NGOs is much lower than Israeli-Palestinian NGO activity, despite the formal peace between the former.[2]

Several factors hamper implementation of joint projects between Jordanian and Israeli NGOs. On the Jordanian side, the anti-normalization movement (the focus of Chapter Nine) has hampered participation by individuals, NGOs and even government ministries in joint projects with Israelis. The influence of this movement, which is deeply entrenched in the country's professional associations, means that individuals who agree to work with Israelis face severe risk to their careers and social standing,[3] preventing many from doing so. There are exceptions to this rule, including the young female law school graduate, who agreed to work for a Jordanian NGO that cooperates with Israelis, despite the risk to her future career, and a few Jordanians who have studied in Israel.

It may be possible that the influence of the anti-normalization movement is overstated, however. A strong movement exists in the Palestinian territories, for example, and yet there is a much higher level of NGO work between Israelis and Palestinians. Events in the region and the failure of the peace to realize the expected benefits have undoubtedly reduced the desire on both sides to cooperate with each other. Though Jordanians are quick to declare that they have no problem with Jews, only the policies of the Israeli government, there is generally a strong psychological resistance to collaboration.

Within Israel, less than a handful of NGOs conduct projects with Jordanian counterparts, though a great many more work with Palestinians. There is little to no governmental support for specifically Israeli-Jordanian projects, and funding must be sought from foundations or other non-governmental sources. As is so often the case in the field of economic cooperation, there is no political will to cut through Israel's extensive bureaucracy to facilitate joint projects. Visa and border crossing issues further hamper projects, since it is much easier for Israelis to come to Jordan than for their colleagues to travel to Israel.

The differential administrative capacity and level of civil society development of both countries are a further obstacle to NGO collaboration. Typically, the Israeli NGOs have much greater experience in writing grant proposals, achieving grant funding and successfully implementing a project. This leads to an asymmetry, where the Jordanian partner, though its participation is crucial for the project, has a limited strategic or management role. The absence of a strong management role typically leads to little funding for administrative or overhead costs, limiting their ability to invest resources in human capital development within their own organizations. Israeli NGOs, when looking for partners in Jordan, often find that few of the organizations willing to collaborate really have the institutional capacity to implement projects. Jordanian-Israeli NGO collaboration is caught in a trap, where Jordanian NGOs often remain dependent on Israeli ones, because they do not have the resources, either in human capital or financial terms, to reduce this dependency. Thus, the Jordanian NGO community beyond the quasi-official royal NGOs stays relatively weak and underdeveloped.

Today, there is little support from the donor community for bilateral projects between Israel and Jordan. For obvious reasons, Israeli-Palestinian projects have been the primary focus of aid in the region for European and United States donors. Recent large scale funding initiatives by the United States, including the Middle East Partnership Initiative, have given poor reviews to bilateral projects designed to foster the Israeli-Jordanian relationship, and are instead funding projects 'that make Muslims like us', in the words of one foreign service officer. There is also an emphasis on region-wide projects.

Jordanian-Israeli NGO Collaboration

Despite these obstacles, some Jordanian-Israeli NGO collaboration is taking place. While certainly any form of large or even medium scale societal contact has not been achieved, small pockets of targeted collaboration exist. Most of the successful projects have taken place directly in the economics field or in areas with economic impact. Collaboration also is kept quiet, with little mention in Jordanian newspapers; names of participants are closely guarded and not put on websites or public reports.

The Culture of Water

This project, implemented by the Peres Centre for Peace in Israel, came out of the recognition of severe water scarcity in the region and the need for collaborative approaches to its management. The goal of this project, which involves Jordanian, Israeli and Palestinian partners, was to create a Centre of Excellence in Jordan, focused on water resources for agricultural and potable needs. The project formed a joint Israeli-Jordanian non-governmental entity responsible for research and development of technical solutions, as well as educational approaches creating a 'Culture of Water' that aims at establishing better water use habits. The project also included the transfer of technology for better economic use of water in Israel, Jordan and the Palestinian territories, and to enhance food security and income generation of farming communities in the region.

Development and promotion of the 'Culture of Water' are a key part of the project:

> Such a concept focuses on the utilization of various educational and social marketing techniques to enhance water usage behaviours in the various sectors, especially agriculture. The concept also promotes

education and training in the field of agriculture through the deployment of low water demanding varieties and crops.[4]

At 70 per cent of total water use, agriculture is the highest consumer of water in the region, and the main focus of the project. It tries to change water use behaviour and attitudes of farmers, and assists them in implementing the Best Management Practices (BMP) to overcome water shortage and create additional resources through savings. Additionally, the utilization of crop varieties resistant to saline water is propagated.[5]

The project includes a research and development unit, the 'Centre of Excellence', located in Jordan and managed by a Jordanian general director. The unit is a joint project of Jordanian and Israeli nonprofit organizations.[6]

Though focused narrowly on water issues, the project relates directly to core issues of the peace treaty. As the droughts of 1997 and 1999 illustrated (Chapter Four), the treaty made no provision for unusual water shortages. Though it hoped to expand the amount of available water through large-scale projects, such as desalinization facilities, these projects have failed to materialize. By better utilizing existing resources, including brackish water, this project may help mitigate friction when water scarcity issues arise.

The Middle East Red Palm Weevil Program

Date palm production is a major economic activity throughout the Middle East, and has strong cultural importance. The Red Palm weevil is an enormous threat to this industry, and thus the livelihoods of many farmers. The insect lays its eggs into the trunk of the palm, and the larvae tunnel into it to feed on plant tissue. Over time the tree is weakened, yield drops, and it eventually dies.

Insects, it has been noted, do not respect national borders. The weevil was recorded for the first time in the region in the United Arab Emirates in 1986; by 1993 it had reached Egypt. The Middle East Red Palm Weevil program was started in 1998, facilitated by the Peres Centre for Peace in Israel, under financial sponsorship of Novartis Agro AG, Switzerland. The goals of the project explicitly included a peace-building objective 'to lay the infrastructure for the development of tomorrow's peace in the region'. This was to be achieved by stimulating cooperation among Middle Eastern countries to control the spread of the weevil and to develop new technologies to control it. Initial participation in the program came from Israel, Palestine, Egypt and Jordan; as the project entered its sixth year in 2004, it was expanding to include Morocco, Tunisia, Spain, Italy, Greece, Cyprus and Malta under the new name 'Middle East Integrated Crop Management, ICM.'[7]

While building local capacity to deal with the pest problem, the project undertook a number of joint activities. In Egypt, a central laboratory was established, with additional research carried out at the Agricultural Research Organization (ARO) in the Beit Shean valley (Israel) and the Plant Protection Centre within the Jordanian Ministry of Agriculture. Several workshops took place in Jordan, Egypt and Israel. The research team also jointly published scientific papers.

Cross Border Cooperation

Perhaps one of the most intensive projects between Israelis and Jordanians is the Cross Border Cooperation (CBC) project in the Northern Jordan Valley-Beit Shean area. It was jointly implemented by two NGOs, the Jordanian Amman Centre for Peace and Development and the Israeli Economic Cooperation Foundation. The project was modelled after cross border projects that took place in Europe after World War II, where areas of cooperation between local communities along the borders in formerly conflicting countries were established. In the Jordan-Israel CBC project, a major goal was to try to create a set of linkages and shared activities at the local level, to serve as a model for the larger national arena. The CBC grew out of an attempt to foster trilateral cross border cooperation between Israel, Jordan and the Palestinians, initiated by the Luxembourg government in 1999. The onset of the *intifada* in 2000 ended trilateral activities, but the bilateral Israel-Jordan cooperation continued.

The CBC's approach is to identify real common interests in order to foster long-term collaboration. It has taken several years to move to the actual project implementation stage, and many more projects are under development. Initial plans were very large scale, calling for the creation of a Jordan Valley Cross Border Cooperation Centre, at a total cost of $400,000. As this early vision proved impossible to realize, because of fund-raising issues, emphasis was placed on more cost-effective projects that would bring people in the two communities in contact with each other. Key funding for specific projects has been provided through donations by the Cleveland (Ohio, USA) Jewish community.

Like the 'Culture of Water' and 'Red Palm Weevil' projects, the CBC projects address tangible needs in the region, including non-chemical means of controlling rodent populations that feed on agricultural stores. Currently, Israelis are training their Jordanian counterparts to use owls as part of an integrated pest management strategy. The main barrier in this project, however, is not based entirely on a reluctance to work with Israelis, but a cultural distaste for owls held by Jordanians. In traditional Islam, owls are considered bad luck, the embodiment of evil spirits. In folklore from some parts of the Arabian Peninsula, owls were believed to carry off children at night. Other cooperation exists between cucumber farmers in Jordan and a pickle manufacturer across the border, which provides technical support to ensure that the produce meets the quality standards required for entry into Israel and for his product specifications.

A main reason for the CBC's success is the combination of support from central and local governments. This is especially important for potential Jordanian participation. The monarchy has sent palace representatives to CBC planning meetings, paving the way for local cooperation. Leadership of the project recently undertook a strategic planning session to identify key priorities. A Mayor's Forum, bringing the mayors of the Israeli and Jordanian municipalities, as well as the Jordanian governor, together to deepen channels of dialog, was set as the highest priority, since good relations between the local authorities are needed to support all other projects. The participants were scheduled to spend two days in Beit Shean; unfortunately, Israeli forces killed the Hamas leader in Gaza, Ahmed Rantisi, the day before the visit. The forum had to be cancelled, and had not yet been rescheduled by summer 2004. A planned visit by female members of local government councils and women's associations from both sides of the border was carried out in July 2004. An innovative set of interfaith discussions has been ongoing since 2003, with meetings between Israeli rabbis and Jordanian imams. The participants have explored subjects such as secularism, the status of women in their respective societies, family relationships and moral codes of behaviour. Hopefully, this dialog will expand to include religious educators and develop a future curriculum on peace education. A slate of other joint projects is planned, funding for which is being sought, including additional activity in agriculture, youth sports (football), and teacher's education.

Despite this success, significant barriers that limit the relationships between the border communities still exist. Of key importance is the need for the mayors of the communities to be in direct contact with each other and establish joint decision-making mechanisms. At present, direct bilateral community contact has not yet been established, and their activities are rather organized by the two NGO partners. In the period since the peace treaty, the local leadership on both sides of the border has never spoken by telephone to their counterparts. Hopefully, after the meeting of the mayors is held, this line of communication can be opened. Effective communication on day-to-day activities, such as coordinating the spraying of pesticides, is the key to the project's the future success.

The ability of this communal experience to serve as a model for national cooperation between Israel and Jordan is still limited. Due to Jordanian sensitivities, the collaboration is kept very quiet, and its successes are not publicly disseminated. For now, the project partners have adopted a strategy of working quietly until the project matures and has deeper roots, while waiting for a possible future where a higher public profile can be reached.

Health Care

The health-care sector has been another area of limited cooperation between Israel and Jordan, despite condemnations of the peace treaty by the doctor's association in Jordan. In May 1998, seven Jordanian physiotherapists participated in training in Israel; similarly, Israeli physiotherapists gave a seminar in Amman. Occasionally, such limited exchanges can lead to larger projects. A one-day joint Israeli-Jordanian conference on the early detection and management of hearing impairment in children and infants led to the formation of the Middle East Association for Managing Hearing Loss (MEHA). Congenital loss of hearing is a widespread problem in the Arab world and among the Arab community in Israel. One in 10 children and 20 per cent of the general population in the region suffer from this affliction.

The Jordanian doctors' professional association was reportedly not too happy about all the exchanges, but support from the monarchy helped MEHA to resist pressure from normalization critics.[8] They established a regional centre in Amman, where Israeli and Jordanian surgeons have performed joint operations. Additional activities include early hearing loss detection projects, neonatal screening, training for families with afflicted children and scientific conferences. MEHA is funded by the Canada International Scientific Exchange Program.[9]

Scientific Collaboration

A number of projects specifically focus on scientific collaboration. Nine Middle Eastern countries (Jordan, Israel, Bahrain, Egypt, Iran, Israel, Palestine Authority, Pakistan, Turkey, and the United Arab Emirates) have united to create the first synchrotron research centre in the region. Under the auspices of the United Nations Educational, Scientific and Cultural Organization (UNESCO), the International Centre for Synchroton-light for Experimental Science Applications in the Middle East (SESAME) is being built in Jordan.[10] Construction began in July 2003; when operational, the synchrotron light source will produce intense beams of x-rays for research in fields such as physics, materials sciences and life sciences. In addition to research, SESAME also conducts training seminars and workshops.[11]

Bridging the Rift

Israel and Jordan recently launched a major joint educational and scientific collaboration project, in cooperation with Cornell and Stanford

Universities. The Bridging the Rift Centre (BTR) will host a databank that will assemble information on all living systems, from microbes to plants to animals. It will be located 50 miles south of the Dead Sea, on the border between Israel and Jordan. Each country will donate land to form a 150-acre site for the research facility. Both Cornell University and Stanford University will offer doctoral degrees at the BTR Centre, which is expected to welcome students from Israel, Jordan and other countries within five years.

Already, a Jordanian anti-normalization group has warned the government against 'dangers posed' by such a project. The statement was signed by the Higher Executive Committee for the Nation's Protection and Resistance to Normalization, which represents opposition parties, including Islamists and trade unions.[12] Indeed, the project, now four years in the making, has faced many obstacles. No Israeli or Jordanian university is formally associated with it, reflecting the tension between the two countries, and the reality is that scientists on both sides cannot afford to be seen as collaborating directly.[13] Groundbreaking ceremonies took place at the site under a cloak of secrecy, with no public guest list.

Role of the Retired Military Leadership

Further limited cooperation takes place between retired generals, who are better equipped to withstand threats from the anti-normalization movement in Jordan. A number of them, many of who were active in creating collaborative military structures prior to and after the peace, are now active in the NGO community. Building on the relationships formed during their military service, they utilize their contacts to pursue collaborative activities in a variety of fields and broaden the circle of connections. As official channels have withered in recent years, the role of these informal meetings has become more important. Despite the high tension created by the *intifada* and Israeli military response, forums have been held at least seven times since 2000, taking place in Israel, Jordan and third country locations. Besides strategic security concerns, issues such as means of conciliation, conflict resolution and broadening societal engagement in the peace have been addressed. The outcome of these meetings can also serve to inform the current political structure about the perception of key issues in the other country.

NGOs Advancing Economic Cooperation

Israeli and Jordanian NGOs have worked together to try to overcome the obstacles to more extensive economic collaboration mentioned in Chapter Six. Key participants in these activities include The Amman Centre for Peace and Development, The Peres Centre for Peace and the Israel-Jordan Chamber of Commerce. Numerous meetings have focused on identifying hindrances to cooperation and defining joint strategies to overcome them. An important seminar on 'Jordanian-Israeli Joint Projects: Past Experience and Future Prospects' in June 2003 examined the post-peace relations to date, focusing on lessons for the future. A pivotal finding of this seminar highlighted the tendency for Israeli bureaucracy to impede collaboration, and called for the creation of a position, perhaps within the Prime Minister's office, to oversee development of relations with Jordan and joint regional projects.[14]

A similar seminar, held in Germany under the sponsorship of Daimler-Chrysler and organized by the Peres Centre for Peace and the Amman Centre for Peace and Development, sought means to improve bilateral business and trade relations especially between businesspeople involved in the lucrative QIZ-led export industry. Issues discussed included the influence of the Israeli-Palestinian conflict, administrative and legal obstacles to collaboration, transportation issues, security issues and the influence of cultural differences. Plans were made to create an ongoing project for joint lobbying of the governmental structures in Jordan and Israel that impact on bilateral trade and cooperation. In addition, joint financial research and specialized seminars were planned.[15]

Peres Centre 'Peace Technology Fund'

In 1999, the Peres Centre announced the launching of a $60 million fund to promote cooperation between Israelis and Jordanians. This fund was similar in design to the Israeli-Palestinian 'Peace Technology Fund', with financing from principally private contributions. A potential area targeted were the 'peace technologies' of telecommunications and high technology, dovetailing with King Abdullah's promise to sponsor joint high-tech projects with Israel to help create a 'Silicon Heights' in Jordan.[16]

Although the peace treaty emphasizes scientific and cultural exchange, very little activity actually takes places. Despite the importance of the projects highlighted here, the magnitude or impact of the NGO sector should not be overestimated. In truth, even in this area, few Jordanians and Israelis have contact with each other, and it is rather a small group of individuals, well known to each other, that sustains this low level of NGO effort.

The experiences of these groups show that successful joint projects must address real needs, which is why economic activities tend to dominate. Such activities have benefited from a history of pragmatic cooperation in key areas (such as fly eradication) prior to the peace. Activities in the educational and cultural realm are more sensitive and therefore much less likely to take place, though exceptions exist.

Several strategies have been utilized by NGOs to facilitate their collaboration within an overall environment that does not support broad societal exchange. Often, Jordanian-Israeli collaboration happens within multilateral projects, rather than through bilateral exchange. In the case of the Bridging the Rift, MEHA and SESAME projects, multiple countries are involved. This multilateral 'umbrella' helps to provide some protection from criticism for the Jordanian participants, as Israel can be portrayed as only one of several partners. Patronage by the Jordanian royal family to Jordanian NGOs is another important factor in enabling them to withstand the onslaught of the anti-normalization movement and protecting individual participants. Also, most joint NGO activity, such as workshops and conferences, takes place in Jordan, rather than Israel. This is in part due to the growing difficulty for Jordanians to obtain Israeli visa, but it also alleviates their concern about travel to Israel and its possible repercussions. However, as long as members of NGOs in both countries are not able or willing to freely travel back and forth, NGO activity will unfortunately remain stunted.

Finally, the potential for Jordanian-Israeli 'people to people' activity has been profoundly affected by the escalation of the Israeli-Palestinian conflict. This created an enormous psychological barrier to cooperation, especially on the Jordanian side, that cannot be breached on a wide scale until at the least the hope of a comprehensive settlement is present. Most of the initial peace-oriented organizations established in Jordan are no longer active or seem to have disappeared. In truth, there are few potential partners, either in Israel or Jordan, to build societal relations at this time.

9

PERCEPTIONS OF PEACE IN JORDAN AND THE ANTI-NORMALIZATION MOVEMENT

Today there is little support for normalization of relations with Israel within either the Jordanian governmental institutions or the general public. Moreover, recent years have witnessed a qualitative change in support for normalization at the highest reaches of government, including the monarchy and top officials, where it is increasingly seen as a choice to be exercised by individuals instead of a concerted government policy. The level of normalized relations, with the limited exception of the QIZ, has grown little beyond where it stood a year or two following the peace treaty. This is particularly noticeable within the sphere of 'people-to-people' contact.

There are several reasons for both the failure of normalized relations to take root and the current attitude in Jordan towards potential future normalization, amongst them a broad perception by the public and many in government that the peace has failed to bring expected benefits and the inability of the Jordanian monarchy to put an end to the anti-normalization movement shortly after the peace treaty. The most significant factor is the failure of the Oslo Accords and the ensuing escalation of conflict between the Palestinian population and the Israeli military under the Sharon government, and the utilization of harsh measures such as targeted assassinations, construction of the separation wall/fence, and house demolitions. The unprecedented level of Palestinian casualties has created greater resistance and anger among Jordanians, especially those of Palestinian origin, towards Israel and any potential relationships, either personal or institutional, with Israelis.[1]

As the various chapters in this volume have illustrated, the last ten years of peace between Jordan and Israel have failed to produce expected benefits. While initial expectations may have been set unrealistically high, particularly the level of anticipated economic impact and the concentration on large 'mega'-projects, favourable attitudes towards the treaty as a whole have diminished:

> Even many who supported the peace process now consider their own country's 1994 agreement with Israel to be unsatisfactory. They balk at normalizing ties with an Israel that has failed to finalise peace agreements with the Palestinians, Syrian and Lebanese and are angered by continuing Israeli settlement building in the West Bank and Gaza. The failure of peace with Israel to bring any obvious economic benefit is another source of irritation; particularly as UN sanctions on Iraq continue to damage Jordan's traditional economic ties with its neighbour.[2]

The tangible lack of economic benefit directly related to the peace treaty, especially at the level of the 'common person', has made it difficult to militate against the growing anger and dismay towards Israel over the deterioration of Israeli-Palestinian relations and growing humanitarian concerns in the Palestinian territories. Though calls to abrogate the treaty remain limited to a small minority in Jordan, the Jordanian public, according to Nevo, 'has not yet become ready for reconciliation and normal relations between the two peoples'.[3]

Surveys of Jordanian Public Opinion

There are very little public opinion polls on Jordanian attitudes towards Israel and the peace treaty. A survey just before the treaty, conducted by the Centre for Strategic Studies at the University of Jordan, showed a high level of support for the Washington Agreement and the subsequent peace treaty, with 80.2 per cent of respondents in favour of the agreement. The survey found that 75.9 per cent expected that Jordan would achieve greater access to water, 68.3 per cent expected improvements in Jordan's security, and 82.8 per cent expected an improved economic situation. Moreover, 40.9 per cent expected economic improvement to take place in the short term, rather than the long run (32.6 per cent).[4]

These high expectations might have contributed to current Jordanian attitudes, which today display a much more pessimistic view of the peace.

A recent groundbreaking survey by the Al-Urdun Al-Jadid Research Centre in Jordan and the Harry S. Truman Institute for the Advancement of Peace at Hebrew University in Israel vividly illustrates the level of disappointment in Jordan and the divergent perceptions of the treaty's effect held by Israelis and Jordanians.[5] The survey assessed Israeli and Jordanian attitudes towards various expected outcomes of the peace, such as security, access to water resources, tourism, economic growth and cooperation between the two states. This level of detail provides insight into Jordanian perceptions of various aspects of the treaty as well as general attitudes towards Israelis.

Security Benefits

Despite the centrality of mutual security as a motivation for the Hashemite monarchy to conclude a peace treaty with Israel, the Jordanian public as a whole does not perceive an increase in security. When asked whether the peace treaty had improved security in Jordan, over 50 per cent of respondents replied 'not at all', as opposed to 6.5 per cent who considered the security dimension to be very worthwhile (Table 9.1). Indeed, over two-thirds of the respondents felt that the peace had little or no impact on security in Jordan.

Even more surprising is the extent to which Jordanians see Israel as a potential threat to their national sovereignty. Thirty-two per cent of respondents strongly agreed with the statement 'Israel would occupy Jordan if it were able to'. Less than 20 per cent of respondents strongly disagreed with this statement. Though not covered by the survey, it would be interesting to know what role the Israeli concept of Jordan as a *watan badil* or alternative homeland for Palestinians plays in this perception. Under what possible circumstances do Jordanians see Israel potentially occupying Jordan? Most scenarios would likely involve the Palestinians, with the *watan badil* as one possibility and Israeli occupation of Jordan following the fall of the Hashemite monarchy to avert control by a militant Palestinian regime as an alternative. While such scenarios may today seem extreme, given the commonality in security interests between the Israeli government and Hashemite monarchy, the fact that 57 per cent of the respondents believe that Israel would occupy Jordan if they could, attests to the fact that while a high level of trust may exist between the two governments, it is certainly not replicated within Jordanian society. Of course, one question not asked in the survey is why, given Israel's great military superiority, it has not yet occupied Jordan.

Also troubling for supporters of the peace in both countries is the Jordanian perception that Israel, unlike Jordan, has accrued significant security benefit from the peace treaty. Over half of the respondents felt that the treaty's contribution to Israel's security had been either 'worthwhile' or 'very worthwhile'. These responses reflect a widely held Jordanian belief that Israel has benefited more greatly from the peace than Jordan. Though the survey asked specifically about security, the idea of disproportional benefit extends to other areas as well, especially economic cooperation.

Conventional wisdom holds that Israel's construction of a separation wall/fence in the West Bank has put a serious strain on Jordanian-Israeli

Table 9.1 Jordanian Perceptions of Security Benefits.

Question: To what extent has the peace treaty improved security in Jordan?

	Response	Frequency	Percent	Valid Percent	Cumulative Percent
Valid	Not at all	412	51.5	52.4	52.4
	A little	123	15.4	15.6	68.0
	To some extent	112	14.0	14.2	82.2
	Worthwhile	89	11.1	11.3	93.5
	Very worthwhile	51	6.4	6.5	100.0
	Total	787	98.4	100.0	
Missing Response		13	1.6		
Total		800	100.0		

Question: Do you believe Israel would occupy Jordan if it were able to?

	Response	Frequency	Percent	Valid Percent	Cumulative Percent
Valid	Strongly disagree	146	18.2	18.2	18.2
	Disagree	95	11.9	11.9	30.1
	Undecided	103	12.9	12.9	43.0
	Agree	200	25.0	25.0	68.0
	Strongly agree	256	32.0	32.0	100.0
	Total	800	100.0	100.0	

Question: To what extent has the peace treaty contributed to Israel's security?

	Response	Frequency	Percent	Valid Percent	Cumulative Percent
Valid	Not at all	116	14.5	14.9	14.9
	A little	116	14.5	14.9	29.9
	To some extent	143	17.9	18.4	48.3
	Worthwhile	190	23.8	24.5	72.7
	Very worthwhile	212	26.5	27.3	100.0
	Total	777	97.1	100.0	
Missing Response		23	2.9		
Total		800	100.0		

relations. Not only does the wall/fence seriously diminish the likelihood of a two-state solution to the Israeli-Palestinian conflict, a necessary prerequisite to a comprehensive peace in the region, but it also increases Jordanian concern regarding a potential flood of Palestinians into Jordan in the event of increased hostilities or an intentional transfer plan. Though Israel has attempted to dispel these concerns among the Jordanian military and monarchy, even conducting tours of the wall for Jordanian retired military officers, discomfort remains high. Jordanians surveyed in the poll are generally divided over the effect of the separation wall/fence on Jordanian relations, but a strong majority saw continued construction as a reason for Jordan to sever relations with Israel (85.3 per cent responding either 'definitely should' or 'should'; Table 9.2).

Water, Tourism and Economic Benefits

In other areas of the treaty, Jordanians surveyed also perceived little or no real benefit. Even in the area of water resources, in which additional transfers of water were guaranteed and Jordan did expand its available water resources, nearly two-thirds of respondents believed that the peace treaty has not improved access to water resources. Only 6 per cent reported that the treaty was 'worthwhile' or 'very worthwhile' in terms of improving the state of water resources (Table 9.3).

Potential economic benefit was the major means by which the peace was marketed to the Jordanian people; the CSS poll in 1994 found higher expectations (82.8 per cent) of an improved economic situation than in any other area of the treaty. In the 2004 poll, nearly two-thirds of respondents saw little tourism benefit to Jordan (responding 'not at all' or 'a little' when asked whether tourism had improved; Table 9.3). These responses are not surprising, given the real challenges that Jordan's tourism industry has faced in the last ten years and the impact of the second Palestinian *intifada*. Both (non-Arab) Israeli and European tourism declined significantly, though an increase in tourists from the region partially offset this decline. On the whole, however, the tourism sector has failed to reap anticipated benefits.

Despite some real economic gains in Jordan over the last ten years, respondents saw little relationship between the peace treaty and an improvement in the Jordanian economy. Fully 87.6 per cent found little or no effect. This may indicate that the Jordanian public does not see a relationship between the QIZ-based export growth, external debt relief, the US Free Trade Agreement and the peace with Israel. It should be noted, however, that the survey did not specifically ask respondents if they believed the economy had improved. It may be possible that they perceived no economic improvement, treaty or no treaty.

Table 9.2 Jordanian Perceptions of the West Bank Security Wall/Fence.

Question: To what extent does the separation wall negatively affect relations between Israel and Jordan?

	Response	Frequency	Percent	Valid Percent	Cumulative Percent
Valid	No effect	126	15.8	16.1	16.1
	A little effect	135	16.9	17.2	33.2
	To a certain extent	176	22.0	22.4	55.7
	Great effect	175	21.9	22.3	78.0
	Definite effect	173	21.6	22.0	100.0
	Total	785	98.1	100.0	
Missing Response		15	1.9		
Total		800	100.0		

Question: Do you believe Jordan should sever relations if Israel continues to construct the separation wall?

	Response	Frequency	Percent	Valid Percent	Cumulative Percent
Valid	Definitely should	426	53.3	55.8	55.8
	Should	225	28.1	29.5	85.3
	Should not	89	11.1	11.6	96.9
	Definitely should not	20	2.5	2.6	99.5
	Don't know / NA	4	0.5	0.5	100.0
	Total	764	95.5	100.0	
Missing Response		36	4.5		
Total		800	100.0		

'People-to-People' Contact

The survey also points out the near total lack of contact between Israelis and Jordanians in the ten years after the peace. 91.5 per cent of respondents had never met an Israeli. With no personal experience to counteract prevailing stereotypes, 'peace' has not penetrated societal relations between Jordan and Israel. The survey further makes clear that any effort to build societal relations will need to overcome severe resistance by Jordanians to the idea of hosting or befriending Israelis. When asked whether they would be willing to host, 91.6 per cent responded 'strongly disagree' or 'disagree'; nearly the

Table 9.3 Jordanian Perception of Water Resource, Tourism and Economic Benefits.

Question: To what extent has the peace treaty improved the state of water resources in Jordan?

	Response	Frequency	Percent	Valid Percent	Cumulative Percent
Valid	Not at all	494	61.8	62.7	62.7
	A little	154	19.3	19.5	82.2
	To some extent	93	11.6	11.8	94.0
	Worthwhile	37	4.6	4.7	98.7
	Very worthwhile	10	1.3	1.3	100.0
	Total	788	98.5	100.0	
Missing Response		12	1.5		
Total		800	100.0		

Question: To what extent has the peace treaty improved tourism to Jordan?

	Response	Frequency	Percent	Valid Percent	Cumulative Percent
Valid	Not at all	365	45.6	46.6	46.6
	A little	147	18.4	18.8	65.4
	To some extent	138	17.3	17.6	83.0
	Worthwhile	89	11.1	11.4	94.4
	Very worthwhile	44	5.5	5.6	100.0
	Total	783	97.9	100.0	
Missing Response		17	2.1		
Total		800	100.0		

Question: To what extent has peace treaty improved the state of the Jordanian economy?

	Response	Frequency	Percent	Valid Percent	Cumulative Percent
Valid	Not at all	591	73.9	74.2	74.2
	A little	106	13.3	13.3	87.5
	To some extent	69	8.6	8.7	96.2
	Worthwhile	20	2.5	2.5	98.7
	Very worthwhile	10	1.3	1.3	100.0
	Total	796	99.5	100.0	
Missing Response		4	0.5		
Total		800	100.0		

same amount (90.8 per cent) would not be willing to befriend an Israeli, and a slightly larger amount would not, in turn, be willing to be hosted by an Israeli (93.3 per cent).

The survey did not explore to what extent these attitudes are linked to feelings about the ongoing Israeli-Palestinian conflict, and if they would change if a just and comprehensive peace were achieved.

Finally, the survey predicts grim prospects for the future of Jordanian-Israeli relations (Table 9.4). Nearly 60 per cent of respondents anticipate that relations between Jordan and Israel will 'deteriorate' or 'deteriorate to a great extent' in the next ten years. This is discouraging news for a peace that has largely failed to take root, much less flourish in its first ten years. Here again, it is not possible to know what scenarios respondents had in mind when predicting a deterioration of relations.

The survey confirms a strong belief in a connection between the Israeli-Palestinian conflict and Jordanian-Israeli bilateral relations. Nearly half of the respondents felt that the Israeli-Palestinian conflict has a 'great' or 'definite' negative effect on Israeli-Jordanian relations. Only 14 per cent felt that the Israeli-Palestinian conflict had no effect on the bilateral relationship. It is very difficult, if not impossible, to separate the Israeli-Jordanian relationship from the Israeli-Palestinian relationship. A key question in the region, that of the potential relationship between Israel and other Arab states following a comprehensive peace, largely remains unanswered. A number of schools of thought exist, both within Israel and the Arab world in general, regarding the ultimate potential for Israeli-Arab relations. The extent of belief throughout the region, that the elimination of the state of Israel is necessary to end the conflict, is a major concern within Israel. In the case of Jordan, the survey found that only a minority (14.3 per cent responding either 'strongly agree' or 'agree') saw the elimination of the Jewish state as a solution to broader Israeli-Arab conflict. Even more significantly, 60.2 per cent strongly disagreed with the idea. Such results are important, as they indicate that the feelings towards Israel are not necessarily existential in nature, but more closely tied to Israeli-Arab relations, namely, the Israeli-Palestinian conflict. This finding may help put the anti-normalization movement, discussed later in this chapter, in perspective, especially the question of its potential influence following a comprehensive settlement between Israel and the Palestinians.

Israeli Perceptions

Generally, Israelis perceived a much greater security benefit to Jordan than Jordanians themselves (Table 9.5). Over 45 per cent of Israelis surveyed felt

Table 9.4 Jordanian Perceptions of Future Jordanian-Israeli Relations.

Question: How do you perceive the direction of relations between Jordan and Israel in the next 10 years?

	Response	Frequency	Percent	Valid Percent	Cumulative Percent
Valid	Improve to great extent	82	10.3	10.3	10.3
	Improve	123	15.4	15.4	25.6
	Remain as now	119	14.9	14.9	40.5
	Deteriorate	217	27.1	27.1	67.6
	Deteriorate to great extent	259	32.4	32.4	100.0
	Total	800	100.0	100.0	

Question: How much does the Israeli-Palestinian Conflict affect Jordanian-Israeli relations?

	Response	Frequency	Percent	Valid Percent	Cumulative Percent
Valid	No effect	110	13.8	14.0	14.0
	A little effect	128	16.0	16.3	30.3
	To a certain extent	169	21.1	21.6	51.9
	Great effect	205	25.6	26.1	78.1
	Definite effect	172	21.5	21.9	100.0
	Total	784	98.0	100.0	
Missing Response		16	2.0		
Total		800	100.0		

Question: Do you agree with the statement that 'The elimination of Israel is a solution to the broader Arab-Israeli conflict'?

	Response	Frequency	Percent	Valid Percent	Cumulative Percent
Valid	Strongly sagree	36	4.4	4.4	4.4
	Agree	79	9.9	9.9	14.3
	Disagree	158	19.8	19.8	34.0
	Strongly disagree	481	60.1	60.2	94.2
	Don't know / NA	46	5.8	5.8	100.0
Total		800	100.0	100.0	

Table 9.5 Israeli Perceptions of Peace Benefits.

Question: To what extent has the peace treaty contributed to an improvement in the security of the Kingdom of Jordan?

	Response	Frequency	Percent	Valid Percent	Cumulative Percent
Valid	Not at all	135	11.2	12.9	12.9
	A little	140	11.7	13.4	26.3
	To some extent	300	25.0	28.7	55.0
	Worthwhile	303	25.2	28.9	83.9
	Very worthwhile	169	14.1	16.1	100.0
	Total	1047	87.2	100.0	
Missing / Don't know		154	12.8		
Total		1201	100.0		

Question: To what extent has the peace treaty has contributed to Israel's overall security?

	Response	Frequency	Percent	Valid Percent	Cumulative Percent
Valid	Not at all	161	13.4	14.2	14.2
	A little	166	13.8	14.7	28.9
	To some extent	307	25.6	27.2	56.1
	Worthwhile	329	27.4	29.1	85.2
	Very worthwhile	167	13.9	14.8	100.0
	Total	1130	94.1	100.0	
Missing / Don't know		71	5.9		
Total		1201	100.0		

Question: To what extent does the separation wall affect Israeli- Jordanian relations?

	Response	Frequency	Percent	Valid Percent	Cumulative Percent
Valid	Very good effect	87	7.2	7.5	7.5
	Good effect	140	11.7	12.0	19.5
	No effect	342	28.5	29.4	49.0
	Bad effect	442	36.8	38.0	86.9
	Very bad effect	151	12.6	13.0	100.0
	Total	1162	96.8	100.0	
Missing / Don't know		39	3.2		
Total		1201	100.0		

that the contribution of the treaty to Jordan's security was 'worthwhile' or 'very worthwhile', whereas only 17.5 per cent of Jordanians gave such a positive assessment. Similarly, though Israelis perceived considerable benefit to Israel's security from the treaty, the assessed benefit was not as high as that perceived by Jordanian respondents. On the issue of the potential impact of the security wall/fence on Israeli-Jordanian relations, the most common responses were either 'bad effect' (38.0 per cent) or 'no effect' (29.4 per cent).

There is great divergence of opinion between Israeli and Jordanian perceptions of the effect of the treaty on Jordan's water resources. While nearly two-thirds of Jordanians indicated that the treaty had created no improvement in their water resources, over half (55.8 per cent) of Israelis felt that the treaty had made a 'worthwhile' or 'very worthwhile' contribution to Jordan's water resources (Table 9.6).

Similar trends are evident in the perception of tourism benefits to Jordan (Table 9.6). While 42.3 per cent of Israelis found the improvement to be 'worthwhile' or 'very worthwhile', nearly half of the Jordanians (46.6 per cent) replied that tourism had improved 'not at all'. Perhaps the greatest divergence of opinion concerns the overall economic benefit of the peace to Jordan. A vast majority (74.2 per cent) of Jordanians felt that the treaty had improved the Jordanian economy 'not at all'; while the Israelis' response to this question was mixed, most respondents indicated either 'some extent' or 'worthwhile', when asked to assess the impact.

Whereas Jordanians generally expect relations with Israel to deteriorate to some degree over the next ten years, Israelis tend to believe relations will stay the same (44.7 per cent) or improve (43.6 per cent; Table 9.7). The survey does not reveal under what possible scenarios this could happen.

Israeli responses to the influence of the Israeli-Palestinian conflict on bilateral relations are much closer to Jordanian responses than other parts of the survey, with just over half of respondents indicating that the conflict had a 'great' or 'very great' effect. If the conflict were to end, 28 per cent feel that reconciliation between Jordan and Israel could take place in a 'few years', however, a sizeable number of respondents felt that it would take a generation or more.

The disparity in perception between Israelis and Jordanians is critical for understanding the role of treaty in past and future societal relations. The results of the survey also point out that the peace, though enjoined by two states, has largely not been implemented as a joint project, with specific emphasis on promoting the peace within their respective governments and populations. Moreover, the survey makes clear that it would be misleading to assume the stability of the Jordanian-Israeli peace, simply because the treaty remains intact.

Table 9.6 Israeli Perceptions of Water Resource and Economic Benefits.

Question: To what extent has the treaty contributed to an improvement in the state of Jordan's water resources?

	Response	Frequency	Percent	Valid Percent	Cumulative Percent
Valid	Not at all	80	6.7	8.4	8.4
	A little	97	8.1	10.2	18.6
	To some extent	244	20.3	25.6	44.2
	Worthwhile	316	26.3	33.2	77.4
	Very worthwhile	215	17.9	22.6	100.0
	Total	952	79.3	100.0	
Missing / Don't know		249	20.7		
Total		1201	100.0		

Question: To what extent has the treaty contributed to an improvement in tourism in Jordan?

	Response	Frequency	Percent	Valid Percent	Cumulative Percent
Valid	Not at all	125	10.4	12.5	12.5
	A little	174	14.5	17.3	29.8
	To some extent	280	23.3	27.9	57.7
	Worthwhile	264	22.0	26.3	84.0
	Very worthwhile	160	13.3	16.0	100.0
	Total	1003	83.5	100.0	
Missing / Don't know		198	16.5		
Total		1201	100.0		

Question: To what extent has the treaty contributed to an improvement in the state of Jordan's economy?

	Response	Frequency	Percent	Valid Percent	Cumulative Percent
Valid	Not at all	103	8.6	11.1	11.1
	A little	170	14.2	18.3	29.4
	To some extent	308	25.6	33.2	62.6
	Worthwhile	232	19.3	25.0	87.6
	Very worthwhile	115	9.6	12.4	100.0
	Total	928	77.3	100.0	
Missing / Don't know		273	22.7		
Total		1201	100.0		

Table 9.7 Israeli Perceptions of Future Israeli-Jordanian Relations.

Question: How do you perceive the direction of relations between Israel and Jordan in the next 10 years?

	Response	Frequency	Percent	Valid Percent	Cumulative Percent
Valid	Improve to great extent	64	5.3	5.7	5.7
	Improve	427	35.6	37.9	43.6
	Remain as now	504	42.0	44.7	88.3
	Deteriorate	124	10.3	11.0	99.3
	Deteriorate to great extent	8	0.7	0.7	100.0
	Total	1127	93.8	100.0	
Missing Response		74	6.2		
Total		1201	100.0		

Question: To what extent does the violent conflict between Israel and Palestinians affect relations between Israel and Jordan?

	Response	Frequency	Percent	Valid Percent	Cumulative Percent
Valid	No effect	115	9.6	9.6	9.6
	A little effect	161	13.4	13.5	23.2
	To a certain extent	351	29.2	29.4	52.6
	Great effect	338	28.1	28.4	81.0
	Very great effect	227	18.9	19.0	100.0
	Total	1192	99.3	100.0	
Missing Response		9	0.7		
Total		1201	100.0		

Question: : If a peace agreement is reached, and a Palestinian state is established and recognized by Israel, how soon do you think full reconciliation between Israel and Jordan will be achieved?

	Response	Frequency	Percent	Valid Percent	Cumulative Percent
Valid	Never	163	13.6	13.6	13.6
	Generations to come	204	17.0	17.0	30.6
	Next generation	198	16.5	16.5	47.1
	Next decade	130	10.8	10.8	57.9
	Few years	336	28.0	28.0	85.8
	Don't know	170	14.2	14.2	100.0
	Total	1201	100.0	100.0	

The Anti-Normalization Movement

The strong negative attitudes held by many Jordanians towards the peace with Israel are projected beyond the individual level into Jordanian politics through the actions of both individuals and organized groups under the general label of the 'anti-normalization movement' (ANM). This movement should not be conceptualized as a single, well-defined formal entity; it rather captures a set of somewhat diverse negative attitudes towards relations with Israel. Various actors include political parties, professional associations and individuals. Generally, attitudes towards normalization broadly fall into two categories, those held by people who espouse a total rejection of the treaty and those whose attitudes towards the peace are shaped primarily by general Arab-Israeli relations, and specifically the Israeli-Palestinian conflict. In mid-1995, George Hawatmeh, editor-in-chief of the Jordanian daily *Al-Rai*, estimated that 20 per cent of Jordanians belonged to the 'rejectionist' camp and 60 per cent to the latter, with the remaining 20 per cent supporting the regime's position, as they do on all other issues.[6] Today, it seems that the 'rejectionist' camp has grown significantly in response to the escalating Israeli-Palestinian conflict.

One may consider that the anti-normalization movement is composed of active and latent elements, all contributing to an environment that discourages contact with Israel.

The 'active' movement is made up of political parties and other groups who work towards the repeal of the treaty and to dissuade other members of society from normalizing with Israel. The Islamic Action Front (IAF), the political arm of the Muslim Brotherhood, is the most influential member of the anti-normalization political parties. Other parties, which routinely join the IAF on its anti-peace platform, include Arab nationalist and leftist parties. The anti-normalization movement coalesced in advance of the treaty signing and long before any 'fruits of peace' could be realized. In May 1994, a coalition of eight political parties launched the 'Popular Arab and Jordanian Committee for Resisting Submission and Normalization'.[7]

The government bureaucracy itself is not immune to anti-normalization activities, reflecting the top–down nature of the peace process that originated from the monarchy.[8]

After the peace treaty, many Jordanian ministers refused to meet with their Israeli counterparts and were critical of the fast rate of normalization and the growing official intolerance of dissent. The Jordanian delegation to the inauguration of the new Israeli embassy in Amman, for example, lacked any senior ministers. Though the Israeli Foreign Minister attended, Jordan was only represented by its Minister of State for foreign affairs.[9] The Ministry of Education is particularly notable for high levels of anti-normalization sentiment. The Minister of Higher Education did not attend an international seminar on education in peaceful coexistence, sending a lower level official instead. Recently, the Minister of Planning appeared at a symposium in Israel on means to increase Israeli-Jordanian cooperation by taped interview.[10] Israelis have also commented on the tendency for 'scheduling conflicts' to keep some high-level Jordanian officials away from joint events, such as the ground-breaking ceremony for the Bridging the Rift Centre.

By holding influence in the Jordanian parliament, and using this as a platform to call for an end to relations with Israel and to forestall normalization efforts, the anti-normalization movement has provided consistent opposition to monarchy-led efforts for normalized relations with Israel. Shortly after the peace treaty, the ANM called for a popular referendum on the treaty. The Islamist-led opposition criticized the secrecy that surrounded drafts of the treaty, arguing that the government intentionally misled the public about its contents.[11] Resolutions, statements and communiqués issued by ANM supporters in Parliament are typical means utilized to express their opposition. Action is often in response to specific events, especially those related to the Israeli-Palestinian conflict. Though most of the opposition to the peace treaty has taken place within the confines of civil society expression, the government has had to deal with more serious challenges in newspapers, at the ballot-box, and within parliamentary debate, such as the arrest of ten members of a group called the Bayat al-Imam (Pledge of Allegiance to the Leader) in September 1995 for subversion and attempted sabotage.[12]

The anti-normalization moment has sought wider public participation in its efforts by holding anti-normalization 'conferences'. Though the government had twice blocked a conference in spring 1995, it was eventually held in September of that year and passed an anti-normalization resolution. The 13 opposition parties in Parliament held a second conference in May 1999. One of this conference's main goals was to target Jordanian businessmen working with Israelis.[13]

As the anti-normalization groups channelled public anger against Israeli actions into protests and demonstrations, especially during the Netanyahu administration, they were able to expand their influence beyond their formal members, increasing the portion of society that could be considered the 'latent' anti-normalization group. The nature of Israel's actions, perceived as both in violation of the Oslo process and militarily aggressive, made it difficult for the government to be too forceful in its attempts to challenge the ANM.

Widespread protests, in addition to calls in Parliament to abrogate the treaty, took place in response to the Israeli operation in Lebanon known as 'Grapes of Wrath' in April 1996. Perhaps the most significant event, however, according to noted Jordanian political analyst Rami Khouri, was the response to Israel's opening of the Hasmonean tunnel in Jerusalem (see Chapter Four).

The leading party in the anti-normalization movement, the IAF, was able to achieve wide-ranging support, including 37 professional associations, political parties and non-governmental organizations, in condemning Israel and calling for resistance to 'all forms of normalization with the Zionist enemy'.[14] The crisis triggered by Israel's failure to redeploy from Hebron, in accord with the Oslo Accords timetable, gave the ANM further opportunity to broaden its base of support in Jordan. They organized large-scale protests against the first Israeli trade fair in Jordan. More than 4,000 protestors turned out, many with banners stating 'A massacre in Hebron and an exhibition in Amman' in reference to Palestinians shot in Hebron. Though the government sent a thousand police officers to control protestors, senior Jordanian officials did not appear at the event.[15] Israel's construction of the Har Homa housing complex later that year brought on renewed calls for abrogating the treaty and public protests. Actions in parliament against the implementation of the treaty were taken throughout the 1990s. In September 1998, 53 (out of 80) deputies presented a statement 'demanding a halt to normalization with Israel, as we see this process only serving Israel's interests'. Three key parliamentary blocs and numerous independents supported the statement in response to a call by the executive committee of the Jordanian Popular Conference for Safeguarding the Homeland and Confronting Normalization, headed by Islamist leader Ishaq al-Farhan.[16]

The ANM exercises control over many of the country's professional organizations by occupying major leadership positions in the associations. These associations represent key professions, including lawyers, doctors, dentists, pharmacists, veterinarians, engineers, nurses and geologists. By 2001, fourteen of the country's professional associations, with a membership of 100,000 strong, had joined the anti-normalization movement.[17] Though the rank-and-file members may not share the political views of the leadership,[18] the ANM has been able to successfully control the associations by securing their positions; often they are the most active membership bloc. Even prior to the peace treaty, the associations adopted resolutions to take disciplinary action (including expulsion) against members engaging in relations with Israelis.[19]

Fear of censure by the professional associations has greatly deterred individuals from collaborating with Israeli institutions and individuals. In 1999, the Jordanian Engineers Association denied membership to engineers that graduated from Israeli universities,[20] making them effectively unemployable. A planned visit by Israel's ambassador to Jordan, Shimon Shamir, to a date palm plantation in the north of the country was cancelled owed to the influence of the ANM. The plantation owner, who would have received 120 saplings from Israel, withdrew his invitation following warnings of disciplinary action from his professional association, the Agricultural Engineer's Syndicate.[21]

Journalists, especially, have often faced reprimand. After a weeklong visit to Israel at the invitation of Haifa University, three journalists, including the editor-in-chief of the English-language daily *The Jordan Times*, were forced to sign statements declaring their support for the anti-normalization movement.[22] In May 1995, the Writers League expelled Hamadah Fara'aneh, a columnist for the well-respected daily *Al-Dustur*, for providing political commentary on Israeli television.[23] In October 2000, shortly after Prime Minister Sharon's highly contested visit to the Temple Mount/Harem Al-Sharif, the Arab Journalists Union conference in Jordan confirmed its anti-normalization stance. Its final statement read: 'The union confirms its firm rejection of normalization with the Zionist entity and condemns the calls of a minority of outsiders who advocate the so-called culture of peace with Israel.'[24] It also called on Arab unions and newspaper federations to supply the AJU with the names of journalists normalizing with Israel in order to issue a special blacklist across the Arab world. Besides problems with their professional associations, Jordanian journalists who have entered Israel have found themselves censured by other Arab states.[25]

In the healthcare field, too, the professional associations have blocked joint efforts, despite the signing of a formal bilateral health accord in 1995. However, in the case physicians and dentists unions the ban against coopera-tion with Israelis has been somewhat balanced by universal medical ethics. In the physicians union, a distinction between cooperation and care exists, and Israelis seeking medical attention in Jordan would not be denied care.[26] The dentists association also agreed to provide emergency, but not routine, care to Israelis. The full effect of these restrictions extended to participation by Jordanian private doctors in a regional Middle East and North Africa economic meeting, which included Israeli participants.[27]

The anti-normalization movement has also targeted its critics. A 1998 seminar on the role of professional associations in Jordan's democratization, organized by the Urdun al-Jadid Research Centre and the Konrad Adenauer Foundation, was postponed 'until further notice'.[28] This action was part of a broader campaign against foreign research centres, led by key figures in Islamist and Communist parties. Foreign organizations, such as the Konrad Adenauer Foundation and the US-affiliated American Centre for Oriental Research (ACOR), have been accused of spying, theft of Jordanian culture, and links with the United States Central Intelligence Agency.

The ANM has actively sought to expose Jordanians accused of working with Israel, using public pressure to stop any individual normalization ac-tions. Blacklists are published, listing the names of people and companies, often in the hotel and agricultural sector, who work with Israelis.[29] If exposed, Jordanians face a loss of business, social standing and individual acts of re-prisal. That may be why the Israeli embassy in Amman was unable to book a hotel for its Independence Day reception in 2000. Faced with potential boycott, the host hotel from the previous year, as well as other major hotels in the city, reported no availability. In a notable example of the power of the professional associations, a Jordanian dentist, who was seeking election to a leadership position in the Amman Dentists' Association, publicly apologized for participating in the previous years' reception. He further declared that he would 'never again make a move that can be construed as normalizing relations with the Zionist enemy.' His apology was prompted by threats from rival dentists to use his participation in the reception as a means to disqualify him for running for office.[30]

The 'Latent' Anti-Normalization Movement

As violence between Israelis and Palestinians increased, the positions held by the formal anti-normalization movement and the general feeling towards Israel among much of Jordan's population have converged. The growth of this 'latent' anti-normalization movement, which includes people who are not necessarily members of anti-normalization political parties or among the leadership of professional associations, is tied to growing resistance to any form of contact with Israelis and growing identification with Palestinian suffering. The early days after the start of the *intifada* in September 2000 saw both a Palestinian solidarity rally, organized by Islamists, and anti-Israeli demonstrations in downtown Amman, attended by thousands.[31] Large demonstrations also took place following the killings of Hamas spiritual leader Sheikh Ahmed Yassin and his successor Gaza Abdel Aziz Rantisi in Spring 2004. Popular anti-Israeli feeling is also expressed through grim humour; on April Fools' Day in 2004, a rumour spread through Jordan that Hamas had killed Israeli Prime Minister Sharon, prompting Jordanians to rush to their televisions for news.[32]

At the same time, Israeli military actions towards the Palestinians discouraged formal bilateral relations; following the start of the *intifada*, Jordan (like Egypt) postponed sending its new ambassador to Israel, tacitly reinforcing the official acceptability of anti-normalization views. Similarly, high reaches of the government are publicly demonstrating sympathy with Palestinian suffering, with the cabinet deciding to deduct one day's salary from approximately 150,000 civil servants to contribute to the Palestinian *intifada*.[33]

Aware of the growing pressure within Jordanian society, the government has been willing to allow marches and demonstrations against violence towards Palestinians, earning them praise from the political opposition dominated by the anti-normalization supporters. In at least one case the opposition aided the government in ending clashes and confrontations between youth demonstrators and Jordanian security forces in Al-Baq'ah, Jordan's largest Palestinian refugee camp.[34]

Governmental Response to Anti-Normalization

The Jordanian government's stance, especially by the monarchy, towards the anti-normalization movement has changed considerably over the last ten years. In the early years after peace, the monarchy under King Hussein did intense battle with the ANM. As the regional situation deteriorated and the rewards of the peace treaty failed to materialize, the monarchy backed off its pressure on the movement in response to domestic sensitivities. Though attempts to restrain the ANM through new press laws in 1997 did not work, electoral reform has been able to reduce the political power of Islamist opposition parties. At the same time, a marked change in the official attitude towards normalization under the reign of King Abdullah II has dramatically scaled-back the governmental role in promoting societal relations with Israel.

Shortly after the treaty, the government took a number of steps to mitigate the power of the professional associations, including attempts to amend laws that require relevant association membership for professionals. Concerned about their potential role in undermining the peace, the government asked prominent members of Hamas leadership leave the country in May 1995. Numerous people were arrested the following year for supporting the group. The government also reacted swiftly to crush the aforementioned group called Bayat al-Imam (Pledge of Allegiance to the Leader). Several individuals were arrested for criticizing normalization and the king.[35]

The pace of normalization, and the suppression of opposition to it, drew concern from within Jordan and the broader Arab world. One influential critic, the editor-in-chief of the influential Pan-Arab newspaper *Al-Hayat*, warned of a 'backlash' from proceeding at such a rapid pace.[36] In numerous public speeches, King Hussein sent strongly worded messages to the opponents of the peace with Israel, warning that powerful measures would be taken if they did not curb their actions.[37] Another concern for Jordan's internal security was the ability of external political forces, either state governments or militant groups, to use the peace and normalization as a wedge to destabilize Jordan domestically. In one speech, King Hussein accused professional unions of having links to foreign groups, noting specifically the Islamist and leftist party leaders who, he said, held 'meetings in neighbouring capitals, especially in Damascus'.[38]

In 1998 there was a rapprochement of sorts between the Islamists and the government, and attempts to repair the rift over the Islamist boycott of the 1997 elections (see following section). Crucially, the Jordanian High Court declared the Press and Publications Law unconstitutional. The government's current relationship with the anti-normalization movement reflects pragmatism on the part of the monarchy, as it tries to maintain balance among domestic constituencies. The ANM has been allowed to operate within confined parameters, but the government is willing to confront it when necessary. Only a few months after the start of the 2000 *intifada*, four lawmakers withdrew their signatures from a petition, demanding cancellation of the peace treaty with Israel, under unidentified 'pressures'.[39] In response to the continued publication of 'blacklists' of Jordanians working with Israel, the government arrested seven anti-normalization activists for affiliation to an 'illegitimate and unlicensed organization'. The published blacklist 'contained the names of 68 journalists, politicians, academics, artists, companies and schools that advocate cross-cultural and economic ties with Israel under the peace treaty. It even listed a politician who helped negotiate the treaty with Israel.'[40] Public actions to support jailed anti-normalization activists were blocked in November 2002,[41] a planned march on the Israeli embassy prohibited,[42] and the Jordanian court of cassation, one of the highest in the country, banned anti-Israel committees linked to the professional trade unions.[43] However, it seems the government's main concern was the threat these actions posed to internal security, rather than their potential effect on relations with Israel.

At the same time, the government made it increasingly clear that normalization was viewed as a personal choice and no one would be forced to have associations with Israel or Israelis. According to Nevo, this stance marks a major distinction between the reign of King Hussein and King Abdullah:

> The gap between the two kings' attitude to normalization was even wider. Hussein considered normalization to be the essence of the peace treaty and refused to regard it as hostage to Israel's good behaviour or as a lever to make more concessions to the Palestinians—as many advised him to do. Abdullah, on the other hand, maintains that normalization has nothing to do with government policy. It should be an independent decision, with discretion accorded to any individual or organization to decide whether or not to visit Israel or to cooperate with Israeli colleagues and counterparts.[44]

Indeed, early in his reign, Abdullah seemed to reach out to the anti-normalization movement, placing a number of its representatives in the cabinet.

Though this shift in governmental policy is associated with Abdullah, it should be noted that King Hussein also made a similar statement: 'Whoever wants to deal with the people in a neighbouring country with which we are at peace can do so, and whoever wishes otherwise is in free.'[45] Nevertheless, Jordanian government officials, while continuing to attack the anti-normalization movement, have consistently reiterated the government's commitment not to force anyone to work with Israel or Israelis.[46]

Electoral Politics

The battle between the government and the ANM also took place within the country's electoral system. In the early 1990s, Jordan embarked on a significant program of political liberalization, largely as a response to political upheaval and riots in the country in 1989.[47] By 1992, two critical steps had been taken that would allow opposition to be voiced in parliament and pave the way for the anti-normalization movement. The first was the adoption of the National Charter, which emphasized political pluralism; the second was the repeal of the ban on political parties dating from 1957. By the time of the 1993 general elections, more than 20 political parties were registered.

At stake in the 1993 elections were the 80 seats in the lower house of Parliament, the House of Deputies. In advance of the elections, the government passed a 'temporary' election law, intensely disliked by many of the political parties. This new law provided for a one-person one-vote system, where a voter could only vote for one candidate to serve as representative for his or her district, even though most districts had more than one representative. The candidate receiving the second largest number of votes would gain the second representative seat and so on. The new law replaced a plurality system, which had been in place for the 1989 elections, where the number of votes each person could cast equalled the number of representatives. This procedure had allowed well-organized parties, especially the Muslim Brotherhood (Ikhwan), to dominate in parliament, as described by Ryan:[48]

> In some areas, the Ikhwan ran lists of candidates up to the exact number of seats for a given district. In this way, the Brotherhood was able to exploit the plurality-based electoral system to win twenty-two out of twenty-six seats it had contested (in the 1989 elections).

In addition to the one-person one-vote system, the new election law also continued to reserve seats for specific ethnic groups (Chechens, Circassians), Christians and Bedouins. Opposition parties charged that the apportioning of seats favoured traditionally pro-government rural areas over urban districts.

The results of the parliamentary elections in 1993 saw a significant decrease in the number of seats held by Islamists. Their representation, now running under the Muslim Brotherhood's new political party, the Islamic Action Front, dropped from 22 to 16 seats. Seats held by independent Islamists dropped from twelve to six.[49]

The Islamists attempted to reassert electoral power in the 1995 municipal elections. In their campaigns, they presented the elections as a referendum on the peace treaty.[50] Overall, the elections were a poor showing for the supporters of anti-normalization, according to Brand:

The turnout was low and the Islamists won only 8 mayorships of the 259 contested, although among the eight were several important ones, including Madaba, Irbid and Karak. Indeed, vocal opposition to normalization remained limited, the most notable exception being the various professional associations, which took an anti-normalization stand and banned their members from visiting Israel or having professional contacts with Israelis.[51]

Demonstrations in advance of the elections were put down by the government as part of the monarchy's campaign against Islamist parties and professional associations.

Reeling from setbacks in the 1993 national and 1995 municipal elections, Islamists made the 1993 electoral law a focal point of the 1997 general elections, increasing the tension between government and opposition. This conflict led to an election boycott by nine opposition parties and thirteen professional associations, in response to a call by the Muslim Brotherhood. In boycotting the election, the Islamists hoped to discredit the electoral process' national and international legitimacy and to pressure the government. Meanwhile, they continued to attack the peace treaty, putting up campaign banners describing Israel as the 'Zionist enemy', which were torn down by Jordanian authorities.[52]

In addition to the refusal to alter the temporary election law, the government adopted a 'temporary' press and publications law in 1997. It was designed to clamp down on Jordan's tabloid press, the main publishing outlet for anti-normalization views. The law required new capital requirements for newspapers, which most tabloids were unable to meet. This served to muffle political debate in the press in the run up to the November 1997 elections.[53]

Results of the 1997 Election

In 2001, an Elections Law was passed that maintained the one-person one-vote formula and increased the number of seats in the Lower House to 104 by reserving seats for specific groups, including women. The total number of seats was later raised to the current 110. Voting irregularities, including the arrest of individuals for 'voting manipulation', marred the 2003 election, but were not thought to have affected its outcome. The IAF ran 30 candidates, but won only 17 seats. Five other seats were won by independent Islamists. Despite this low number of seats, Islamists represented the largest bloc in parliament. Pan-Arab and leftist parties fared poorly, winning only two seats.[54] The election was largely seen as favourable for the monarchy, since pro-royal elements emerged as the most significant force.

Three trends typify the Jordanian perception of the peace treaty at the ten-year mark: strong disillusionment among the general population combined with general anger towards Israel, the institutionalization and entrenchment of the anti-normalization movement and the retreat of the government's efforts to promote normalization. As early as 1997, Rami Khouri documented the connection between a shift of perception among the general population and the strengthening of the ANM:

> We are witnessing qualitative changes and new elements in the political landscape, rather than reruns of old scenarios. One, two and four years ago, the anti-normalization camp in Jordan sought to stop the peace treaty and its implementation, but achieved very little; today, anti-normalization sentiment permeates much of society. We should not deny the association between the extreme new attitudes in Jordan and the extreme new policies in Israel.[55]

The growth of these 'extreme new attitudes' not only threatens the peace, but also the stability of the nation as a whole, prompting warnings from the government against attempts to use popular anger at Israelis to 'endanger national unity'.[56] Such statements illustrate the tightrope the Jordanian government walks between maintaining its treaty commitments and internal stability. While the government at first enthusiastically promoted normalized relations with Israel, especially under the reign of King Hussein, they had reduced their efforts as early as 1996:

> The passion that once defined the government's peacemaking with Israel has dimmed measurably. This is clear in several different forms: the government no longer actively opposes or significantly obstructs the anti-normalization campaign, as it did in 1994–95; public meetings with Israeli officials and Jewish delegations from around the world are few and far between, and not as loudly trumpeted as they used to be; and despite my frequent naps, I have not heard any government minister, including our prime ministers, speak passionately or wax eloquently about peace with Israel, for about, oh, two years now.[57]

Today, the government no longer speaks of normalization as an intentional governmental policy, but as a 'personal choice' to be exercised by Jordanians at their will.

10
LESSONS FROM AN INCOMPLETE PEACE

In February 1995, 29 of the 120 members of the Knesset shared dinner with King Hussein at Hashimiyeh Palace in Amman. The Israeli delegation reflected the full spectrum of Israel's political life, including members from Labour, Likud, Meretz, Shas, Yi'ud, the National Religious Party, United Torah, Moledet, the Arab Democratic Party and the Democratic Front for Peace and Equality.[1] One can hardly imagine such an event happening today.

At that dinner, King Hussein expressed this wish that 'Hopefully the peace between two countries and peoples will be an example to others throughout the region.' Though the Jordanian-Israeli peace cannot and should not be considered a failure, it remains an incomplete peace in many ways, its expected potential unrealized and its future outlook disheartening. In sum, Jordan and Israel largely failed to make the transition from peace making to peace building. In this regard, the Jordanian-Israeli experience may indeed provide important lessons for the region and provide key lessons for future peace-making efforts.

Reflections on the Current Relationship

Ten years after making peace, the Jordanian-Israeli relationship is both strong and quite fragile. The degree to which the parties themselves appreciate the extent of its weakness is not clear. This is especially true for the Israeli government and people, which tend to place the highest value on security, the treaty's main area of success. But even there, the 'Voice of Israel' was warning of 'continuing deterioration of ties between Israel and Jordan' by 2001. A classified Israeli Foreign Ministry document stated that 'cooperation between Israel and Jordan is almost completely frozen'. The program further asserted that 'unless there is real change in Israel's political stands, the deterioration in relations with Jordan is inevitable'.[2]

Satloff also warned that the Jordanian-Israeli relationship risked being one-dimensional:

> The bottom line is that, unless it is nurtured, the Jordan-Israel relationship could slide into what one could call 'pre-treaty-plus'—close security and military relations (which Abdullah is firmly committed to maintain and even expand) at the expense of economic, political, and cultural 'normalization.'[3]

The centrality of security remains a strength and a weakness of the treaty, providing a strong motivation to both parties to cooperate, while at the same time overshadowing other areas of potential cooperation. Although both militaries have been able to forge a strong reciprocal security relationship, success on the security front has not been linked to efforts to forge broader bilateral economic and societal relations.

Public enthusiasm for the peace and official cooperation in fields beyond security began to wane as early as 1996, and declined along a trajectory that largely paralleled the disintegration of the Oslo process, the rise of right-wing politics in Israel and the outbreak of the second Palestinian *intifada*. Few references to cooperation between Israel and Jordan have been mentioned in published accounts over the last six years. Even the 10-year anniversary of the peace went largely unnoticed in the Israeli and Jordanian press. Though Jordan's Foreign Minister, Marwan Muasher, did reaffirm that 'the Israeli-Jordanian peace treaty was sacred and that Jordan would uphold it even if bilateral relations were hurt',[4] Jordanian government officials, in statements through the semiofficial newspaper *Al-Dustur*, also denied rumours that an official Israeli Foreign Ministry delegation had visited Amman on the anniversary of the treaty.[5]

A lack of confidence marks the relationship between the two parties at the governmental and societal level. Though it would have been unrealistic to expect future leadership to bring the same passion to the peace as its main architects, Yitzakh Rabin and King Hussein, neither government has taken the key steps required to institutionalize the peace beyond its security and—to a limited extent—economic parameters. This is partly a result of how quickly the prospects for normal bilateral relations dimmed in the face of renewed regional conflict. As Israel made no structural provisions within the government for comprehensive bilateral relations with Jordan, and the Jordanian government seemed to abandon its policy of active, dynamic normalization with Israel by 1996,[6] the peace never became deeply embedded in either government or society.

While the negative repercussions of the Israeli-Palestinian conflict on Jordanian attitudes towards the peace may be unavoidable, the absence of a highly visible set of concrete outcomes leaves little possibility to create a more multi-dimensional image of Israel inside Jordan. The close linkage between Jordan's peace with Israel and the Arab-Israeli conflict is apparent even at the highest reaches of government; a senior Jordanian official noted in 2001: 'The biggest failure (of the treaty) was not the lack of fruits of peace. The biggest failure was not achieving comprehensive peace.'[7]

The ability of the Israeli-Palestinian conflict to constrain the perception of the Israeli-Jordanian peace was evident very soon after the signing of the treaty. Marwan Muasher, Jordan's first ambassador to Israel, observed in 1995:

> In short, the lag between peacemaking and the achievement of prosperity associated with stability, as well as hitherto unresolved political problems (i.e. the Palestinian issue), have prevented many Jordanians from viewing the future with confidence. The reluctance that many Jordanians exhibit toward full normalization with Israel is not necessarily an indication of opposition to the peace process, but rather a reaction to harsh realities that are still being encountered in their daily lives.[8]

This sentiment does raise the question how much progress can actually be made between Jordan and Israel as long as the Israeli-Palestinian conflict rages with no prospect of a negotiated solution in sight. In reality, the Hashemite monarchy faces enormous domestic constraints in its relationship with Israel. Yet, it would be a mistake for Israel to presume that Jordanian domestic resistance to the peace and normalization is solely a 'Jordanian problem'. Rather, this issue affects the overall potential for bilateral relations; if Jordan and Israel are truly 'partners in peace', joint approaches to overcome societal resistance in both countries are needed.

What is the future of Jordanian-Israeli relations? Logically, there are three possible scenarios: status quo, disintegration of bilateral relations or deepening and broadening of the bilateral relationship.

Status Quo

The most likely situation is continuation of the relationship at the current level. Because it is in their mutual best interest, both parties will maintain a strong security relationship, especially in the face of increased instability in the region coming from both the occupied territories and Iraq. Under this option, however, security cooperation remains largely functional and does not further develop to the strategic level. Limited economic cooperation continues, focused on the QIZ, and challenges to the treaty are handled as they arise, rather than through a process that attempts to anticipate future

problems and militate against them. Neither government encourages more societal interaction or supports the creation of ties between the two peoples.

Deterioration

As societal relations currently do not exist, the deterioration option would
entail, at the very least, a further curtailment of relations between the two
governments. Mechanisms for cooperation, many of which have atrophied
in recent years, would remain idle or formally disband. The cessation of
routine security cooperation, if it occurred, would be a strong indicator of
deterioration. Official statements and reports given to media outlets would
be marked by greater criticism and hostility, and freer reign would be given
to critics in both governments and societies. However, barring regime change
in Jordan, it remains unlikely that either party would formally abrogate the
treaty, as its security guarantees can continue even without joint mechanisms.
As long as the two parties share a fundamental agreement on security, the
treaty will likely remain intact. However, the potential for water resource
allocations to precipitate a conflict and potential abrogation of the treaty
remains very high.

Though at present the option of military conflict between Israel and
Jordan seems remote, its future potential should not be ignored. Most conflict scenarios are based on either a forced movement of Palestinians from
the West Bank or a dramatic regime change inside Jordan.

Improvement

Can the Jordanian-Israeli relationship improve, and reach the level of
'good neighbourly relations' articulated in the treaty? Is it possible to overcome external pressures, namely, the Israeli-Palestinian conflict, to increase
bilateral relations? Does either party have the political will to do this? Today,
an improvement of the Jordanian-Israeli relationship seems very unlikely,
unless serious conflict resolution efforts are renewed.

Recommendations

Returning for a moment to that dinner in 1995, the words of Crown
Prince Hassan take on more significance today: 'our ability to deliver du-
rable peace and prosperity to future generations is still dependent on our
willingness for compromise and sacrifice'.

Certainly, compromise has played a part in maintaining the Jordanian-
Israeli peace, as in water allocations and the Mish'al incident. The question

remains as to what extend Jordan and Israel are willing to engage in compromise and sacrifice today in order to broaden and deepen the peace.

It is clear that 'peace-building' must be an intentional act; it cannot be expected as a natural outcome of the conclusion of a treaty, no matter how detailed or well intentioned. In some ways, Jordan and Israel face a more difficult task of peacemaking today than they did in 1994. They must overcome a track record of disappointments and unmet expectations, at a time when there is no active negotiating process between Israel and the Palestinians and the very concept of the two-state solution is in doubt. Like the Oslo process, the Jordanian-Israeli peace suffers from having no current vision of what the peace could or should look like. It may be that both parties are content with the status of the relationship, which can best be described as a robust security arrangement with some economic activity; if they do, however, wish to go beyond this relatively narrow set of contacts, a concerted effort will be required to transform the relationship beyond its current level and prevent potential future deterioration.

The following steps will likely need to be part of any process:

Assessment of the Current Relationship[9]

Both parties must conduct a comprehensive assessment of the Jordanian-Israeli bilateral relationship, in order to gain a clear understanding of its strengths and weaknesses. This task should be approached in a manner that does not encourage assigning blame to either party, but in a sincere effort to assess the relationship between these strategic partners. This step, best undertaken in joint meetings, is a prerequisite before the parties can establish a comprehensive set of goals and a vision for their future relations.

The assessment process should acknowledge the existence of unmet expectations by both parties and their impact on relations at the governmental and societal level. They should also identify internal and external factors that affect the state of current relations. Such factors may include, but are not limited to, the influence of domestic politics and the collapse of the Israeli-Palestinian peace process. Factors and processes that promote the peace, such as economic activity in the QIZ, as well as those that discourage joint activities, such as confusing visa procedures, need to be identified, so that both parties will have a greater understanding of the resources available to further the peace, as well as the obstacles that its further development faces.

Creating A New Vision of the Peace

The parties must decide if they want to pursue deeper, more normalized relations. If both are satisfied with the current level of interaction, then the status of the treaty as 'security plus' should be acknowledged publicly, so that societal expectations can abate.

Key questions each party needs to evaluate independently include: To what extent is the bilateral relationship important? What are the potential benefits and drawbacks to deeper relations?

Israel has traditionally conceptualized Jordan primarily as a security buffer; such an assessment tends to minimize the potential role of economic and cultural relations, despite the fact that these relations are necessary to cultivate broader societal support for the peace in Jordan. This support would reduce domestic friction and strengthen the position of the very regime that delivers the security guarantees that Israel needs. Fundamentally, Israel needs to decide if the relationship with Jordan, beyond basic security, is really a priority.

Both parties need to engage in a frank and systematic discussion of how the Jordanian-Israeli relationship relates to the Israeli-Palestinian relationship. Such a discussion will not be easy, especially given the high level of emotion the conflict elicits in Jordan and the prevailing sensitivity to Israeli governmental stances in the territories:

> Israel cannot expect to enjoy the benefits of tourism in Petra and industrial joint projects in Irbid, on the one hand, while on the other hand it bombs Palestinian towns, picks off Palestinian children with sniper fire and sends its most predatory right-wing ideologues on missions of political provocation to the most important Palestinian, Islamic and Arab holy sites in Jerusalem.[10]

And yet, the Israeli-Palestinian conflict cannot continue to be the two-ton elephant in the room that no one talks about. An attempt to move the Jordanian-Israeli relationship forward, without acknowledging the role of the Israeli-Palestinian conflict, places it in an artificial context and will only produce unrealistic and unworkable outcomes.

Identifying 'Spaces' Within the Current Situation

Conventional wisdom dictates that many of the goals envisioned in the peace treaty between Jordan and Israel will remain on hold until there is a comprehensive peace in the region, or at least a strong expectation that peace is coming soon. If the Jordanian-Israeli relationship is to improve before this takes place, 'spaces' for additional cooperation within the current political situation must be identified.

It would also be a mistake to believe that a just and comprehensive peace would automatically lead to improvement of the weakened Jordanian-Israeli relationship. Identification of such spaces now, while the conflict still rages, can be considered a preparatory step for the time when the Jordanian-Israeli relationship is better able to move forward.

Expanding the Security Relationship

The Jordanian-Israeli security relationship needs to move to the level of a strategic dialogue, rather than stay a functional relationship largely focused on responding to events. Recent developments in the region, including the US occupation of Iraq, the rise of Al Qaeda influenced groups, the Israeli construction of the security wall/fence, and the Gaza disengagement plan, are all issues for which there should be comprehensive consultation between the two parties. The emphasis needs to be on dialogue that feeds back into the policy process in both governments, not on simply informing the other party of a plan of action (often after the fact). In a best-case scenario, such a consultative process could form the nucleus of a regional security process, which would benefit the Arab states as much as Israel.

The Jordan Anti-Normalization Movement

The parties need to decide if the anti-normalization movement is solely a Jordanian problem, or a more general barrier to the peace that needs to be addressed by both Jordan and Israel. As Jordan continues with political reforms, societal voices—including those in the opposition—will continue to be heard. Just as members of Israeli society and its political body will continue to speak of 'the Jordan option', some in Jordan will call for abrogation of the treaty.

The most effective means to address the anti-normalization movements in both countries is to build bridges between political actors in the centre of the political spectrum. At this point, only a few liberal Jordanian politicians have ever met with their Israeli colleagues, and the same is true for Israeli politicians. Without direct contact between the centres, judgments about the other country and its motives are largely based on media reports and stereotype. As the remaining politicians and military officials who were involved in the peace treaty retire and leave public life, the situation will become even more acute. Building bridges between the centres can facilitate the clear articulation of the essential interests between Jordan and Israel.

The sad truth is that, even in this day of building the wall and increased travel restrictions on Palestinians, it is more likely that Israeli and Palestinian politicians will meet than Israeli and Jordanian ones. Success on this front will require political pressure from the top levels in both the Jordanian monarchy and the Israeli government.

Utilizing the Second Track

Though second-track meetings, typically associated with the negotiating process leading up to an agreement, have been used extensively by Israelis and Palestinians, most notably in the Oslo Agreement breakthrough, they have not been systematically used by Jordan and Israel, in order to maintain and grow peaceful relations between them. Track-two dialogues are shielded from the public view and typically involve participants who do not hold official positions in government (or current officials acting in a private capacity); therefore, they can move beyond political posturing and address sensitive issues.

Track-two dialogs could be used in the Jordan-Israel relationship to explore the questions of what can be gained from a more comprehensive bilateral relationship and how this could be reached. In the optimal case, the track-two process should be linked to the policy process in both countries and provide information and feedback into it. Retired generals, academics, NGO specialists and entrepreneurs all provide a rich source of potential track-two participants with detailed knowledge of the other country.

Recognizing the Asymmetry in Israeli-Jordanian Relations

It is inaccurate to believe that the peace was made between two equal partners and that relations between them must proceed along a highly reciprocal 'tit for tat' process, with each side demonstrating equal 'compromise and sacrifice'. The fundamental reality is that for a variety of reasons, the growth of the peace and deeper normalization is dependent on significant tangible benefits accruing in Jordan.

This asymmetry is the result of significant economic and political differences in the stature of the two countries, as well as the greatly different domestic environments. In the economic area, for example, Israel's economic relationship with Jordan is largely insignificant compared to its relationship with the United States or the European Union, but Jordan's relationship with Israel, and especially its future potential, is significant. Politically, Israel's stature in the international arena is far more influential, largely because of its relationship with the United States. To be quite frank, when Israel speaks, the US administration and—more importantly—the US public listens. In the internal political dimension, the Hashemite regime walks a tightrope, especially today, and the relationship with Israel is often a liability. While Israelis may not be consistently satisfied with Jordan's actions, the issue does not figure prominently in parliamentary debate or public protests.

A key question for Israel to consider is: why, in light of the continued Israeli-Palestinian conflict and Israel's use of harsh military tactics, should Jordan try to deepen normalization and risk greater internal destabilization.

Is it in Israel's best national interest to assist Jordan in finding a way to turn the peace from a domestic liability to a neutral issue, at the very least? As Satloff observed:

> Those Israelis who think that Abdullah needs to replicate his father's penchant for iconoclastic peacemaking before they are willing to 'reward' him, have the equation backwards; they should be offering Jordan an array of enticements to build a multifaceted alliance—political, economic, intelligence and military.[11]

Closer relations with Jordan should not be viewed as a 'gift' to the Jordanians, but as a component of Israeli national security, since Jordan is the one Arab state with which Israel shares real common interests. Jordan will continue to be an influential player in any eventual peace process, as well as in alternative approaches such as the Gaza disengagement, which entailed the efforts of not only Jordan, but also Egypt, in key security issues and diplomatic processes.

Overcoming this asymmetry is important even at the symbolic level, and much could be gained through Israel's willingness to consult with Jordan, even when they don't need to.

Reduction of Administrative and Bureaucratic Hurdles

It is important in this area as well to recognize the difference between the nature of Israel and Jordan's governmental systems. Within Jordan, the relationship is largely driven and maintained by the monarchy, which is able to move things forward when they choose to, despite societal resistance.

Within Israel, however, the relationship with Jordan, like many other political issues, is subject to the changeable winds of domestic politics. Is there a desire to create a strategic relationship with Jordan that is insulated from or can rise above the tactical aspects of Israeli internal politics? Is the relationship with Jordan central enough to be given a core status and recognized as a central component of Israel's interests? In the absence of such status, there is little coordination within the Israeli bureaucracy to effectively carry out a full spectrum of relations with Jordan.

If there is an attempt to deepen relations, addressing the bureaucratic hurdles will be necessary to reinvigorate the types of projects that could lead to greater societal support for the peace in Jordan and increased overall activity. Potential projects include the Red Sea–Dead Sea Canal, expansion of the Sheikh Hussein crossing and opening of the West Bank to Jordanian trade.

Jordan should also reassess its lack of representation in Tel Aviv at the ambassadorial level. While the ambassador was originally withdrawn to express concern about Israeli military actions in the occupied territories, the political point has been made. Representation, while symbolically reaffirming the peace, would provide an important channel for transmitting Jordanian views on both the conflict and bilateral relations.

Empowering the NGO Sector

The ability of nongovernmental organizations in Jordan and Israel to complete projects must be increased, if significant societal relations are to develop. Currently the NGO sector suffers from a lack of funds for projects and little government support to break through complicated bureaucracies and challenge critics. Third party donors have largely ignored bilateral Jordanian-Israeli projects, perhaps assuming that they were not needed, as peace had already been legally achieved. The United States and the European Union, as well as Jordan and Israel themselves, need to provide financial support for greater activity in this area.

Education of the Public

Both publics lack comprehensive knowledge of the peace, the details of the agreement and the process of peacemaking that took place ten years ago. Neither government undertook an extensive peace education campaign at the societal level during the early years of the peace. The failures of recent years have left a strong negative impression.

Members of both societies hold attitudes that limit the potential for broader normalized relations. For example, even the most knowledgeable Israelis contend that Israel's concessions to the peace were material, while those of the Jordanians were only psychological, implying that Jordan's concessions were not important. Similarly, it is inexcusable that Jordanians do not know the role of Israeli entrepreneurs in the QIZ.

A public peace education campaign will only be successful if there is a new, collaborative effort to build the peace, with clear, achievable goals. Unfortunately, the record of the first ten years is not good enough to be able to build excitement about the future. Without goals and plans for the next decade, and no hope of better relations, there is little chance of increasing public engagement in 'good neighbourly relations'.

Appendix

TREATY OF PEACE BETWEEN THE STATE OF ISRAEL AND THE HASHEMITE KINGDOM OF JORDAN

PREAMBLE

The Government of the State of Israel and the Government of the Hashemite Kingdom of Jordan:

Bearing in mind the Washington Declaration, signed by them on 25th July, 1994, and which they are both committed to honour;

Aiming at the achievement of a just, lasting and comprehensive peace in the Middle East based on Security Council resolutions 242 and 338 in all their aspects;

Bearing in mind the importance of maintaining and strengthening peace based on freedom, equality, justice and respect for fundamental human rights, thereby overcoming psychological barriers and promoting human dignity;

Reaffirming their faith in the purposes and principles of the Charter of the United Nations and recognizing their right and obligation to live in peace with each other as well as within all states, within secure and recognized boundaries;

Desiring to develop friendly relations and cooperation between them in accordance with the principles of international law governing international relations in times of peace;

Desiring as well to ensure lasting security for both their States and in particular to avoid threats and the use of force between them;

Bearing in mind that in their Washington Declaration of 25th July 1994, they declared the termination of the state of belligerency between them;

Deciding to establish peace between them in accordance with this treaty of peace;

Have agreed as follows:

ARTICLE 1—ESTABLISHMENT OF PEACE

Peace is hereby established between the State of Israel and the Hashemite Kingdom of Jordan (the "parties") effective from the exchange of the instruments of ratification of this treaty.

ARTICLE 2—GENERAL PRINCIPLES

The parties will apply between them the provisions of the Charter of the United Nations and the principles of international law governing relations among states in times of peace. In particular:

1. They recognize and will respect each other's sovereignty, territorial integrity and political independence;

2. They recognize and will respect each other's right to live in peace with in secure and recognized boundaries;

3. They will develop good neighbourly relations of cooperation between them to ensure lasting security, will refrain form the threat of use of force against each other and will settle all disputes between them by peaceful means;

4. They respect and recognize the sovereignty, territorial integrity and political independent of every state in the region;

5. They respect and recognize the pivotal role of human development and dignity in regional and bilateral relationships;

6. They further believe that within their control, involuntary movements of persons in such a way as to adversely prejudice the security of either party should not be permitted.

ARTICLE 3—INTERNATIONAL BOUNDARY

1. The international boundary between Israel and Jordan is delimited with reference to the boundary definition under the Mandate.

2. The boundary, as set out in Annex I(a), is the permanent, secure and recognized international boundary between Israel and Jordan, without prejudice to the status of any territories that came under Israeli military government control in 1967.

3. The parties recognize the international boundary, as well as each other's territory, territorial waters and airspace, as inviolable, and will respect and comply with them.

4. The demarcation of the boundary will take place as set forth in Appendix (I) to Annex I and will be concluded not later than nine months after the signing of the treaty.

5. It is agreed that where the boundary follows a river, in the event of natural changes in the course of the flow of the river as described in Annex I (a), the boundary shall follow the new course of the flow. In the event of any other changes, the boundary shall not be affected unless otherwise agreed.

6. Immediately upon the exchange of the instruments of ratification of this treaty, each party will deploy on its side of the international boundary as defined in Annex I (a).

7. The parties shall, upon the signature of the treaty, enter into negotiations to conclude, within nine months, an agreement on the delimitation of their maritime boundary in the Gulf of Aqaba.

8. Taking into account the special circumstances of the Naharayim/ Baqura area, which is under Jordanian sovereignty, with Israeli private ownership rights, the parties agreed to apply the provisions set out in Annex I(b).

9. With respect to the Tsofar/Al-Ghamer area, the provisions set out in Annex I© will apply.

ARTICLE 4—SECURITY

1. (a) Both parties, acknowledging that mutual understanding and cooperation in security-related matters will form a significant part of their relations and will further enhance the security of the region, take upon themselves to base their security relations on mutual trust, advancement of joint interests and cooperation, and to aim towards a regional framework of partnership in peace.

   (b) Towards that goal the parties recognize the achievements of the European Community and European Union in the development of the Conference on Security and Cooperation in Europe (CSCE) and commit themselves to the creation, in the Middle

East, of a Conference on Security and Cooperation in the Middle East (CSCME).

This commitment entails the adoption of regional models of security successfully implemented in the post-World War era (along the lines of the Helsinki process) culminating I a regional zone of security and stability.

2. The obligations referred to in this Article are without prejudice to the inherent right of self-defence in accordance with the United Nations Charter.

3. The parties undertake, in accordance with the provisions of this Article, the following:

(a) to refrain from the threat or use of force of weapons, conventional, non-conventional or of any other kind, against each other, or of other actions or activities that adversely affect the security of the other party;

(b) to refrain from organizing, instigating, inciting, assisting or participating in acts or threats of belligerency, hostility, subversion or violence against the other party;

(c) to take necessary and effective measures to ensure that acts of threats of belligerency, hostility, subversion or violence against the other party do not originate from, and are not committed within, through or over their territory (hereinafter the terms "territory" includes the airspace and territorial waters).

4. Consistent with the era of peace and with the efforts to build regional security and to avoid and prevent aggression and violence; the parties further agree to refrain from the following:

(a) joining or in any way assisting, promoting or cooperating with any coalition, organization or alliance with a military or security character with a third party, the objectives or activities of which include launching aggression or other acts of military hostility against the other party, in contravention of the provisions of the present treaty;

(b) allowing the entry, stationing and operating on their territory, or through it, of military forces, personnel or materiel of a third party, in circumstances, which may adversely prejudice the security of the other party.

5. Both parties will take necessary and effective measures, and will cooperate in combating terrorism of all kinds. The parties undertake:

(a) to take necessary and effective measures to prevent acts of terrorism, subversion or violence from being carried out from their territory or through it and to take necessary and effective measures to combat such activities and all their perpetrators;

(b) without prejudice to the basic rights of freedom of expression and association, to take necessary and effective measures to prevent the entry, presence and cooperation in their territory of any groups or organization, and their infrastructure, which threatens the security of the other party by the use of or incitement to the use of violent means;

(c) to cooperate in preventing and combating cross-boundary infiltrations.

6. Any question as to the implementation of this article will be dealt with through a mechanism of consultations with will include a liaison system, verification, supervision, and where necessary, other mechanisms, and higher-level consultations. The details of the mechanism of consultations will be contained in an agreement to be concluded by the parties within three months of the exchange of instruments of ratification of this treaty.

7. The parties undertake to work as a matter of priority, and as soon as possible in the context of the Multilateral Working Group on Arms Control and Regional Security, and jointly towards the following:

(a) the creation in the Middle East of a region free from hostile alliances and coalitions

(b) the creation of a Middle East free from weapons of mass destruction, both conventional and non-conventional, in the context of a comprehensive, lasting and stable peace, characterized by the renunciation of the use of force, reconciliation and goodwill.

ARTICLE 5—DIPLOMATIC AND OTHER BILATERAL RELATIONS

1. The parties agree to establish full diplomatic and consider relations and exchange resident ambassadors within one month of the exchange of the instruments of ratification of this treaty.

2. The parties agree that the normal relationship between them will further include economic and cultural relations.

ARTICLE 6—WATER

With the view to achieving a comprehensive and lasting settlement of all the water problems between them:

1. The parties agree mutually to recognize the rightful allocations of both of them in Jordan River and Yarmouk River waters and Araba/Arava ground water in accordance with the agreed acceptable principles, quantities and quality as set out in Annex II, which shall be fully respected and complied with.

2. The parties, recognizing the necessity to find a practical, just and agreed solution to their water problems and with the view that the subject of water can form the basis for the advancement of cooperation between them, jointly undertake to ensure that the management and development of their water resources do not, in any way, harm the water resources of the other party.

3. The parties recognize that their water resources are not sufficient to meet their needs. More water should be supplied for their use through various methods, including projects of regional and international cooperation.

4. In light of paragraph three of this Article, with the understanding that cooperate in water-related subjects would be to the benefit of both parties, and will help alleviate their water shortages, and that water issues along their entire boundary must be dealt with in their totality, including the possibility of transboundary water transfers, the parties agree to search for ways to alleviate water shortages and to cooperate in the following fields:

(a) development of existing and new water resources, increasing the water availability, including cooperation on a regional basis as appropriate, and minimizing wastage of water resources through the chain of their uses;

(b) prevention of contamination of water resources;

(c) mutual assistance in the alleviation of water resources;

(d) transfer of information and joint research and development in water-related subjects, and review of the potentials for enhancement of water resources development and use.

ARTICLE 7 –ECONOMIC RELATIONS

1. Viewing economic development and prosperity as pillars of peace, security and harmonious relations between states, peoples and individual human being, the parties, taking note understandings reached between them, affirm their mutual desire to promote economic cooperation between them, as well as within the framework of wider regional economic cooperation.

2. In order to accomplish this goal, the parties agree to the following:

(a) to remove all discriminatory barriers to normal economic relations, to terminate economic boycotts directed at each other, and to cooperate in terminating boycotts against either party by third parties;

(b) recognizing that the principle of free and unimpeded flow of goods and services should guide their relations, the parties will enter into negotiations with a view to concluding agreements on economic cooperation, including trade and the establishment of a free-trade area or areas, investment, banking, industrial cooperation and labour, for the purpose of promoting beneficial economic relations, based on principles to be agreed upon, as well as on human development consideration on a regional basis. These negotiations will be concluded no later than six months from the exchange of the instruments of ratification of this treaty;

(c) to cooperate bilaterally, as well as in multilateral forums, towards the promotion of their respective economies and of their neighbourly economic relations with other regional partners.

ARTICLE 8—REFUGEES AND DISPLACED PERSONS

1. Recognizing the massive human problems caused to both parties by the conflict in the Middle East, as well as the contribution made by them towards the alleviation of human suffering, the parties will seek to further alleviate those problems arising on a bilateral level.

2. Recognizing that the above human problems caused by the conflict in the Middle East cannot by fully recognized on the bilateral level, the parties will seek to resolve them in appropriate forums, in accordance with international law, including the following:

   (a) in the case of displaced persons, in a quadripartite committee together with Egypt, and the Palestinians;

   (b) in the case of refugees,

   > (i) in the framework of the Multilateral Working Group on Refugees;

   > (ii) in negotiations, in a framework to be agreed, bilateral or otherwise, in conjunction with and at the same time as the permanent status negotiations pertaining to the territories to in Article 3 of this treaty;

   (c) through the implementation of agreed United Nations programs and other international economic programs concerning refugees and displaced persons, including assistance to their settlement.

ARTICLE 9—PLACES OF HISTORICAL AND RELIGIOUS SIGNIFICANCE AND INTERFAITH RELATIONS

1. Each party will provide freedom of access to places of religious and historical significance.

2. In this regard, in accordance with the Washington Declaration, Israel respects the present special role of the Hashemite Kingdom of Jordan in Muslim holy shrines in Jerusalem. When negotiations on the permanent status will take place, Israel will give high priority to the Jordanian historic role in these shrines.

3. The parties will act together to promise interfaith relations among the three monotheistic religions, with the aim of working towards religious understanding, moral commitment, freedom of religious worship, and tolerance and peace.

ARTICLE 10-CULTURAL AND SCIENTIFIC EXCHANGE

The parties, wishing to remove biases developed through periods of conflict, recognize the desirability of cultural and scientific exchanges in all fields, and agree to establish normal cultural relations between them. Thus, they shall, as soon as possible and not later than nine months from the exchange of the instruments of ratification of this treaty, conclude the negotiations on cultural and scientific agreements.

ARTICLE 11—MUTUAL UNDERSTANDING AND NEIGHBOURLY RELATIONS

1. The parties will seek to foster mutual understanding and tolerance based on shared history values, an accordingly undertake:

   (a) to abstain from hostile or discriminatory propaganda against each other, and to take all possible legal and administrative measures to prevent the dissemination of such propaganda by any organization or individual present in the territory of either party;

   (b) as soon as possible, and not later than three months from the exchange of the instruments of ratification of this treaty, to repeal all adverse or discriminatory references and expressions of hostility in their respective legislation;

   (c) to refrain in all government publications from any such references or expressions;

   (d) to ensure mutual enjoyment by each other's citizens of due process of law within their respective legal systems and before their courts.

2. Paragraph 1(a) of this Article is without prejudice to the right to freedom of expression as contained in the International Covenant on Civil and Political Rights.

3. A joint committee shall be formed to examine incidents where one party claims there has been a violation of this Article

ARTICLE 12—COMBATING CRIME AND DRUGS

The parties will cooperate in combating crime, with an emphasis on smuggling, and will take all necessary measures to combat an prevent such activities as the production of, as well as the trafficking of illicit drugs, and will bring to trail perpetrators of such acts. In this regard, they will take note of the understandings reached between them in the above spheres, in accordance with Annex III and undertake to conclude all relevant agreements not later than nine months from the date of the exchange of instruments of ratification of this treaty.

ARTICLE 13—TRANSPORTATION

Taking note of the progress already made in the area of transportation, the parties recognize the mutuality of interest in good neighbourly relations in the area of transportation and agree to the following means to promote relations between them in this sphere:

1. Each party will permit the free movement of nationals and vehicles of the other into and within its territory according to the general rules applicable to nationals and vehicles of other states. Neither party will impose discriminatory taxes or restrictions on the free movement of persons and vehicles from its territory to the territory of the other.

2. The parties will open and maintain roads and border crossings between their countries and will consider further road and rail links between them.

3. The parties will continue their negotiations concerning mutual transportation agreements in the above and other areas, such as joint projects, traffic safety, transport standards and norms, licensing of vehicles, land passages, shipment of goods and cargo, and meteorology, to be concluded not later than six months from the exchange of the instruments of ratifications of this treaty.

4. The parties agree to continue their negotiations for a highway to be constructed and maintained between Egypt, Israel and Jordan near Eilat.

ARTICLE 14—FREEDOM OF NAVIGATION AND ACCESS TO PORTS

1. Without prejudice to the provisions of paragraph three, each party recognizes the right of the vessels of the other party to innocent passage through its territorial waters in accordance with the rules of international law.

2. Each party will grant normal access to its ports for vessels and cargoes of the other, as well as vessels and cargoes destined for or coming from the other party. Such access will be granted on the same conditions as is generally applicable to vessels and cargoes of other nations.

3. The parties consider the Strait of Tiran and the Gulf of Aqaba to be international waterways open to all nations for unimpeded and non-suspendable freedom of navigation and overflight. The parties will respect each other's right to navigation and overflight for access to either party through the Strait of Tiran and the Gulf of Aqaba.

ARTICLE 16—CIVIL AVIATION

1. The parties recognize as applicable to each other the rights, privileges and obligations provided for by the multilateral aviation agreements to which they are both party, particularly by the 1944 Convention on International Civil Aviation (The Chicago Convention) and the 1944 International Air Services Transit Agreement.

2. Any declaration of national emergency by a party under Article 89 of the Chicago Convention will not be applied to the other party on a discriminatory basis.

3. The parties take note of the negotiation on the international air corridor to be opened between them in accordance with the Washington Declaration. In addition, the parties shall, upon ratification of this treaty, enter into negotiations for the purpose of concluding a Civil Aviation Agreement. All the above negotiations are to be concluded not later than six months from the exchange of the instruments of ratification of this treaty.

ARTICLE 16—POSTS AND TELECOMMUNICATIONS

The parties take note of the opening between them, in accordance with the Washington Declaration, of direct telephone and facsimile lines. Postal links, the negotiations on which having been concluded will be activated upon the signature of this treaty. The parties further agree that normal wireless and cable communications and television relay, services by cable, radio and satellite, will be established between them, in accordance with all relevant international conventions and regulations. The negotiations on these subjects will be concluded not later than nine months from the exchange of the instruments of ratification of this treaty.

ARTICLE 17—TOURISM

The parties affirm their mutual desire to promote cooperation between them in the field of tourism. In order to accomplish this goal, the parties taking note of the understandings reached between them concerning tourism agree to negotiate, as soon as possible, and to conclude not later than three months from the exchange of the instruments of ratification of this treaty, an agreement to facilitate and encourage mutual tourism and tourism from third countries.

ARTICLE 18—ENVIRONMENT

The parties will cooperate in matters relating to the environment, a sphere to which they attach great importance, including conservation of nature and prevention of pollution, as set forth in Annex IV. They will negotiate an agreement on the above, to be concluded not later than six months from the exchange of the instruments of ratification of this treaty.

ARTICLE 19—ENERGY

1. The parties will cooperation in the development of energy resources, including the development of energy-related projects such as the utilization of solar energy.

2. The parties, having concluded their negotiations on the interconnecting of their electric grids in the Eilat-Aqaba area, will implement the interconnecting upon the signature of this treaty. The parties view this step as a part of wider binational and regional concept. They agree to continue their negotiations as soon as possible to widen the scope of their interconnected grids.

3. The parties will conclude the relevant agreements in the field of energy within six months from the date of exchange of the instruments of ratification of this treaty.

ARTICLE 20—RIFT VALLEY DEVELOPMENT

The parties attaché great importance to the integrated development of the Jordan Rift Valley area, including joint projects in the economic, environmental, energy-related and tourism fields. Taking note of the terms of reference developed in the framework of the Trilateral Israel-Jordan-US Economic Committee towards the Jordan Rift Valley Development Master Plan, they will vigorously continue their efforts towards the completion of planning and towards implementation.

ARTICLE 21—HEALTH

The parties will cooperate in the area of health and shall negotiate with a view to the conclusion of an agreement within nine months from the exchange of instruments of ratification of this treaty.

ARTICLE 22—AGRICULTURE

The parties will cooperate in the area of agriculture, including veterinary services, plant protections, biotechnology and marketing, and shall negotiate with a view to the conclusion of an agreement within six months from the date of the exchange of instruments of ratification of this treaty.

ARTICLE 23-AQABA AND EILAT

The parties agree to enter into negotiations, as soon as possible, and not later than one month from the exchange of the instruments of ratification of this treaty, on arrangements that would enable the joint development of the towns of Aqaba and Eilat with regard to such matters, *inter alia,* as joint tourism development, joint customs posts, free trade zone, cooperation in aviation, prevention of pollution, maritime matters, police, customs and health cooperation. The parties will conclude all relevant agreements within nine months from the exchange of the instruments of ratification of the treaty.

ARTICLE 24—CLAIMS

The parties agree to establish a claims commission for the mutual settlement of all financial claims.

ARTICLE 25—RIGHTS AND OBLIGATIONS

1. This treaty does not affect and shall not be interpreted as affecting, in any way, the rights and obligations of the parties under the Charter of the United Nations.

2. The parties undertake to fulfil in good faith their obligations under this treaty without regards to action or inaction of any other party and independently of any instrument inconsistent with the treaty. For the purposes of this paragraph, each party represents to the other that in its opinion and interpretation there is not inconsistency between their existing treaty obligations and the treaty.

3. They further undertake to take all the necessary measures for the application in their relations of the provisions of the multilateral conventions to which they are parties, including the submission of appropriate notification to the Secretary General of the United Nations and other depositories of such conventions.

4. Both parties will also take the necessary steps to abolish all pejorative references to the other party, in multilateral conventions to which they are parties, to the extent that such references exist.

5. The parties undertake not to enter into any obligation in conflict with this treaty.

6. Subject to Article 103 of the United Nations Charter, in the event of a conflict between the obligations of the parties under the present treaty and any of their other obligations, the obligations under this treaty will be binding and implemented.

ARTICLE 26—LEGISLATION

Within three months of the exchange of ratifications of this treaty, the parties undertake to enact any legislation necessary in order to implement the treaty, and to terminate any international commitments and to repeal any legislation that is inconsistent with the treaty.

ARTICLE 27—RATIFICATION

1. This treaty shall be ratified by both parties in conformity with their respective national procedures. It shall enter into force on the exchange of the instruments of ratification.

2. The annexes, appendices, and other attachments to this treaty shall be considered integral parts thereof.

ARTICLE 28—INTERIM MEASURES

The parties will apply, in certain spheres, to be agreed upon, interim measures pending the conclusion of the relevant agreements in accordance with this treaty, as stipulated in Annex V.

ARTICLE 29—SETTLEMENT OF DISPUTES

1. Disputes arising out of the application or interpretation of this treaty shall be resolved by negotiations.

2. Any such disputes, which cannot be settled by negotiations, shall be resolved by conciliations or submitted to arbitration.

ARTICLE 30—REGISTRATION

The treaty shall be transmitted to the Secretary General of the United Nations for registration in accordance with the provisions of Article 102 of the Charter of the United Nations.

Done at the Arava/Araba crossing point this day, Heshvan 21, 5755/Jumada Al-Ula 21, 1415, which corresponds to October 26, 1994, in Hebrew, English and Arabic languages, all texts being equally authentic. In the case of divergence of interpretation, the English text shall prevail.

For the State of Israel: For the Hashemite Kingdom of Jordan:
Yizhak Rabin   *Abdul Salam Majali*
Prime Minister   Prime Minister

Witnessed by:
William J. Clinton
President of the United States of America

ANNEX I(A)

ISRAEL-JORDAN INTERNATIONAL BOUNDARY DELIMITATION AND DEMARCATION

I. It is agreed that, in accordance with Article 3 of the treaty, the international boundary between the two states consists of the following sectors:

    A.   The Jordan and Yarmouk Rivers

    B.   The Dead Sea

    C.   The Emek Ha'arava/Wadi Araba

    D.   The Gulf of Aqaba

II. The boundary is delimited as follows:

A. JORDAN AND YARMOUK RIVERS

1. The boundary shall follow the middle of the main course of the flow of the Jordan and Yarmouk Rivers.

2. The boundary shall follow natural changes (accretion or erosion) in the course the rivers unless agreed. Artificial changes in or of the course of the rivers shall not affect the location of the boundary unless otherwise agreed. No artificial changes may be made except by agreement between both parties.

3. In the even of a future sudden natural change in or of the course of the rivers (avulsion or cutting of a new bed) the Joint Boundary Commission (Article 3 below) shall meet as soon as possible, to decide on necessary measures, which may include physical restoration of the prior location of the river course.

4. The boundary line in the two rivers is shown on the 1:10,000 orthophoto maps dated 1994.

5. Adjustment to the boundary line in any of the rivers due to natural changes (accretion or erosion) shall be carried out whenever it is deemed necessary by the Joint Boundary Commission or one every five years.

6. The lines defining the special Naharayim/Baqura area are shown on the 1:10,000 orthophoto map.

7. The orthophoto maps and image maps showing the line separating Jordan from the territory that came under Israeli military government control in 1967 shall have that line indicated in a different presentation and the legend shall carry on it the following disclaimer: "This line is the administrative boundary between Jordan and the territory which came under Israeli military government control in 1967. Any treatment of this line shall be without prejudice to the status of the territory."

B. DEAD SEA AND SALT PANS

The boundary line is shown on the 1:50,000 image maps. The list of geographic and Universal Transverse Mercator (UTM) coordinates of this boundary line shall be based on Israel-Jordan Boundary Datum (IJBD 1994) and, and when completed and agreed upon by both parties, this list of coordinates shall be binding and take precedence over the maps as to the location of the boundary line in the Dead Sea and salt pans.

C. EMEK HA'ARAVA/WADI ARABA

1. The boundary line is shown on 1:20,000 orthophoto maps.

2. The land boundary shall be demarcated, under a joint boundary demarcation procedure, by boundary pillars which will be jointly located, erected, measured and documented on the basis of the boundary shown in the 1:20,000 orthophoto maps referred to in Article 2-C-(1) above. Between each two adjacent boundary pillars, the boundary line shall follow a straight line.

3. The boundary pillars shall be defined in a list of geographic and UTM coordinates based on joint boundary datum (IJBD 4) to be agreed upon by the Joint Team of Experts appointed by the two parties (hereinafter the JTE) using joint Global Positioning System (GPS) Measurements. The list of coordinates shall be prepared, signed and approved by both parties as soon as possible and not later than nine months after this treat enters into force and shall become part of this annex. This list of geographic and UTM coordinates when completed and agreed upon by both parties shall be binding and shall take precedence over the maps as to the location of the boundary line of this sector.

4. The boundary pillars shall be maintained by both parties in accordance with a procedure to be agreed upon. The coordinates

in article 2-C-(3) above shall be used to reconstruct boundary pillars in case they are damaged, destroyed or displaced.

5. The line defining the Tsofar/al-Ghamr area is shown on the 1:20,000 Emek Ha'Araba/Wadi Araba orthophoto map.

D. THE GULF OF AQABA

The parties shall act in accordance with article 3.7 of the treaty.

III. Joint Boundary Commission

A.   For the purpose of the implementation of this annex, the parties will establish a Joint Boundary Commission comprised of three members of each country.

B.   The commission will, with the approval of the respective governments, specify its work procedures, the frequency of its meetings, the details of its scope of work. The Commission may invite experts and/or advisors as may be required.

C.   The commission may form, as it deems necessary, specialized teams or committees and assign them to technical tasks.

ANNEX I(B)

THE NAHARAYIM/BAQURA AREA

1. The two parties agree that a special regime will apply to the Naharayim/Baqura area ("the area") on a temporary basis, as set out in this annex. For the purpose of this annex, the area is detailed in Appendix IV.

2. Recognizing that in the area which is under Jordan's sovereignty with Israeli private land ownership right and property interests ("land-owners") in the land comprising the area ("the land") Jordan undertakes:

(a) to grant without charge unimpeded freedom of entry to, exit from, land usage and movement within the areas to the land-owners and to their invitees or employees and to all the land-owners to freely dispose of their land in accordance with applicable Jordanian law;

(b) not to apply its customs or immigration legislation to land-owners, their invitees or employees crossing from Israel directly to the area for the purpose of gaining access to the land for agricultural or any agreed purposes;

(c) not to impose discriminatory taxes or charges with regard to the land or activities within the area;

(d) to take all necessary measures to protect and prevent harassment of or harm to any person entering the area under this annex;

(e) to permit with the minimum of formality, uniformed officers of the Israeli police force access to the area for the purpose of investigating crime or dealing with other incidents solely involving the land-owners, their invites or employees.

3. Recognizing Jordanian sovereignty over the area, Israel undertakes:

(a) not to carry out or allow to be carried out in the area activities prejudicial to the peace or security of Jordan;

(b) not to allow any person entering the area under this annex (other than uniformed officers referred to in paragraph 2(e) of this Annex) to carry weapons of any kind in the area; unless authorized by the licensing authorities in Jordan after being processed by the liaison committee referred to in Article 8 of this annex;

(c) not to allow the dumping of wastes from outside this area into the area.

4. (a) Subject to this annex, Jordanian law will apply to this area;

(b) Israeli law applying to the extra-territorial activities of Israelis may be applied to Israelis and their activities in the area, and Israel may take measures in the area to enforce such laws;

(c) Having regard to this annex, Jordan will not apply its criminal laws to activities in the areas which involve only Israeli nationals.

5. In the event of any joint projects to be agreed and developed by the parties in the area, the terms of this annex may be altered for the purpose of the joint project by agreement between the parties at any time. One of the options to be discussed in the context

of the joint projects would be the establishment of a free-trade zone.

6. Without prejudice to private rights of ownership of land within the area, this annex will remain in force for twenty-five years, and shall be renewed automatically for the same periods, unless one year prior notice of termination is given by either party, in which case, at the request of either party, consultations shall be renewed automatically for the same periods, unless one year prior notice of termination is given by either party, in which case, at the request of either party, consultations shall be entered into.

7. In addition to the requirement referred to in Article 4(a) of this annex, the acquisition of land in the area by persons who are not Israeli citizens shall take place only with the prior approval of Jordan.

8. An Israeli-Jordanian Liaison Committee is hereby established in order to deal with all matters arising under this annex.

ANNEX 1 (C)

THE TSOFAR/AL-GHAMR AREA

1. The two parties agree that a special regime will apply to the Tso-far/al-Ghamr area ("the area") on a temporary basis, as set out in this annex. For the purpose of this annex, the area is detailed in Appendix V.

2. Recognizing that in the area which is under Jordan's sovereignty with Israeli private land use rights ("land-users") in the land comprising the area ("the land"), Jordan undertakes:

   (a) to grant without charge unimpeded freedom of entry to, exit from, land usage and movement within the areas to the land users and their invitees or employees and to allow the land-users freely to dispose of their land in accordance with applicable Jordanian law;

   (b) not to apply its customs or immigration legislation to land-users, their invitees or employees crossing from Israel directly to the area for the purpose of gaining access to the land for agricultural or any agreed purposes;

(c) not to impose discriminatory taxes or charges with regard to the land or activities within the area;

(d) to take all necessary measures to protect and prevent harassment of or harm to any person entering the area under this annex;

(e) to permit with the minimum of formality, uniformed officers of the Israeli police force, access to the area for the purpose of investigating crime or dealing with other incidents solely involving the land-users, their invitees or employees.

3. Recognizing Jordanian sovereignty over the area Israel undertakes:

(a) not to carry out or allow to be carried out in the area activities prejudicial to the peace or security of Jordan;

(b) not to allow any person entering the area under this annex (other than the uniformed officers referred to in Article 8 of this annex;

(c) not to allow the dumping of wastes from outside the area into the area.

4. (a) Subject to this Annex, Jordanian law will apply to this area.

(b) Israeli law applying to the extra-territorial activities of Israel may be applied to Israelis and their activities in the area, and Israel may take measures in the area to enforce such law.

(c) Having regard to this Annex, Jordan will not apply its criminal law to activities which involved only Israeli nationals.

5. In the event of any joint projects to be agreed and developed by the Parties in the area, the terms of this Annex may be altered for the purpose of the joint project by agreement between the Parties at any time.

6. Without prejudice to private rights of use of land within the area, this Annex will remain in force for twenty-five years, and shall be renewed automatically for the same periods, unless one-year prior notice of termination is given by either Party, in which case, at the request of either Party, consultations shall be entered into.

7. In addition to the requirement referred to in Article 4(a) of this Annex, the acquisition of land in the area by persons who are not Israeli citizens shall take place only with the prior approval of Jordan.

8. Any Israeli-Jordanian Liaison Committee is hereby established in order to deal with all matters arising under this Annex.

ANNEX II

WATER-RELATED MATTERS

Pursuant to Article 6 of the Treaty, Jordan and Israel agreed on the following articles on water-related matters:

ARTICLE 1—ALLOCATION

1. Water from the Yarmouk River

(a) Summer period—15th May to 15th October of each year, Israel pumps twelve million cubic meters (mcm) and Jordan gets the rest of the flow.

(b) Winter period—16th October to 14th May of each year. Israel pumps 13 mcm and Jordan is entitled to the rest of the flow subject to provisions outlined herein below: Jordan concedes to Israel pumping an additional 20 mcm from the Yarmouk in winter in return for Israel conceding to transferring to Jordan during the summer period the quantity specified in paragraph 2(a) below from the Jordan River.

(c) In order that waste of water will be minimized, Israel and Jordan may use, downstream of point 121/Adassiya Diversion, excess floodwater that is not usable and will evidently go to waste unused.

2. Water from the Jordan River

(a) Summer period—15th May to 15th October of each year. In return for the additional water that Jordan concedes to Israel in winter in accordance with paragraph 1 (b) above, Israel concedes to transfer to Jordan in the summer period 20 mcm from the

Jordan River directly upstream from the Deganya gates on the river. Jordan shall pay the operation and maintenance cost of such transfer through existing systems (not including capital cost) and shall bear the total cost of any new transmission system. A separate protocol shall regulate this transfer.

(b) Winter period—16th October to 14th May of each year. Jordan is entitled to store for its use a minimum average of 20 mcm of the floods in the Jordan River south of its confluence with the Yarmouk (as outlined in Article II below). Excess floods that are not usable and that will otherwise be wasted can be utilized for the benefit of the two Parties including pumped storage of the course of the river.

(c) In addition to the above, Israel is entitled to maintain its current uses of the Jordan River waters between its confluence with the Yarmouk and its confluence with Tirat Zvi/Wadi Yabis. Jordan is entitled to an annual quantity equivalent to that of Israel, provided however, that Jordan's use will not harm the quantity or quality of the above Israeli uses. The Joint Water Commission (outlined in Article VII below) will survey existing uses for documentation and prevention of appreciable harm.

(d) Jordan is entitled to an annual quantity of 10 mcm of desalinated water from the desalination of about 20 mcm of saline springs now diverted to the Jordan River. Israel will explore the possibility of financing the operation and maintenance cost of the supply to Jordan of this desalinated water (not including capital cost). Until the desalination facilities are operation, and upon the entry into fore of the Treaty, Israel will supply Jordan 10 mcm of Jordan River water from the same location as in paragraph 2(a) above, outside the summer period and during dates Jordan selects, subject to the maximum capacity of transmission.

3. Additional Water

Israel and Jordan shall cooperate in finding sources for the supply to Jordan of an additional quantity of 50 mcm/year of water of drinkable standards. To this end, the Joint Water Committee will develop, within one year from the entry into force of the Treaty, a plan for the supply to Jordan of the above-mentioned additional water. This plan will be forwarded to the respective governments for discussion and decision.

4. Operation and Maintenance

(a) Operation and maintenance of the systems on Israeli territory that supply Jordan with water, and their electricity supply, shall be Israel's responsibility. The operation and maintenance of the new systems that serve only Jordan will be contracted at Jordan's expense to authorities or companies selected by Jordan.

(b) Israel will guarantee easy unhindered access of personnel and equipment to such new systems for operation and maintenance. This subject will be further detailed in the agreements to be signed between Israel and the authorities or companies selected by Jordan.

ARTICLE II—STORAGE

1. Israel and Jordan shall cooperate to build a diversion/storage dam on the Yarmouk River directly downstream of the point 121/Adassiya Diversion. The purpose is to improve the diversion efficiency into the King Abdullah Canal of the water allocation of the Hashemite Kingdom of Jordan, and possibly for the diversion of Israel's allocation of the river water. Other purposes can be mutually agreed.

2. For this purpose, Israel and Jordan will jointly monitor the quality of water along their boundary, by use of jointly established monitoring stations to be operated under the guidance of the Joint Water Committee.

3. Israel and Jordan will each prohibit the disposal of municipal and industrial wastewater into the course of the Yarmouk or the Jordan Rivers before they are treated to standards allowing their unrestricted agricultural use. Implementation of this prohibition shall be completed within three years from the entry into force of the Treaty.

4. The quality of water supplied from one country to the other at any given location shall be equivalent to the quality of the water used from the same location by the supplying country.

5. Saline springs currently diverted to the Jordan River are earmarked for desalination within four years. Both countries shall cooperate to ensure that the resulting bring will not be disposed of in the Jordan River or in any of its tributaries.

6. Israel and Jordan will each protect water systems in its own territory, supplying water tot eh other, against any pollution, contamination, harm, or unauthorized withdrawal from each other's allocations.

ARTICLE IV—GROUNDWATER IN EMEK HA'ARAVA/WADI ARABA

1. In accordance with the provisions of this Treaty, some wells drilled and used by Israel along with their associated systems fall on the Jordanian side of the borders. These wells and systems are under Jordan's sovereignty. Israel shall retain the use of these wells and systems in the quantity and quality detailed in an Appendix to this Annex that shall be jointly prepared by 31st December 1994. Neither country shall take, nor cause to be taken, any measure that may appreciably reduce the yields or quality of these wells and systems.

2. Throughout the period of Israel's use of these wells and systems, replacement of any well that may fail among them shall be licensed by Jordan in accordance with the laws and regulations then in effect. For this purpose, the failed well shall be treated as though it was drilled under license from the competent Jordanian authority at the time of its drilling. Israel shall supply Jordan with the log of each of the wells and the technical information about it to be kept on record. The replacement well shall be connected to the Israeli electricity and water systems.

3. Israel may increase the abstraction rate from wells and systems in Jordan by up to 10 mcm/year above the yields referred to in paragraph 1 above, subject to a determination by the Joint Water Committee that this understanding is hydrogeologically feasible and does not harm existing Jordanian uses. Such increase is to be carried out within five years from the entry into force of the Treaty.

4. Operation and Maintenance

    (a) Operation and maintenance of the wells and systems on Jordanian territory that supply Israel with water, and their electricity supply shall be Jordan's responsibility. The operation and maintenance of these wells and systems will be contracted at Israel's expense to authorities or companies selected by Israel.

(b) Jordan will guarantee easy unhindered access of personnel and equipment to such wells and systems for operation and maintenance. This subject will be further detailed in the agreements to be signed between Jordan and the authorities or companies selected by Israel.

ARTICLE V—NOTIFICATION AND AGREEMENT

1. Israel and Jordan undertake to exchange relevant data on water resources through the Joint Water Committee.

2. Israel and Jordan shall cooperate in developing plans for purposes of increasing water supplies and improving water use efficiency, within the context of bilateral, regional, or international cooperation.

ARTICLE VII—JOINT WATER COMMITTEE

1. For the purpose of the implementation of this Annex, the Parties will establish a Joint Water Committee comprised of three members from each country.

2. The Joint Water Committee will, with the approval of the respective governments, specify its work procedures, the frequency of its meetings, and the details of its scope of work. The committee may invite experts and/or advisers as may be required.

3. The committee may form, as it deems necessary, a number of specializes subcommittees and assign them technical tasks. In this context, it is agreed that these subcommittees will include a northern subcommittee and a southern subcommittee, for the management on the ground of the mutual water resources in the sectors.

ANNEX III

COMBATING CRIME AND DRUGS

Pursuant to Article 12 of the Treaty of Peace, Israel and Jordan have decided to cooperate in the following fields:

A. Cooperation on Combating Dangerous Drugs

1. The two Parties shall cooperate in fighting illicit drugs according to the legal systems of their countries.

2. The two Parties shall take all necessary measures to prevent drug smuggling between the two countries.

3. The two Parties shall exchange information regarding drug trafficking and dealers' activities concerning the two countries.

4. Information given by one of the Parties may not be shared with a third Party without the consent of the Party, which provided the information.

5. The two Parties shall exchange and share the experience of fighting against drugs, including anti-drug education, prevention, treatment, rehabilitation programs, technical means, and methods of concealment.

6. In order to identify the persons involved in drug archives, the two Parties shall facilitate controlled deliveries of drugs between the two countries according to their law.

7. Drug law enforcement officer from both sides shall meet periodically to coordinate efforts pertaining to drug problems concerning the two countries.

8. The two Parties shall maintain open channels of communication such as fax, telephone, and telex for liaison purposes in drug matters concerning the two countries.

9. The two Parties shall cooperate with the multilateral forums, which deal with drug issues in the area.

10. The two Parties shall cooperate in investigating procedures necessary for collecting evidence and indictment in cases against drug dealers which concern either or both countries.

11. The two parties shall exchange information regarding statistics on the type and number of drug crimes committed in each country including detailed information regarding suspected and convicted persons involved in these cases.

12. The two Parties shall exchange all relevant information regarding the narcotic drug producing laboratories if revealed in either of the two countries, including structure, working methods, and technical features of the laboratory as well as the type and mark of the product.

13. The cooperation described in this document will be carried out in accordance with the legal systems of the two countries.

B. Crime

The Parties have agreed that the Agreements to be negotiated pursuant to Article 12 of the Treaty shall cover the following issues:

1. Crime

- Exchange of information concerning all aspects of smuggling, theft (including art objects, vehicles, national treasures, antiquities, and documents), etc.:
- Apprehension of criminals and exchange of information including transmission of evidence in order to carry out judicial procedures in each of the two countries, subject to the relevant treaties and regulations.

2. General Cooperation

- Exchange of information regarding technical matters;
- Exchange of information regarding training and research;
- Joint police research projects on topics of mutual interest to both countries.

3. Additional Issues

- Rescue;
- Unintentional border crossing, fugitives from justice;
- Notification of detention of nationals of the other country;
- Establishment of a liaison mechanism between the sides.

C. Cooperation in Forensic Science

1. The two Parties shall cooperate on the subjects of criminal identification and forensic science.

2. The two Parties shall share and exchange professional experience and training programs, *inter alia:*

    (a) Use of field kits for preliminary examinations;

    (b) Analysis of illicit drugs;

    (c) Analysis of poison and toxic materials;

    (d) Forensic biology and DNA examinations;

    (e) Toolmarks and materials examinations;

(f) Questionable documents examinations;

(g) Analysis of voice prints;

(h) Analysis of firearms;

(i) Detection of latent fingerprints;

(j) Analysis of explosive traces;

(k) Examination for arson in laboratories;

(l) Identification of victims in mass disasters;

(m) Research and development in forensic science.

NOTES

Notes to Chapter 1 – The Challenge to Create 'Good Neighbourly Relations'

1. Collins, Liat, 'A day like no other', *The Jerusalem Post*, 27 October 1994, p. 2
2. Pinkas, Alon, 'Israel, Jordan sign treaty', *The Jerusalem Post*, 27 October 1994, p. 1
3. Satloff, Robert B., (1995) 'The Jordan-Israel Peace Treaty: A Remarkable Document', *Middle East Quarterly*, http://www.meforum.org/meq/issues/19950 (27 June 2005)
4. 'Three Israelis indicted for vandalizing Rabin memorial', *Xinhua News Agency*, 4 November 2003
5. 'Jordan's new king', *The Economist*, 13 February 1999, p. 43
6. Meital, Yoram, 'Peace with Israel in Egypt's Policy', in J. Ginat et al. (eds), *The Middle East Peace Process: Vision Versus Reality* (Norman, Oklahoma, 2002), p. 145
7. Frucht, Leora Eren, 'A chill wind from the Nile', *The Jerusalem Post*, 13 April 2001, p. 3B
8. Gold, Dore, 'One step forward, one step backward', *The Jerusalem Post*, 20 January 1995, p. 8
9. Abou El-Magd, Nadia, '25 years after Sadat's Jerusalem visit, no real peace, but no war either', *The Associated Press*, 19 November 2002
10. Satloff: 'The Jordan-Israel Peace Treaty'
11. Satloff: 'The Jordan-Israel Peace Treaty'
12. *Treaty of Peace Between the State of Israel and the Hashemite Kingdom of Jordan*, Article 11
13. Thomas, Evan and Dickey, Christopher, 'Farewell to the King', *Newsweek*, 15 February 1999, p. 36
14. For more information on conflict management and assessment see: Miall, Hugh, *Contemporary Conflict Resolution: The Prevention, Management and Transformation of Deadly Conflicts* (Malden, MA, 1999); Tidwell, Alan, *Conflict Resolved?: A Critical Assessment of Conflict Resolution* (London, 1998); Hauss, Charles, *International Conflict Resolution* (London, 2001)
15. For detailed accounts of the implementation of the peace agreement in the first years after it was signed, see two reports by the Washington Institute: Cook, Steven A., *Jordan-Israel Peace, Year One: Laying the Foundation* (The Washington Institute, Washington DC, 1995) and Plotkin, Lori, *Jordan-Israel Peace: Taking Stock, 1994–1997* (The Washington Institute, Washington DC, 1997)
16. Zak, Moshe, 'Quietly, they talked about water, borders', *The Jerusalem Post*, 21 October 1994
17. The Jordanian parliament is divided into two bodies; the Upper House (senate) has 55 members appointed by the King, the 110 member Chamber of Deputies is elected by the population. Following the June 2003 elections, pro-Royal elements

became the dominant force, though 30 candidates ran for the Islamic Action Front. Other Islamic parties were banned from running by the government. For more see Pelham, Nicolas, 'Islamists join election contest', *The Financial Times*, 16 June 2003, p. 6 and Halaby, Jamal, 'Kings allies triumph in Jordan's elections, Islamists return to Parliament', *The Associated Press*, 18 June 2003. This is discussed in more detail in Chapter Nine.

18. Goldberg, Andy, 'Netanyahu in charge: Mideast enters new phase of uncertainty', *Deutsche Presse-Agentur*, 18 June 1996

19. Hirst, David, 'Netanyahu keeps Arabs on the boil', *The Guardian* (London), 20 June 1996

20. 'King Hussein "very worried" about Mideast situation', *Agence France Presse*, 24 October 1996

21. Nevo, Joseph, 'The Jordanian-Israeli Peace: the View from Amman', in J. Ginat et al. (eds), *The Middle East Peace Process: Vision Versus Reality* (Norman, Oklahoma, 2002), p. 169

22. Thomas and Dickey: 'Farewell to the King', p. 36

23. Both the Jordanian and Egyptian ambassadorial posts in Israel were filled in March 2005, presumably in response to the Gaza disengagement plan. 'Egypt's, Jordan's first Ambassadors in years present credentials in Israel', *Financial Times Information*, 21 March 2005.

24. Salibi, Kamal, *The Modern History of Jordan* (London, 1993), p. 261

25. Hider, James, 'Benny Elon, settler envoy who backs "transfer" of Palestinians, heads to US', *Agence France Presse*, 4 May 2003

26. Estimates on the size of the Palestinian population in Jordan vary, but may be as high as 65–70 per cent; the size of the Palestinian population increased by approximately 10 per cent in 1992, when 300,000 Palestinians returned from Kuwait and other Gulf countries; *Middle East Review of World Information*, 28 September 2000

27. 'Jordan, Palestinians sign accord', *The Jerusalem Post*, 27 January 1995, p. 2

28. Susser, Asher, *Jordan: Case Study of a Pivotal State* (Washington, 2000), p. 92

29. Haddad, Mohanna, 'Jordan's Perspective of Peace', in J. Ginat et. al (eds), *The Middle East Peace Process: Vision Versus Reality* (Norman, Oklahoma, 2002)

30. Haddad: 'Jordan's Perspective', p. 162

31. Satloff, Robert B., *From Hussein to Abdullah: Jordan in Transition*, (Washington, DC, 1999)

32. Nevo: 'The Jordanian-Israeli Peace', p. 170

33. Benn, Aluf and Levi-Stein, Revital, 'Abdullah envisions an "open Jerusalem" on his first visit to Israel, Jordanian king stresses Amman's interest in success of Palestinian track', *Ha'aretz*, 24 April, 2000

34. Http://www.jewishvirtuallibrary.org/jsource/US-Israel/U.S._Assistance_to_Is-rael1.html (27 June 2005)

Notes to Chapter 2 – The Road to Peace Between Jordan and Israel

1. Noor, Queen, *Leap of Faith: Memoirs of an Unexpected Life* (New York, 2003)

2. The relationship between the Hashemite leadership and the state of Israel are long and complex. A more detailed review can be found in Garfinkle, Adam,

Israel and Jordan in the Shadow of War: Functional Ties and Futile Diplomacy in a Small Place (New York, 1992); Joseph, Uri, *The best of enemies: Israel and Transjordan in the war of 1948* (London, 1987); Shlaim, Avi, *Collusion across the Jordan* (New York, 1988); Wilson, Mary C., *King Abdullah, Great Britain and the Making of Jordan* (New York, 1988)

3. Zak, Moshe, (1995) 'Thirty years of clandestine meetings: the Jordan-Israel peace treaty' *Middle East Quarterly*. Http://www.meforum.org/article/241 (27 June 2005)

4. Zak: 'Thirty years'

5. Lukacs, Yehuda, *Israel, Jordan and the Peace Process* (Syracuse, 1997), p. 63

6. Salibi, Kamal, *The Modern History of Jordan* (London, 1993), p. 220

7. Kissinger, Henry, *Years of Upheaval* (Boston, 1982), p. 506

8. Lukacs: *Israel, Jordan*, pp. 25–26

9. Salibi: *The Modern History*, pp. 250–251

10. Kimmerling, Baruch and Migdal, Joel S., *The Palestinian People: A History* (Cambridge MA, 2003), p. 262

11. Noor, Queen: *Leap of Faith*, p. 119

12. 'Hussein asked for Israel's help during Black September: British Documents', *Agence France Presse*, 1 January 2001

13. Dobson, Christopher, *Black September: Its Short, Violent History* (New York, 1974)

14. Salibi: *The Modern History*, p. 266

15. See Beilin, Yossi, *Touching Peace: from the Oslo Accord to a final agreement* (London, 1999), pp. 30–31

16. Halaby, Jamal, 'Jordanian king calls for direct talks with Israel', *The Associate Press*, 2 June 1991

17. Zak: 'Thirty years'

18. Bligh, Alexander, *The political legacy of King Hussein* (Brighton, 2002), p. 158

19. Amro, Rateb M., 'The peace process: a Jordanian perspective', in J. Ginat et al. (eds), *The Middle East Peace Process: Vision Versus Reality* (Norman, Oklahoma, 2002), p. 179

20. Satloff, Robert B., 'A US strategic opening: Americans and the Jordan-Israeli peace treaty, five years on' *The Jerusalem Post*, 22 October 1999, p. 13

21. Nevo, Joseph, 'The Jordanian-Israeli Peace: the View from Amman', in J. Ginat et al. (eds), *The Middle East Peace Process: Vision Versus Reality* (Norman, Oklahoma, 2002), p. 168

22. *The Israel-Jordan Common Agenda*, 14 September 1993

23. Ryan, Curtis R., *Jordan in Transition: from Hussein to Abdullah* (Boulder, 2002)

24. 'Jordan: non-combattant loser', *The Economist*, 6 April 1991; Vulliamy, Ed, 'US punishes Jordan by cutting aid', *The Guardian* (London), 12 April 1991

25. Satloff, Robert B., *From Hussein to Abdullah: Jordan in Transition* (Washington DC, 1999)

26. Makovsky, David, 'Jordanian debts not eased by peace', *The Jerusalem Post*, 19 January 1995, p. 2

27. Steele, Jonathan, 'War in the Gulf: Pressure on the king to denounce invasion: Jordan's leader falls short of direct criticism of the US', *The Guardian* (London), 5 April 2003

28. 'United States grants $138.5 million in economic assistance to Jordan', Embassy of the United States of America – Amman, http://www.usembassy-amman.org. jo/mil2004.html, 23 March 2004; 'Jordan receives 18.5 M dollar installment for development, reforms from USA', *Financial Times Information*, 24 February 2004
29. Haddad, Mohanna, 'Jordan's Perspective of Peace', in J. Gilat et al. (eds), *The Middle East Peace Process: Vision Versus Reality* (Norman, Oklahoma, 2002)
30. Http://www.kingabdullah.jo
31. Cook, Steven A., *Jordan-Israel Peace, Year One: Laying the Foundation* (Washington DC, 1995), p. 16
32. Nevo: 'The Jordanian-Israeli Peace', p. 169

Notes to Chapter 3 – The Jordanian-Israeli Security Relationship

1. Alpher, Joseph, 'Israel's security concerns in the Peace Process', *International Affairs* 70/2 (1994), p. 236
2. Zunes, Stephen, 'The Israeli-Jordanian Agreement: Peace or Pax Americana?', *Middle East Policy* 3.4 (1995), pp. 57–68
3. Salibi, Kamal, *The Modern History of Jordan* (London, 1993), p. 228–29
4. Kimmerling, Baruch and Migdal, Joel S., *The Palestinian People: A History* (Cambridge MA, 2003), p. 216
5. See Bar-Joseph, Uri, *The Best of Enemies: Israel and Transjordan in the War of 1948* (London, 1987); Shlaim, Avi, *Collusion across the Jordan* (New York, 1988); Wilson Mary C., *King Abdullah, Great Britain and the Making of Jordan* (New York, 1988)
6. Inbar, Efraim and Sadler, Shmuel, 'The Arab-Israeli relationship: from deterrence to security regime', in E. Inbar (ed), *Regional Security Regimes: Israel and Its Neighbors* (New York, 1995), pp. 273–98
7. Kimmerling and Migdal: *The Palestinian People*, p. 251
8. Salibi: *The Modern History*, pp. 237–38
9. Bligh, Alexander, *The political legacy of King Hussein* (Brighton, 2002).
10. 'Jordanian premier says Yassin's murder "demolishes" peace process', *Deutsche Presse-Agentur*, 24 March 2004
11. 'Jordanian opposition urges government to sever ties with Israel', *Deutsche Presse-Agentur*, 22 March 2004
12. 'Demonstrators detained in Jordan for alleged rioting', *Deutsche Presse-Agentur*, 26 March 2004; 'Incident at Wahdat camp', *Mideast Mirror*, 5 April 2004
13. 'Army brass meet and exchange gifts', *The Jerusalem Post*, 27 October 1994, p. 2
14. Bligh: *The Political Legacy*, p. 185
15. Gazit, Shlomo, 'The Gulf War – Main Political and Military Developments', in J. Alpher (ed), *War in the Gulf: Implications for Israel* (Boulder, 1992), p. 41
16. 'Israel, Jordan, Palestinians to make joint efforts to combat flies', *Xinhua News Agency*, 29 July 1994
17. Cook, Steven A., *Jordan-Israel Peace, Year One: Laying the Foundation* (Washington DC, 1995)

18. 'Israeli Parliament questions legality of return of land to Jordan', *Agence France Presse*, 31 January 1995
19. Collins, Liat, 'Israel returns Arava land to Jordan', *The Jerusalem Post*, 31 January 1995, p. 1
20. 'Jordan Assists Israeli army', *Sunday Times* (London), 30 December 2001
21. See Bligh: *The Political Legacy*,
22. 'Jordan assists Israeli army', *Sunday Times* (London), 30 December 2001
23. 'Jordan assists Israeli army', *Sunday Times* (London), 30 December 2001
24. Keyser, Jason, 'Shooting attack rattles calm at Israel's Red Sea "escape" town', *The Associated Press*, 20 November 2003; 'Jordanian governor ends Israel visit, says border shooting probe ongoing', *Financial Times Information*, 26 November 2003
25. Plotkin, Lori, *Jordan-Israel Peace: Taking Stock, 1994-1997* (Washington, 1997), p. 19
26. Plotkin: *Jordan-Israel Peace*, p. 19
27. 'Jordan, Israel hold joint naval exercises', *Deutsche Presse-Agentur*, 26 November 1997
28. O'Sullivan, Arieh, 'Keeping it quiet', *The Jerusalem Post*, 26 December 2001, p. 1
29. 'Israeli firm to sell arms to Jordan', *Xinhua News Agency*, 18 October 1999
30. Mahnaimi, Uzi, 'Mossad took urine sample from Assad', *The Times* (London), 9 January 2000
31. 'Jordan assists Israeli army', *The Times* (London), 30 December 2001
32. Bligh, *The Political Legacy*,
33. Lavie, Mark, 'Israeli soldier, two assailants killed in Jordan border clash; Israel lifts restrictions on West Bank town', *The Associated Press*, 26 December 2001
34. 'Jordan silent on reported talks with Israel', *Xinhua News Agency*, 9 September 1998
35. 'Syria blasts Jordan's participation in maneouvre', *Deutsche Presse-Agentur*, 6 January 1998
36. 'Is Jordan joining the Israel-Turkey axis?' *Mideast Mirror*, 7 September 1998

Notes to Chapter 4 – A Relationship Challenged

1. *The Treaty of Peace Between the State of Israel and the Hashemite Kingdom of Jordan*, Article 10, Paragraph 2
2. Abdallah, Sana, 'Jordan's king leaves for Washington', *United Press International*, 30 September 1996
3. Khouri, Rami G., 'Gas masks and lost passion in Jordanian-Israeli relations', *The Jordan Times*, reproduced in *Mideast Mirror*, 15 October 1996
4. 'Jordan: Israel plays down Jordan's objection to tunnel issue', *The Jordan Times*, 2 October 1996
5. 'The Tunnel Crisis', *The Journal of Palestine Studies* 26/2 (1997), pp. 95–101
6. Abdallah, Sana, 'Jordan's king to meet Arafat, Weizman', *United Press International*, 13 October 1996
7. Plotkin, Lori, *Jordan-Israel Peace: Taking Stock, 1994-1997* (Washington, 1997), p. 22

8. 'Israeli FM to visit Jordan', *Xinhua News Agency*, 11 December 1996
9. 'Israel: Netanyahu on Ties with Jordan, Other Issues', *The Jordan Times*, 17 October 1996
10. 'Jordanian king visits bereaved families in Israel, plans return in "10 days"', *BBC Summary of World Broadcasts* (source: Voice of Israel, Jerusalem, in English), 16 March 1997
11. Keinon, Herb, 'Hussein visit shows strength of peace with Jordan', *The Jerusalem Post*, 17 March 1997
12. Makovsky, David, 'The Prince of Peace', *The Jerusalem Post*, 17 March 1997
13. 'Reciprocity is Vital', *The Jordan Times*, 17 March 1997
14. Rodan, Steve, 'Only Jordan is promoting the peace process, says ambassador', *The Jerusalem Post*, 1 April 1997
15. 'Deaths on the Island of Peace', *The Jerusalem Post*, 3 April 1997
16. 'New Jordanian PM expected to improve ties with Israel', *The Jerusalem Post*, 21 March 1997
17. Al-Kilani, Musa, 'Only Israel to benefit from shooting incident', *The Jordan Times*, 15 March 1997
18. Al Kilani-Musa: 'Only Israel'
19. 'Jordan gunman says girls mocked him', *The Jerusalem Post*, 28 March 1997
20. Sommer, Allison Kaplan, 'Ceremony cancellation shocks, angers Beit Shemesh', *The Jerusalem Post*, 7 May 1997
21. Rodan, Steven, 'Jordanian envoy: no water, no talks, *The Jerusalem Post*, 7 May 1997
22. 'Jordan condemns Israel's new settlement plan, *Xinhua News Agency*, 26 July 1997
23. 'Jordanian, Israeli army officers meet, agree to change Naharayim regulations', *BBC Summary of World Broadcasts* (source: 'Hatzofe', Tel Aviv, in Hebrew), 25 March 1997
24. 'Jordan says Mossad chief should have gone months ago', *Agence France Presse*, 25 February 1998
25. 'King Husayn says his trust in Netanyahu has all but evaporated', *BBC Summary of World Broadcasts* (source: Jordanian TV, Amman), 2 November 1997
26. Zak, Moshe, 'A missed opportunity', *The Jerusalem Post*, 15 October 1997.
27. Bukhari, Natasha, 'King Hussein voices trust in Netanyahu after months of suspicion', *Deutsche Presse-Agentur*, 13 August 1997
28. Bushinksy, Jay, 'Israel denies Jordanian security freeze', *The Jerusalem Post*, 12 October 1997
29. Rabin, Eitan (et al.), 'Israel, Jordan in quiet talks: PM attempts to placate Hussein, *The Jerusalem Post*, 17 February 1998
30. 'King rejects security ties with Israel until Mossad heads replaced', *BBC Summary of World Broadcasts* (text of Yediot Aharonot, in Hebrew), 16 January 1998
31. Harris, David, 'Sharon, Hussein discuss projects as Mashaal-affair wounds heal', *The Jerusalem Post*, 9 March 1998
32. 'Jordanian Official: Jordanian Foreign Minister Accepts Sharon Clarifications', *The Jordan Times*, 24 March 1998
33. 'Israel: Israel's Mordekhay on Withdrawal, Peace Issues', *The Jordan Times*, 15 April 1998

34. Ayyub, Tariq, 'Jordan: Jordan Protests to Israel over Sharon's Statement', *The Jordan Times*, 16 March 1998

35. Ayyub, Tariq, 'Jordan: Jordan Officials Comment on Israeli Report in Misha'al Case', *The Jordan Times*, 17 February 1998

36. 'People-Peace in the Air', *The Jerusalem Report*, 27 November 1997

37. Ibrahim, Youssef M., 'Jordan is angered by Israeli findings on assassination fiasco', *The New York Times*, 18 February 1998, p. 7

38. 'Jordan: Lawyers to file international lawsuit against Ariel Sharon', *The Jordan Times*, 3 May 1998

39. Zak, Moshe, 'Crisis proof peace treaty', *The Jerusalem Post*, 10 October 1997, p. 4

40. Bligh, Alexander, *The political legacy of King Hussein* (Brighton, 2002), p. 199

41. Katz, Samuel M., 'Still Partners', *The Jerusalem Report*, 27 November 1997

42. 'Israel: Netanyahu on ties with Jordan, other issues', *The Jordan Times*, 17 October 1996

43. 'Jordan's premier criticizes Netanyahu', *Xinhua News Agency*, 1 December 1996

44. Khouri: 'Gas masks and lost passion'

45. 'Mish'al affair prompts Jordan to suspend all security cooperation with Israel', *BBC Summary of World Broadcasts* (source: Voice of Palestine, Ramallah, in Arabic), 11 October 1997

46. 'King Husayn says his trust in Netanyahu has all but evaporated', *BBC Summary of World Broadcasts* (source: Jordanian TV, Amman), 2 November 1997

47. 'With slogans left behind' Editorial, *The Jordan Times*, 20 November 1997

48. 'King rejects security ties with Israel until Mossad head replaced', *BBC Summary of World Broadcasts* (source: Yediot Aharonot, in Hebrew), 16 January 1998

49. 'Jordanians on Dani Yatom's appointment', *Jerusalem Al-Quds* (in Arabic), 24 August 1999

50. Brand, Laurie, 'The effects of the peace process on political liberalization in Jordan', *Journal of Palestine Studies* 28 (1999), pp. 52–67

51. Habib, Randa, 'Islamist poll boycott shuts out opponents of Jordan-Israel treaty', *Agence France Presse*, 1 November 1997

Notes to Chapter 5 – 'The Fruits of Peace'

1. For more extensive analyses of water issues in the Jordan basin, see: Allan, John A., *Water, Peace and the Middle East: Negotiating Resources in the Jordan Basin* (London, 1996); Starr, Joyce R. and Stoll, Daniel C., *The Politics of Scarcity: Water in the Middle East* (Boulder, 1987); Wolf, Aaron T., *Hydropolitics along the Jordan River: Scarce Water and its Impact on the Arab-Israeli Conflict* (Tokyo, 1996); Amery, Hussein A. and Wolf, Aaron T. (eds), *Water in the Middle East: A Geography of Peace* (Austin, 2000)

2. Dodge, Toby and Tell, Tariq, 'Peace and the Politics of water in Jordan', in John A. Allan (ed), *Water, Peace and the Middle East: Negotiating Resources in the Jordan Basin* (London, 1996), pp. 169–84

3. Reproduced after Beaumont, Peter, 'Dividing the Waters of the River Jordan: An Analysis of the 1994 Israel-Jordan Peace Treaty', *Water Resources Development* xiii/5 (1997), p. 421
4. Haddadin, Munther, 'Negotiated Resolution of the Jordan-Israel Water Conflict', *International Negotiations* v (2000), pp. 263–88
5. Dodge and Tell: 'Peace and the Politics', p. 178
6. Haddad: 'Negotiated Resolution', pp. 277–81
7. Dodge and Tell; 'Peace and the Politics', pp. 178–80
8. Beaumont, Peter, 'Conflict, Coexistence and Cooperation: A Study of Water Use in the Jordan basin', in Hussein A. Amery and Aaron T. Wolf (eds), *Water in the Middle East: A Geography of Peace* (Austin, 2000), p. 21
9. Beaumont: 'Conflict, Coexistence and Cooperation', p. 21
10. Http://www.usembassy-amman.org.jo/USAID/water.htm, (13 March 2004)
11. Http://www.jordanembassyus.org/agricult.htm, (13 March 2004)
12. 'Report views projects to boost Jordan's water resources', *The Jordan Times*, 25 December 2000
13. Beaumont: 'Conflict, Coexistence and Cooperation', pp. 26–27
14. Cockburn, Patrick, 'Israeli drought cuts off Jordan's water supply', *The Independent* (London), 16 March 1999, p. 13
15. Beaumont: 'Conflict, Coexistence and Cooperation', pp. 28–33
16. Elmusa, Sharif S., 'The Jordan-Israel water agreement: a model or exception?' *Journal of Palestine Studies*, xxiv/3 (1995), pp. 63–73
17. Beaumont: 'Dividing the waters', pp. 415–24
18. Beaumont: 'Dividing the waters', pp. 418-423; Elmusa: 'The Jordan-Israel water agreement', p. 69
19. Rodan, Steve, 'Jordanian envoy: No water, no talks', *The Jerusalem Post*, 7 May 1997, p. 4
20. 'New crises with Jordan as Weizman takes gov't plan to Arafat', *Mideast Mirror* xi/86 (6 May 1997)
21. Rodan: 'Jordanian envoy', p. 4
22. Yudelman, Michal (et al.), 'Hussein, Netanyahu try to resolve water crisis', *The Jerusalem Post*, 7 May 1997, p. 1
23. Walker, Christopher, 'Israel has secret Jordan meeting on water crisis', *The Times* (London), 10 May 1997
24. 'Israel to open consulate in Jordanian Red Sea port', *Agence France Presse*, 25 May 1997
25. 'King Husayn says supply of water by Israel "fruit of peace"', *BBC Summary of World Broadcasts* (source: Hashemite Kingdom of Jordan Radio, Amman, in Arabic), 29 May 1997
26. 'Officials deny Israeli "claims" about agreement on changing dam site', *BBC Summary of World Broadcasts* (source: Al-Arab-al-Yawm, in Arabic), 26 August 1997
27. Bukhari, Natasha, 'Jordan blasts Israel over allegations on joint dam project', *Deutsche Presse-Agentur*, 26 August 1997
28. 'Israeli government confirms dam to be built on land claimed by Syria', *Agence France Presse*, 24 August 1997

29. 'Jordan declares drought, aid for farmers', *The Associated Press*, 17 January 1999

30. Cotenta, Sandro, 'In the Middle East, the next conflict will likely flow from water', *The Toronto Star*, 26 June 1999

31. 'Jordan to unveil water "Emergency Plan" in next few days', *The Jordan Times*, 17 March 1999

32. Cockburn, Patrick, 'Israeli drought', p. 13

33. Harman, Danna, 'Jordan: Israeli decision to cut water supply casts suspicion on peace process', *The Jerusalem Post*, 18 March 1999, p. 1

34. 'Jordan threatens "appropriate" response if Israel reduces water share', *BBC Summary of World Broadcasts* (source: *Al-Sharq al-Awsat*, London, Arabic), 19 March 1999

35. 'King threatens "other means to pressure" Israel over water', *BBC Summary of World Broadcasts* (source: 'Al-Bayan' Website, Dubai, in Arabic), 20 March 1999

36. 'Israeli ambassador comments on cutting of water supply to Jordan', *BBC Summary of World Broadcasts* (source: Jordanian TV, Amman, in English), 15 March 1999

37. 'Israel to give Jordan full water share', *Deutsche Presse-Agentur*, 21 April 1999

38. Coren, Ora, 'Israel approves acceleration of Adasiya Dam construction by Jordan at Hamat Gader; agreement has been reached on the water quotas Israel will transfer to Jordan next summer', *Globes Publisher Itonut*, 27 May 1999

39. Hala, Jamal, 'Israel, Jordan revise water distribution deal', *The Jerusalem Post*, 18 August 1999, p. 5

40. Though the government stated that Israel provided its full water share, Mahashneh, head of the Jordan Valley Authority, contended that Israel was still not providing the required share, and says he was forced to resign because of his attacks on Israel at the time. Cotenta, Sandro, 'In the Middle East, the next conflict will likely flow from water: Water flows just once a week', *The Toronto Star*, 26 June 1999

41. 'Country to receive emergency UN food aid to counter effects of drought', *The Jordan Times*, 4 August 1999

42. 'Syria begins to supply water to Jordan', *Xinhua News Agency*, 15 May 1999

43. 'Syria to increase water supply to Jordan', *Financial Times Information*, 21 August 2002

44. 'Is there a dam in Jordan's future?', *Mideast Mirror* xiii/89 (12 May 1999)

45. Rubinstein, Danny, 'A bridge over troubled waters: how Israel's plan to cut water supplies helped build new ties between Jordan and Syria', *Ha'aretz Daily Newspaper*, 25 May 1999

46. 'Report on Jordanian-Syrian Dam Accord', *BBC Summary of World Broadcasts* (source: *Al-Dustur*, in Arabic), 21 May 1999

47. 'New moves on Jordan Valley projects', *Middle East Economic Digest*, 8 January 1999, p. 20

48. *Treaty of Peace Between the State of Israel and the Hashemite Kingdom of Jordan*, Annex II, Article III, Paragraph 5

49. 'New moves on Jordan Valley project', *Middle East Economic Digest*, 8 January 1999, p. 20

50. 'Jordan has plan to save Dead Sea from dying', *Agence France Presse*, 29 August 2002

51. 'Foreign Minister pushes "Red–Dead" canal to US Jews', *The Jerusalem Post*, 16 March 2001, p. 2A

52. Swarns, Rachel, 'Israelis and Jordanians cast an accord upon the Dead Sea's waters', *The New York Times*, 2 September 2002, p. A9; Friedman, Ina, 'Stench threatens new Israel-Jordan Dead Sea water project', *The Jerusalem Post*, 12 August 2002

53. Boncompagni, Hala, 'Dead Sea to disappear in 50 years unless linked to Red Sea canal: Jordan', *Agence France Presse*, 1 June 2004

54. 'Arabs oppose Jordan's Dead Sea canal scheme', *Agence France Presse*, 30 August 2002

55. 'Egypt-Jordan differences over Dead–Red canal', *Mideast Mirror*, 23 September 2002

56. 'Jordanian parliament says Israeli water cut plans "serious threat" to peace', *Petra-JNA news agency Website*, Amman, Arabic, 17 May 1999

57. Cotenta: 'In the Middle East'

Notes to Chapter 6 – Economic Cooperation and Trade

1. *Treaty of Peace Between the State of Israel and the Hashemite Kingdom of Jordan*, Article 7, Paragraph 1

2. Astorino-Courtois, Allison, 'Transforming International Agreements into National Realities: Marketing Arab Israeli Peace in Jordan', *The Journal of Politics* lviii/4 (1996), pp. 1036–37

3. Makovsky, David, 'Jordanian debts not eased by peace', *The Jerusalem Post*, 19 January 1995, p. 2

4. Zunes, Stephen, 'The Israeli-Jordanian Agreement: Peace or Pax Americana?', *Middle East Policy* iii/4 (1995), pp. 57–68

5. Plotkin, Lori, *Jordan-Israel Peace: Taking Stock, 1994–1997* (Washington, 1997), p. 33

6. 'US grants $138.5 million in economic assistance to Jordan', Press Release, Embassy of the USA-Amman, 23 March 2004, http://www.usembassy-amman.org.jo/mil2004.html

7. 'Jordan to receive U.S. military equipment', *The Jordan Times*, 13 December 1996

8. 'Disappointment with peace gains hits Amman stocks', *The Jerusalem Post*, 2 January 1995, p. 9

9. Bukhari, Natasha and Goldberg, Andy, 'In Jordan and Israel, peace dividends lag behind expectations', *Deutsche Presse-Agentur*, 23 October 1995

10. Khouri, Rami G., 'Assessing two years of Jordanian-Israeli peacemaking', *Mideast Mirror*, 6 August 1996

11. Khouri, Rami G., 'Some Jordanians gain, many do not', *The Jerusalem Post*, 22 October 1999, p. 2B

12. 'Jordan times year end report views "ailing economy"', *The Jordan Times*, 20 December 2000

13. Ibrahim, Youssef M., 'Jordan is angered by Israeli findings on assassination fiasco', *The New York Times*, 18 February 1998, p. 7

14. 'Jordan begins new air route to Israel', *United Press International*, 6 January 1997

15. 'The second KAS-IJCC meeting: regional trade relations and cooperation with the EU and US', 21 October 2003, Konrad Adenauer Foundation, Jerusalem

16. 'Jordanian minister: regional projects halted for political reasons', *Deutsche Presse-Agentur*, 13 November 1996

17. 'Annual economic conference with Israel finds few Arab takers', *Agence France Presse*, 12 November 1997

18. 'Jordan, Israel agree to establish industrial zone', *Xinhua News Agency*, 16 November 1997

19. 'Jordan-Israel Industrial estate faces criticism', *The Star* (Beirut), 4 December 1997

20. Chmaytelli, Maher, 'WEF meet in Jordan rekindles hopes of prosperous, peaceful Mideast', *Agence France Presse*, 19 June 2003

21. Stern, Bazelal, 'Olmert: keep politics and business matters separate', *The Jerusalem Post*, 8 July 2003

22. 'Israeli envoy on "cautious optimism" at world economic forum', *Financial Times Information*, 22 June 2003

23. 'Jordanian businessmen refuse cooperation with Israel in Iraq's reconstruction', *Xinhua News Agency*, 30 June 2003

24. CIA World Factbook, http://www.cia.gov (15 January 2004)

25. 'Jordan Data Profile', 'Israel Data Profile', The World Bank Group, World Development Indicators database, April 2004

26. Kardoush, Marwan, 'Economics of peace', reprint in *The Jerusalem Post* (from *The Jordan Times*), 25 September 2002

27. 'Jordan: Special Report country table', *Middle East Economic Digest* (MEED), Weekly Special Report, 29 May 1998

28. 'Interview: Mohammed Abu Hammour, Jordan Finance Minister', *Middle East Economics Digest*, 2 July 2004, p. 8

29. MEED Weekly Special Report, 9 June 2000, p. 21

30. Susser, Asher, *Jordan: Case Study of a Pivotal State* (Washington, 2000)

31. 'Jordan times year-end report views "ailing economy"', *The Jordan Times*, 20 December 2000

32. *Treaty of Peace between the State of Israel and the Hashemite Kingdom of Jordan*, Article 7, Paragraph 1

33. *Treaty of Peace between the State of Israel and the Hashemite Kingdom of Jordan*, Article 7, Paragraph 2

34. Mishal, Shaul; Kuperman, Ranan D. and Boas, David, *Investment in Peace: The Politics of Economic Cooperation between Israel, Jordan and the Palestinian Authority* (Brighton, 2001), pp. 119–20

35. Gal, Yitzhak, 'Sheikh Hussein-Jordan River Crossing: Working Paper', 2 May 2004

36. Cook, Steven A., *Jordan-Israel Peace, Year One: Laying the Foundation* (Washington DC, 1995), p. 4

37. Shamir, Shimon (ed), *Israel-Jordan Relations, Projects, Economics, Business* (Tel Aviv, 2004), p. 133
38. 'A winning formula', *Middle East Economic Digest*, 8 June 2001
39. 'Jordan: Jordanian investors try to reduce Israeli interest in zones, *The Jordan Times*, 15 July 1998; 'Jordan: Jordanians investors urged to have "open mind" on QIZ', *The Jordan Times*, 7 August 1998
40. Manneh, Jane, 'Qualifying Industrial Zones: Sector Report', Export and Finance Bank, Jordan, 10 June 2003
41. Manneh: 'Qualifying Industrial Zones'
42. 'Jordan: Exports Witness 25% growth in 2001, US largest consumer', *The Jordan Times*, 2 February 2002
43. Joha, Ghassan, 'Economic performance of 2003, in retrospect', *The Star*, 5 January 2004
44. 'A Winning Formula', *Middle East Economic Digest*, 8 June 2001
45. 'Jordan: Government plans to replace foreign workers in QIZ with Jordanians', *The Jordan Times*, 7 January 2002
46. 'Israeli firm invests $1.5 million in Jordan factories; 2000 trade figures noted', *The Jordan Times*, 22 February 2001. However, the Kingdom of Jordan's Department of Statistics figures showed a higher number for Jordanian exports to Israel of $57.7 million during the same period of 2000, and $34.7 million in 1999. Jordan imported $46 million worth in the 9-month period, compared to $16 million in 1999. When examining Israeli and Jordanian trade data, differences in data compilation must be noted. Israeli figures report core trade data, while Jordanian governmental figures include goods in transit, such as products that are partially processed in Jordan and then sent to Israel for additional processing, as exports. As a result the Jordanian trade value overestimates actual exports.
47. 'Jordan: 47 Jordanian, Israeli Companies Cooperating in Exportations', *The Jordan Times*, 16 March 1998
48. 'Business Chronicle: Israeli companies flourish in Jordan, *Emerging Markets Datafile*, 17 July 1997
49. Manor, Hadas, 'Israel-Jordan-EU agreement depends on solving territories export problem', *Globes Publisher Itonut*, 17 May 2004
50. 'Israel gives into EU calls to label goods from occupied territories', *AFX News Limited*, 5 August 2004
51. 'Jordanian business leaders deny launch of joint chamber of commerce with Israel', *BBC Summary of World Broadcasts* (source: *Al-Dustur*, Amman, in Arabic, 13 September 1998), 22 September 1998
52. Awad, Rana, 'Jordanian businessmen urge severing of trade ties with Israel', *The Jordan Times*, 1 April 2002
53. Henderson, Amy, 'Jordanian-Israeli Industrial Complex to Expand QIZ', *The Jordan Times*, 31 May 1998
54. For an extensive discussion of the Jordan Gateway project see Mishal (et al.): *Investment in Peace*, pp. 127–30
55. Http://www.foeme.org/
56. Mishal (et al.): *Investment in Peace*, p. 130
57. Mishal (et al.): *Investment in Peace*, p. 135

58. Danon, Yitzhak, 'Petition to liquidate Jordan Gate projects', *Globes Publisher Itonut*, Israel's Business Arena, 5 July 2004

59. 'Jordan pins high hopes on FTA', *The Jordan Times*, 9 November 2000

60. 'Special Report Jordan QIZ', *Quest Economics Data base, MEED Weekly Special Report*, 8 June 2001

61. 'Jordan: Projects with Israel Infeasible', *Financial Times Information*, 27 August 2002

62. Kardoush: 'Economics of peace'

63. Plotkin: *Jordan-Israel Peace*, p. 3

64. 'Jordanian official: trade with Israel "modest in volume", "limited in nature"', *The Jordan Times*, 26 October 2001

65. 'Joint project agreed with Israel', *Middle East Economic Digest*, 20 March 1998, p. 28

66. 'Minister suggests extending Israel-Jordan trade protocol, meet with counterpart', *Ma'ariv* (Tel Aviv), in Hebrew, 16 April 2001, p. 7

67. 'Jordan and Israel sign trade pact', World Economic Forum Press Release, 16 May 2004, http://www.weforum.org

68. For a short time, door-to-door delivery was allowed

69. Gal: 'Sheikh Hussein-Jordan River Crossing'

70. Gal: 'Sheikh Hussein-Jordan River Crossing', p. 4

71. Shamir: *Israel-Jordan Relations*, p. 133

72. 'Jordan, Israel agree to boost economic cooperation', *Deutsche Presse-Agentur*, 23 November 1998

73. 'Jordan Keen to Expand Trade with Israel, Palestinian Areas', *The Jordan Times*, 27 February 1999

74. Henderson, Amy, 'Joint Jordanian-Israeli Transport Committee meets today', *The Jordan Times*, 6 September 1999

75. According to Mishal (et al.), cement and fuel are delivered through a door-to-door method

76. 'Jordan: Jordanian columnist on trade with Israel, PA', *The Jordan Times*, 31 May 1998

77. Henderson: 'Joint Jordanian-Israeli Transport'

78. 'Jordan: Jordanian columnist on trade with Israel, PA', *The Jordan Times*, 31 May 1998

79. Shamir: *Israel-Jordan Relations*, p. 134

80. Hirst, David, 'For Jordan, the peace treaty with Israel has been far from warm and offered few improvement for its citizens', *The Guardian* (London), 3 April 1995, p. 20

Notes to Chapter 7 – Tourism

1. *Tourism Sector, Key Indicators 1994–2002*, Jordanian Ministry of Tourism, Information & Statistics Department.

2. 'Peace brings Jordan record tourism boom', *The Jerusalem Post*, 10 December 1995

3. 'King Hussein and Crown Prince Hassan host a quarter of the Knesset at dinner', *Mideast Mirror*, 6 February 1995

4. Prusher, Ilene R., 'Despite peace, Jordan sees tourist no-show', *The Christian Scientist Monitor*, 14 August 1996, p. 7

5. Rudge, David, 'Children's group are the first Jordanian visitors', *The Jerusalem Post*, 29 November 1994, p. 1

6. Cook, Steven A., *Jordan-Israel Peace, Year One: Laying the Foundation* (Washington DC, 1995), p. 14

7. Bukhari, Natasha, 'Jordan caught in a crisis over peace', *Deutsche Presse-Agentur*, 17 April 1998

8. *Tourism Sector, Key Indicators 1994–2002*, Jordanian Ministry of Tourism, Information & Statistics Department

9. 'Israel and Jordan in joint tourism boost', *Deutsche Presse-Agentur*, 11 November 1996

10. 'Israel, Jordan Collaborate on 2000 Plans, *Info-Prod Research Ltd.*, 1 July 1999

11. *Financial Times*, 8 September 1999

12. Boncompagni, Hala, 'With violence rocking Mideast, Jordan to host "peace through tourism" forum', *Agence France Presse*, 30 October 2000

13. 'Minister discusses Israeli tourism, calls for alcohol ban', *BBC Summary of World Broadcasts*, 16 September 2000

14. *Tourism Sectors, Key Indicators 1994–2002*, Jordanian Ministry of Tourism, Information & Statistics Department; tourism receipt figures for 2000 and 2001 are preliminary.

15. 'Israeli offensive's impact on Jordanian economy bad, but manageable', *Financial Times News*, 19 April 2002

16. 'Jordan's national carrier back in black in 2002', *Agence France Presse*, 16 December 2002

17. 'Jordan's tourism: another casualty', *Financial Times Information*, 30 April 2002

18. 'Jordan's tourism industry is intifada's latest casualty: minister', *Agence France Presse*, 28 May 2001

19. 'European Tour Operators Shocked by Ze'evi's Posting', *Ha'aretz Daily News*, 7 March 2001

20. Shapiro, Haim, 'Jordanians say Israel delays visas', *The Jerusalem Post*, 20 November 1994, p. 2

21. Plotkin, Lori, *Jordan-Israel Peace: Taking Stock, 1994–1997* (Washington, 1997), p. 6

22. Plotkin, *Jordan-Israel Peace*, p. 6

23. Prusher: 'Despite peace'

24. Levinson, Jay, 'Jordan is trying to keep Israeli tourists coming', *The Jerusalem Post*, 20 October 1997, p. 7

25. 'Minister discusses Israeli tourism'

26. Rudge, David, 'Israeli tourist stabbed in Jordan', *The Jerusalem Post*, 1 May 1997

27. 'Israeli ministers urge Jordan to make arrests over embassy shooting', *Voice of Israel*, Tel Aviv, in Hebrew, 24 September 1997

28. Dudkevitch, Margot, 'Unknown group claims Amman attack', *The Jerusalem Post*, 22 September 1997, p. 1

29. O'Sullivan, Arieh, 'Israelis urged not to travel to Arab countries', *The Jerusalem Post*, 9 August 2001, p. 1

30. Shapiro, Haim, 'Jordan seen as more dangerous for Israelis than Egypt', *The Jerusalem Post*, 9 August 2001

31. Zacharia, Janine, 'Jordanian foreign minister to "Post": It's safe for Israelis to visit', *The Jerusalem Post*, 22 August 2001

32. 'Peace City to be built, *The Jerusalem Post*, 19 October 1994, p. 2

33. 'US gives two million dollars for Red Sea peace park', *Agence France Presse*, 18 December 1997

34. 'Israeli planes to land at Jordan's Aqaba airport', *Agence France Press*, 10 November 1997

35. 'Jordan, Israel sign an agreement on the use of Aqaba airport', *BBC Summary of World Broadcasts* (source: Hashemite Kingdom of Jordan Radio, Amman, in Arabic), 31 August 1997

36. Mishal, Shaul; Kuperman, Ranan D. and Boas, David, *Investment in Peace: The Politics of Economic Cooperation between Israel, Jordan and the Palestinian Authority* (Brighton, 2001), p. 122

37. 'Jordanian transport minister, Israeli counterpart discuss "peace" airport', *BBC Summary of World Broadcasts* (source: Jordanian TV, Amman), 14 September 1999

38. Cook: *Jordan-Israel Peace*, p. 14

39. 'Special Report Jordan: Aqaba: the Economic Transformation Begins', *MEED Weekly Special Report*, 15 August 2003, p. 26

40. 'Business at Large, Jordan', *Financial Times Information*, 5 July 2002

41. 'ASEZA 2003 Achievements Highlighted', *Info-Prod Research Ltd.*, 11 March 2004

42. 'Investments in Aqaba private economic zone estimated at $2 billion', *Info-Prod Research, Ltd.*, 15 June 2003

43. Greenbaum, Lior, 'Eilat's next door nemesis', *Financial Times Information*, 6 October 2002

Notes to Chapter 8 – Building Peace Between the People

1. *Treaty of Peace between the State of Israel and the Hashemite Kingdom of Jordan*, Article 10

2. It should be noted, though, that the construction of the separation wall/fence in the West Bank and associated travel restrictions have seriously impaired joint NGO activity.

3. Individuals targeted by the anti-normalization movement have faced expulsion from professional associations, threats, blacklisting in newspapers and, in at least one case, had a child fail key comprehensive educational exams because of his parent's association with Israelis.

4. *Culture of Water, Jordan-Israel Center of Excellence* (Tel Aviv, 2002), p. 8

5. *Culture of Water, Jordan-Israel Center of Excellence* (Tel Aviv, 2002)

6. Because of sensitivity inside Jordan to such collaborative projects, the specific NGOs will not be named here.

7. *The Middle East Red Palm Weevil Program, 5-Year Summary: 1998–2003* (Tel Aviv, 2003)
8. Kersherner, Isabel, 'Though other ties are under strain, Israeli-Jordanian medical cooperation is flourishing', *The Jerusalem Report*, p. 17
9. For more information see http://www.cisepo.ca/
10. 'Jordan's king inaugurates Mideast science project grouping Iran, Israel', *British Broadcast Corporation* (source: Petra JNA news agency web site), 6 January 2003
11. Http://www.sesame.org.jo
12. 'Jordan, Israel to lay cornerstone for international science centre', *The Jordan Times*, 8 March 2004, p. 2
13. Krajick, Kevin, 'Science Center on Jordan-Israel Border Aims to Bridge the Rift', *Science Magazine*, 5 March 2004
14. It is interesting to note that in the summary produced by the Peres Center for Peace on this seminar, no Jordanians in attendance are identified by name and that the Jordanian Minister of Planning delivered his speech via a recorded video message. *The Jordanian-Israeli Projects: Past Experience and Future Prospects* (Tel Aviv, 2003)
15. 'Forum on Economic Cooperation, A Jordanian-Israeli Joint Initiative', 9–13th March 2003, Wittenberg, Germany
16. 'Peres declares Israel-Jordan fund: King Abdullah agreed to sponsor high-tech endeavors; World Bank to assist too', *Financial Times Information*, 19 September 1999

Notes to Chapter 9 – Perceptions of Peace in Jordan

1. Israelis generally refer to the separation wall as a 'fence', pointing out that a system of multiple fences is in place most of its length. Some third parties, such as the United States government, have adopted the term 'barrier' to refer to the wall/fence. The term 'wall' is used here, as it most accurately reflects Jordanian perception.
2. *MEED Weekly Special Report*, 9 June 2000
3. Nevo, Joseph, 'The Jordanian-Israeli Peace: the View from Amman', in J. Ginat et al. (eds), *The Middle East Peace Process: Vision Versus Reality* (Norman, Oklahoma, 2002), p. 167
4. *Public Opinion Poll concerning Israeli-Jordanian Negotiations*, Amman, Center for Strategic Studies, 1994
5. The survey in Jordan included 800 participants and was conducted under the supervision of Hani Hourani in association with Ismail Abus Sundus of the Dar al-Arab Research and Study Center. The survey in Israel included 1201 participants, interviewed by phone. The project leader at the Truman Institute was Gadi Wolfsfeld. It is interesting to note that although 37.8 per cent of the Jordanian respondents reporting having relatives in the Palestinian territories, ethnic identification as a Palestinian is not a significant factor in overall responses by Jordanian participants.
6. Plotkin, Lori, *Jordan-Israel Peace: Taking Stock, 1994–1997* (Washington, 1997), p. 27

7. 'Born: A Jordanian Committee to "resist normalization with Israel"', *Mideast Mirror*, 16 May 1994

8. See Andoni, Lamis and Schwedler, Jillian, 'Bread Riots in Jordan' *Middle East Report* 26 (1996), p. 42

9. Khouri, Rami G., 'Reading Jordanian Rage, Arab attitudes and Israeli policies', *Mideast Mirror*, 7 January 1997

10. 'The Jordanian-Israeli Projects: Past Experience and Future Prospects", Peres Center for Peace, June 2003

11. 'Jordan's Islamist-led opposition calls for referendum on treaty with Israel', *Mideast Mirror*, 2 November 1994

12. *The Jordan Times*, 2 September 1995

13. 'Jordanians opposing peace with Israel campaign against normalization', *Deutsche Presse-Agentur*, 18 May 1999

14. Plotkin: *Jordan-Israel Peace*, p. 29

15. 'Odds for Hebron deal stay the same', *Mideast Mirror*, 8 January 1997

16. 'Lobbying group, deputies call for freeze in ties with Israel', *BBC Summary of World Broadcasts* (source: *The Jordan Times* Website), 6 October 1998

17. 'Unions publish list of Jordanians dealing with Israel', *Agence France Presse*, 21 January 2001

18. A 1996 opinion poll conducted by the University of Jordan's Centre for Strategic Studies suggested that public support for the professional associations' political role was not so widespread: 43.3 per cent of those polled said they supported limiting professional associations solely to work-related (i.e. non-political) matters; 27.5 per cent were in opposition; see Plotkin: *Jordan-Israel Peace*, p. 31

19. Plotkin: *Jordan-Israel Peace*, p. 27

20. 'Engineers body denies membership to graduates of Israeli universities', *BBC Monitoring Middle East* (source: *al-Arab al-Yawm*, in Arabic), 1 August 1999

21. 'Jordanian opponents of normalization with Israel score symbolic victory', *Mideast Mirror*, 1 November 1996

22. 'Jordanian guild expels writer for ITV interview', *The Jerusalem Post*, 10 May 1995

23. 'Jordanian guild expels writer for ITV interview', *The Jerusalem Post*, 10 May 1995

24. 'Arab Journalists Union conference in Jordan condemns normalization with Israel', *BBC Monitoring Middle East* (source: *The Jordan Times* Website), 29 October 2000

25. 'Syria reportedly bars entry to several Jordanians for contacts with Israel', *BBC Summary of World Broadcasts* (source: *Al-Sabil*, in Arabic) 9 February 2000

26. Indeed, on a number of occasions Israelis have been treated in Jordan

27. Abdallah, Sana, 'Jordan doctors boycott economic meeting', *United Press International*, 8 October 1995

28. '"New McCarthyism" feared as anti-normalization campaign heightens', *The Jordan Times*, 21 July 1998

29. 'Unions publish list of Jordanians dealing with Israel', *Agence France Presse*, 21 January 2001

30. Ba'rel, Zvi, 'Normalization is not for public consumption', *Ha'aretz Daily*, 3 May 2000

31. 'Peaceful demos in Jordan vent anti-Israeli anger', *Agence France Presse*, 27 October 2000
32. 'Jordan's April Fool: Sharon Killed', *United Press International*, 1 April 2004
33. 'Jordan's civil servants to chip in one day's salary to intifada', *Agence France Presse*, 23 October 2000
34. 'Jordanian Opposition praises government's decision not to interfere with marches', *Financial Times Information* (source: *Al-Dustur*, 3 April), 4 April 2002
35. Plotkin: *Israel-Jordan Peace*, see list of incidents on p. 20
36. 'Hussein warned he's moving too fast on normalization with Israel', *Mideast Mirror*, 1 August 1995
37. 'King Hussein warns local opponents of peace process', *Mideast Mirror*, 10 November 1995
38. 'King Hussein lashes out at union leaders', *Agence France Presse*, 8 June 1997
39. Ayyub, Tariq, 'Four deputies renege on petition to cancel Jordan-Israel treaty', *The Jordan Times*, 22 December 2000
40. Halaby, Jamal, 'Authorities in Jordan arrest hard-line activists opposed to peace with Israel', *The Associated Press*, 27 January 2001
41. 'Jordan bans unions from holding solidarity rally for anti-Israel activists', *Agence France Presse*, 22 November 2002
42. 'Jordanian minister warns against "illegal march" on the Israeli embassy', *Financial Times Information*, 12 April 2002
43. 'Top Jordanian court bands trade union anti-Israeli committees', *Agence France Presse*, 29 November 2002
44. Nevo: 'The Jordanian-Israeli Peace', p. 170
45. 'Sparks fly in Amman', *Mideast Mirror*, 14 June 1995
46. 'Jordanian PM blasts opponents of relations with Israel', *Ha'aretz Daily News*, 30 August 2000
47. For more on this subject see Ryan, Curtis R., *Jordan in Transition: from Hussein to Abdullah* (Boulder, 2002)
48. Ryan: *Jordan in Transition*, p. 27
49. 'Jordan polls: the best possible birthday gift for King Hussein', *Mideast Mirror*, 10 November 1993
50. Habib, Randa, 'Jordanians vote in local elections, first test for peace deal', *Agence France Presse*, 11 July 1995
51. Brand, Laurie, 'The effects of the peace process on political liberalization in Jordan', *Journal of Palestine Studies* 28 (1999), p. 60
52. Habib, Randa, 'Islamist poll boycott shuts out opponents of Jordan-Israel treaty', *Agence France Presse*, 1 November 1997
53. 'Jordan', *MEED Weekly Special Report*, 29 May 1998
54. 'Islamists accuse Jordanian government of vote rigging', *Deutsche Presse-Agentur*, 19 June 2003
55. Khouri: 'Reading Jordanian Rage'
56. 'Jordan warns on bids to use pro-Palestinian anger to destabilize country', *Agence France Presse*, 1 November 2000
57. Khouri, Rami G., 'Gas masks and lost passion in Jordanian-Israeli relations', *Mideast Mirror*, 15 October 1996

Notes to Chapter 10 – Lessons from an Incomplete Peace

1. 'King Hussein and Crown Prince Hassan host a quarter of the Knesset at dinner', *Mideast Mirror*, 6 February 1995
2. 'Document warns of "continuing deterioration" in ties with Egypt, Jordan', *BBC Summary of World Broadcasts* (source: Voice of Israel, Jerusalem, 3 January 2001), 4 January 2001
3. Satloff, Robert, 'A US strategic opening: Americans and the Jordan-Israeli peace treaty, five years on', *The Jerusalem Post*, 22 October 1999, p. 7
4. 'Jordanian foreign minister comments on peace treaty with Israel, Road Map', *BBC Monitoring Middle East* (source: Voice of Israel, Jerusalem, in Hebrew), 13 October 2004
5. 'Jordan denies Israeli foreign ministry delegation visit to Amman', *BBC Monitoring Middle East* (source: MENA news agency, Cairo, in English), 14 October 2004
6. Khouri, Rami G., 'Gas masks and lost passion in Jordanian-Israeli relations', *The Jordan Times*, 15 October 1996, as reported in *Mideast Mirror*, 15 October 1996
7. 'Jordan-Israel peace depends on Israel-Palestinian solution: ambassador', *Agence France Presse*, 26 October 2001
8. Cook, Steven A., *Jordan-Israel Peace, Year One: Laying the Foundation* (Washington DC, 1995), p. 9; quoted from *Building on Peace: Toward Regional Security and Economic Development in the Middle East*, Proceedings of an International Policy Conference (Washington, DC: Washington Institute for Near East Policy, 1995) p. 11
9. 'King Hussein and Crown Prince Hassan host a quarter of the Knesset at dinner', *Mideast Mirror*, 6 February 1995
10. 'Six years later', *The Jordan Times*, 26 October 2000
11. Satloff: 'A US strategic opening ', p. 8

BIBLIOGRAPHY

Abdallah, Sana. 'Jordan doctors boycott economic meeting', *United Press International*, 8 October 1995
———. 'Jordan's king leaves for Washington', *United Press International*, 30 September 1996
———. 'Jordan's king to meet Arafat, Weizman', *United Press International*, 13 October 1996

Abou El-Magd, Nadia. '25 years after Sadat's Jerusalem visit, no real peace, but no war either', *The Associated Press*, 19 November 2002

AFX News Limited. 'Israel gives into EU calls to label goods from occupied territories', 5 August 2004

Agence France Presse. 'Israeli Parliament questions legality of return of land to Jordan', 31 January 1995
———. 'King Hussein "very worried" about Mideast situation', 24 October 1996
———. 'Israel to open consulate in Jordanian Red Sea port', 25 May 1997
———. 'King Hussein lashes out at union leaders', 8 June 1997
———. 'Israeli government confirms dam to be built on land claimed by Syria', 24 August 1997
———. 'Israeli planes to land at Jordan's Aqaba airport', 10 November 1997
———. 'Annual economic conference with Israel finds few Arab takers', 12 November 1997
———. 'US gives two million dollars for Red Sea peace park', 18 December 1997
———. 'Jordan says Mossad chief should have gone months ago', 25 February 1998
———. 'Jordan's civil servants to chip in one day's salary to intifada', 23 October 2000
———. 'Peaceful demos in Jordan vent anti-Israeli anger', 27 October 2000
———. 'Jordan warns on bids to use pro-Palestinian anger to destabilize country', 1 November 2000
———. 'Hussein asked for Israel's help during Black September: British Documents', 1 January 2001
———. 'Unions publish list of Jordanians dealing with Israel', 21 January 2001

Agence France Presse (cont.). 'Jordan's tourism industry is intifada's latest casualty: minister', 28 May 2001

———. 'Jordan-Israel peace depends on Israel-Palestinian solution: ambassador', 26 October 2001

———. 'Jordan has plan to save Dead Sea from dying', 29 August 2002

———. 'Arabs oppose Jordan's Dead Sea canal scheme', 30 August 2002

———. 'Jordan bans unions from holding solidarity rally for anti-Israel activists', 22 November 2002

———. 'Top Jordanian court bands trade union anti-Israeli committees', 29 November 2002

———. 'Jordan's national carrier back in black in 2002', 16 December 2002

Allan, John A. *Water, Peace and the Middle East: Negotiating Resources in the Jordan Basin* (London, 1996)

Al-Kilani, Musa. 'Only Israel to benefit from shooting incident', *The Jordan Times*, 15 March 1997

Alpher, Joseph. 'Israel's security concerns in the Peace Process', *International Affairs* 70/2 (1994), pp. 229–41

Amery, Hussein A. and Wolf, Aaron T. (eds). *Water in the Middle East: A Geography of Peace* (Austin, TX, 2000)

Amro, Rateb M. 'The peace process: a Jordanian perspective', in J. Ginat et al. (eds), *The Middle East Peace Process: Vision Versus Reality* (Norman, OK, 2002), pp. 178–89

Andoni, Lamis and Schwedler, Jillian. 'Bread Riots in Jordan' *Middle East Report* 26 (1996), pp. 40–42

Astorino-Courtois, Allison. 'Transforming International Agreements into National Realities: Marketing Arab Israeli Peace in Jordan', *The Journal of Politics* lviii/4 (1996), pp. 1036–37

Awad, Rana. 'Jordanian businessmen urge severing of trade ties with Israel', *The Jordan Times*, 1 April 2002

Ayyub, Tariq. 'Jordan: Jordan Officials Comment on Israeli Report in Misha'al Case', *The Jordan Times*, 17 February 1998

———. 'Jordan: Jordan Protests to Israel over Sharon's Statement', *The Jordan Times*, 16 March 1998

———. 'Four deputies renege on petition to cancel Jordan-Israel treaty', *The Jordan Times*, 22 December 2000

Bar-Joseph, Uri. *The Best of Enemies: Israel and Transjordan in the War of 1948* (London, 1987)

Ba'rel, Zvi. 'Normalization is not for public consumption', *Ha'aretz Daily*, 3 May 2000

BBC Monitoring Middle East. 'Engineers body denies membership to graduates of Israeli universities' (source: *al-Arab al-Yawm*, in Arabic), 1 August 1999

———. 'Arab Journalists Union conference in Jordan condemns normalization with Israel' (source: *The Jordan Times* Website), 29 October 2000

———. 'Jordanian foreign minister comments on peace treaty with Israel, Road Map' (source: Voice of Israel, Jerusalem, in Hebrew), 13 October 2004

———. 'Jordan denies Israeli foreign ministry delegation visit to Amman' (source: MENA news agency, Cairo, in English), 14 October 2004

BBC Summary of World Broadcasts. 'Jordanian king visits bereaved families in Israel, plans return in "10 days"' (source: Voice of Israel, Jerusalem, in English), 16 March 1997

———. 'Jordanian, Israeli army officers meet, agree to change Naharayim regulations' (source: 'Hatzofe', Tel Aviv, in Hebrew), 25 March 1997

———. 'King Husayn says supply of water by Israel "fruit of peace"' (source: Hashemite Kingdom of Jordan Radio, Amman, in Arabic), 29 May 1997

———. 'Officials deny Israeli "claims" about agreement on changing dam site' (source: *Al-Arab-al-Yawm*, in Arabic), 26 August 1997

———. 'Jordan, Israel sign an agreement on the use of Aqaba airport' (source: Hashemite Kingdom of Jordan Radio, Amman, in Arabic), 31 August 1997

———. 'Mish'al affair prompts Jordan to suspend all security cooperation with Israel' (source: Voice of Palestine, Ramallah, in Arabic), 11 October 1997

———. 'King Husayn says his trust in Netanyahu has all but evaporated', (source: Jordanian TV, Amman), 2 November 1997

———. 'King rejects security ties with Israel until Mossad heads replaced' (source: Yediot Aharonot, in Hebrew), 16 January 1998

———. 'Jordanian business leaders deny launch of joint chamber of commerce with Israel' (source: *Al-Dustur*, Amman, in Arabic, 13 September 1998), 22 September 1998

———. 'Lobbying group, deputies call for freeze in ties with Israel' (source: *The Jordan Times* Website), 6 October 1998

———. 'Israeli ambassador comments on cutting of water supply to Jordan' (source: Jordanian TV, Amman, in English), 15 March 1999

———. 'Jordan threatens "appropriate" response if Israel reduces water share' (source: *Al-Sharq al-Awsat*, London, Arabic), 19 March 1999

BBC Summary of World Broadcasts (cont.). 'King threatens "other means to pressure" Israel over water' (source: 'Al-Bayan' Website, Dubai, in Arabic), 20 March 1999

———. 'Report on Jordanian-Syrian Dam Accord' (source: *Al-Dustur*, in Arabic), 21 May 1999

———. 'Jordanian transport minister, Israeli counterpart discuss "peace" airport' (source: Jordanian TV, Amman), 14 September 1999

———. 'Syria reportedly bars entry to several Jordanians for contacts with Israel' (source: *Al-Sabil*, in Arabic) 9 February 2000

———. 'Minister discusses Israeli tourism, calls for alcohol ban', 16 September 2000

———. 'Document warns of "continuing deterioration" in ties with Egypt, Jordan' (source: Voice of Israel, Jerusalem, 3 January 2001), 4 January 2001

———. 'Jordan's king inaugurates Mideast science project grouping Iran, Israel' (source: Petra JNA news agency web site), 6 January 2003

Beaumont, Peter. 'Dividing the Waters of the River Jordan: An Analysis of the 1994 Israel-Jordan Peace Treaty', *Water Resources Development* xiii/5 (1997), pp. 415–25

———. 'Conflict, Coexistence and Cooperation: A Study of Water Use in the Jordan basin', in Hussein A. Amery and Aaron T. Wolf (eds), *Water in the Middle East: A Geography of Peace* (Austin, TX, 2000), pp. 19–44

Beilin, Yossi. *Touching Peace: from the Oslo Accord to a final agreement* (London, 1999)

Benn, Aluf and Levi-Stein, Revital. 'Abdullah envisions an "open Jerusalem" on his first visit to Israel, Jordanian king stresses Amman's interest in success of Palestinian track', *Ha'aretz*, 24 April, 2000

Bligh, Alexander. *The political legacy of King Hussein* (Brighton, 2002)

Boncompagni, Hala. 'With violence rocking Mideast, Jordan to host "peace through tourism" forum', *Agence France Presse*, 30 October 2000

———. 'Dead Sea to disappear in 50 years unless linked to Red Sea canal: Jordan', *Agence France Presse*, 1 June 2004

Brand, Laurie. 'The effects of the peace process on political liberalization in Jordan', *Journal of Palestine Studies* 28 (1999), pp. 52–67

Bukhari, Natasha. 'King Hussein voices trust in Netanyahu after months of suspicion', *Deutsche Presse-Agentur*, 13 August 1997

———. 'Jordan blasts Israel over allegations on joint dam project', *Deutsche Presse-Agentur*, 26 August 1997

———. 'Jordan caught in a crisis over peace', *Deutsche Presse-Agentur*, 17 April 1998

Bukhari, Natasha and Goldberg, Andy. 'In Jordan and Israel, peace dividends lag behind expectations', *Deutsche Presse-Agentur*, 23 October 1995

Bushinksy, Jay. 'Israel denies Jordanian security freeze', *The Jerusalem Post*, 12 October 1997

Center for Strategic Studies. *Public Opinion Poll concerning Israeli-Jordanian Negotiations* (Amman, 1994)

Chmaytelli, Maher. 'WEF meet in Jordan rekindles hopes of prosperous, peaceful Mideast', *Agence France Presse*, 19 June 2003

CIA World Factbook. http://www.cia.gov (15 January 2004)

Cockburn, Patrick. 'Israeli drought cuts off Jordan's water supply', *The Independent* (London), 16 March 1999

Collins, Liat. 'A day like no other', *The Jerusalem Post*, 27 October 1994
————. 'Israel returns Arava land to Jordan', *The Jerusalem Post*, 31 January 1995

Cook, Steven A. *Jordan-Israel Peace, Year One: Laying the Foundation* (The Washington Institute, Washington, DC, 1995)

Coren, Ora. 'Israel approves acceleration of Adasiya Dam construction by Jordan at Hamat Gader; agreement has been reached on the water quotas Israel will transfer to Jordan next summer', *Globes Publisher Itonut*, 27 May 1999

Cotenta, Sandro. 'In the Middle East, the next conflict will likely flow from water', *The Toronto Star*, 26 June 1999

Danon, Yitzhak. 'Petition to liquidate Jordan Gate projects', *Globes Publisher Itonut*, Israel's Business Arena, 5 July 2004

Deutsche Presse-Agentur. 'Israel and Jordan in joint tourism boost', 11 November 1996
————. 'Jordanian minister: regional projects halted for political reasons', 13 November 1996
————. 'Jordan, Israel hold joint naval exercises', *Deutsche Presse-Agentur*, 26 November 1997
————. 'Syria blasts Jordan's participation in maneouvre', 6 January 1998
————. 'Jordan, Israel agree to boost economic cooperation', 23 November 1998
————. 'Israel to give Jordan full water share', 21 April 1999
————. 'Jordanians opposing peace with Israel campaign against normalization', 18 May 1999
————. 'Islamists accuse Jordanian government of vote rigging', 19 June 2003

Deutsche Presse-Agentur (cont.). 'Jordanian opposition urges government to sever ties with Israel', 22 March 2004

———. 'Jordanian premier says Yassin's murder "demolishes" peace process', 24 March 2004

———. 'Demonstrators detained in Jordan for alleged rioting', 26 March 2004

Dobson, Christopher. *Black September: Its Short, Violent History* (New York, 1974)

Dodge, Toby and Tell, Tariq. 'Peace and the Politics of water in Jordan', in John A. Allan (ed), *Water, Peace and the Middle East: Negotiating Resources in the Jordan Basin* (London, 1996), pp. 169–84

Dudkevitch, Margot. 'Unknown group claims Amman attack', *The Jerusalem Post*, 22 September 1997

Elmusa, Sharif S. 'The Jordan-Israel water agreement: a model or exception?' *Journal of Palestine Studies*, xxiv/3 (1995), pp. 63–73

Embassy of the United States-Amman. 'US grants $138.5 million in economic assistance to Jordan', Press Release, 23 March 2004, http://www.usembassy-amman.org.jo/mil2004.html

Emerging Market Datafile. 'Business Chronicle: Israeli companies flourish in Jordan, 17 July 1997

Financial Times Information. 'Peres declares Israel-Jordan fund: King Abdullah agreed to sponsor high-tech endeavors; World Bank to assist too', 19 September 1999

———. 'Jordanian Opposition praises government's decision not to interfere with marches' (source: *Al-Dustur*, 3 April), 4 April 2002

———. 'Jordanian minister warns against "illegal march" on the Israeli embassy', 12 April 2002

———. 'Jordan's tourism: another casualty', 30 April 2002

———. 'Business at Large, Jordan', 5 July 2002

———. 'Syria to increase water supply to Jordan', 21 August 2002

———. 'Jordan: Projects with Israel Infeasible', 27 August 2002

———. 'Israeli envoy on "cautious optimism" at world economic forum', 22 June 2003

———. 'Jordanian governor ends Israel visit, says border shooting probe ongoing', 26 November 2003

———. 'Jordan receives 18.5 M dollar installment for development, reforms from USA', 24 February 2004

———. 'Egypt's, Jordan's first Ambassadors in years present credentials in Israel', 21 March 2005

Financial Times News. 'Israeli offensive's impact on Jordanian economy bad, but manageable', 19 April 2002

Friedman, Ina. 'Stench threatens new Israel-Jordan Dead Sea water project', *The Jerusalem Post*, 12 August 2002

Frucht, Leora Eren. 'A chill wind from the Nile', *The Jerusalem Post*, 13 April 2001

Gal, Yitzhak, 'Sheikh Hussein-Jordan River Crossing: Working Paper', 2 May 2004

Garfinkle, Adam. *Israel and Jordan in the Shadow of War: Functional Ties and Futile Diplomacy in a Small Place* (New York, NY, 1992)

Gazit, Shlomo. 'The Gulf War – Main Political and Military Developments', in J. Alpher (ed), *War in the Gulf: Implications for Israel* (Boulder, CO, 1992), p. 41

Gold, Dore. 'One step forward, one step backward', *The Jerusalem Post*, 20 January 1995

Goldberg, Andy. 'Netanyahu in charge: Mideast enters new phase of uncertainty', *Deutsche Presse-Agentur*, 18 June 1996

Greenbaum, Lior. 'Eilat's next door nemesis', *Financial Times Information*, 6 October 2002

Ha'aretz Daily News. 'Jordanian PM blasts opponents of relations with Israel', 30 August 2000
———. 'European Tour Operators Shocked by Ze'evi's Posting', 7 March 2001

Habib, Randa. 'Jordanians vote in local elections, first test for peace deal', *Agence France Presse*, 11 July 1995
———. 'Islamist poll boycott shuts out opponents of Jordan-Israel treaty', *Agence France Presse*, 1 November 1997

Haddad, Mohanna, 'Jordan's Perspective of Peace', in J. Ginat et. al (eds), *The Middle East Peace Process: Vision Versus Reality* (Norman, OK, 2002), pp. 151–66

Haddadin, Munther. 'Negotiated Resolution of the Jordan-Israel Water Conflict', *International Negotiations* v (2000), pp. 263–88

Hala, Jamal. 'Israel, Jordan revise water distribution deal', *The Jerusalem Post*, 18 August 1999

Halaby, Jamal. 'Jordanian king calls for direct talks with Israel', *The Associate Press*, 2 June 1991
———. 'Authorities in Jordan arrest hard-line activists opposed to peace with Israel', *The Associated Press*, 27 January 2001
———. 'Kings allies triumph in Jordan's elections, Islamists return to Parliament', *The Associated Press*, 18 June 2003

Harman, Danna . 'Jordan: Israeli decision to cut water supply casts suspicion on peace process', *The Jerusalem Post*, 18 March 1999

Harris, David. 'Sharon, Hussein discuss projects as Mashaal-affair wounds heal', *The Jerusalem Post*, 9 March 1998

Hauss, Charles. *International Conflict Resolution* (London, 2001)

Henderson, Amy. 'Jordanian-Israeli Industrial Complex to Expand QIZ', *The Jordan Times*, 31 May 1998
———. 'Joint Jordanian-Israeli Transport Committee meets today', *The Jordan Times*, 6 September 1999

Hider, James. 'Benny Elon, settler envoy who backs "transfer" of Palestinians, heads to US', *Agence France Presse*, 4 May 2003

Hirst, David, 'For Jordan, the peace treaty with Israel has been far from warm and offered few improvement for its citizens', *The Guardian* (London), 3 April 1995
———. 'Netanyahu keeps Arabs on the boil', *The Guardian* (London), 20 June 1996

Ibrahim, Youssef M. 'Jordan is angered by Israeli findings on assassination fiasco', *The New York Times*, 18 February 1998

Inbar, Efraim and Sadler, Shmuel. 'The Arab-Israeli relationship: from deterrence to security regime', in E. Inbar (ed), *Regional Security Regimes: Israel and Its Neighbors* (New York, NY, 1995), pp. 273–98

Info-Prod Research Ltd. 'Israel, Jordan Collaborate on 2000 Plans, 1 July 1999
———. 'Investments in Aqaba private economic zone estimated at $2 billion', 15 June 2003
———. 'ASEZA 2003 Achievements Highlighted', 11 March 2004

Jerusalem Al-Quds (in Arabic). 'Jordanians on Dani Yatom's appointment', 24 August 1999

Joha, Ghassan. 'Economic performance of 2003, in retrospect', *The Star*, 5 January 2004

Jordan-Israel Center of Excellence. *Culture of Water* (Tel Aviv, 2002)

Jordanian Ministry of Tourism. *Tourism Sector, Key Indicators 1994–2002*, Information & Statistics Department

Joseph, Uri. *The best of enemies: Israel and Transjordan in the war of 1948* (London, 1987)

Journal of Palestine Studies. 'The Tunnel Crisis', IPS Forum, *The Journal of Palestine Studies* 26/2 (1997), pp. 95–101

Kardoush, Marwan. 'Economics of peace', reprint in *The Jerusalem Post* (from *The Jordan Times*), 25 September 2002

Katz, Samuel M. 'Still Partners', *The Jerusalem Report*, 27 November 1997

Keinon, Herb. 'Hussein visit shows strength of peace with Jordan', *The Jerusalem Post*, 17 March 1997

Kersherner, Isabel. 'Though other ties are under strain, Israeli-Jordanian medical cooperation is flourishing', *The Jerusalem Report*,

Keyser, Jason. 'Shooting attack rattles calm at Israel's Red Sea "escape" town', *The Associated Press*, 20 November 2003

Khouri, Rami G. 'Assessing two years of Jordanian-Israeli peacemaking', *Mideast Mirror*, 6 August 1996
———. 'Gas masks and lost passion in Jordanian-Israeli relations', Jordan Times, reproduced in *Mideast Mirror*, 15 October 1996
———. 'Reading Jordanian Rage, Arab attitudes and Israeli policies', *Mideast Mirror*, 7 January 1997
———. 'Some Jordanians gain, many do not', *The Jerusalem Post*, 22 October 1999

Kimmerling, Baruch and Migdal, Joel S. *The Palestinian People: A History* (Cambridge, MA, 2003)

Kissinger, Henry. *Years of Upheaval* (Boston, MA, 1982)

Krajick, Kevin. 'Science Center on Jordan-Israel Border Aims to Bridge the Rift', *Science Magazine*, 5 March 2004

Lavie, Mark. 'Israeli soldier, two assailants killed in Jordan border clash; Israel lifts restrictions on West Bank town', *The Associated Press*, 26 December 2001

Levinson, Jay. 'Jordan is trying to keep Israeli tourists coming', *The Jerusalem Post*, 20 October 1997

Lukacs, Yehuda. *Israel, Jordan and the Peace Process* (Syracuse, NY, 1997)

Ma'ariv (Tel Aviv). 'Minister suggests extending Israel-Jordan trade protocol, meet with counterpart', in Hebrew, 16 April 2001

Mahnaimi, Uzi. 'Mossad took urine sample from Assad', *The Times* (London), 9 January 2000

Makovsky, David. 'Jordanian debts not eased by peace', *The Jerusalem Post*, 19 January 1995
———. 'The Prince of Peace', *The Jerusalem Post*, 17 March 1997

Manneh, Jane. 'Qualifying Industrial Zones: Sector Report', Export and Finance Bank, Jordan, 10 June 2003

Manor, Hadas. 'Israel-Jordan-EU agreement depends on solving territories export problem', *Globes Publisher Itonut*, 17 May 2004

Meital, Yoram. 'Peace with Israel in Egypt's Policy', in J. Ginat et al. (eds), *The Middle East Peace Process: Vision Versus Reality* (Norman, OK, 2002), pp. 140–50

Miall, Hugh. *Contemporary Conflict Resolution: The Prevention, Management and Transformation of Deadly Conflicts* (Malden, MA, 1999)

Middle East Economic Digest. 'Joint project agreed with Israel', 20 March 1998

———. 'Jordan: Special Report country table', Weekly Special Report, 29 May 1998

———. 'New moves on Jordan Valley projects', 8 January 1999

———. Weekly Special Report, 9 June 2000

———. 'A winning formula', 8 June 2001

———. 'Special Report Jordan QIZ', Quest Economics Data base, MEED Weekly Special Report, 8 June 2001

———. 'Special Report Jordan: Aqaba: the Economic Transformation Begins', MEED Weekly Special Report, 15 August 2003

———. 'Interview: Mohammed Abu Hammour, Jordan Finance Minister', 2 July 2004

Mideast Mirror. 'Jordan polls: the best possible birthday gift for King Hussein', 10 November 1993

———. 'Born: A Jordanian Committee to "resist normalization with Israel"', 16 May 1994

———. 'Jordan's Islamist-led opposition calls for referendum on treaty with Israel', 2 November 1994

———. 'King Hussein and Crown Prince Hassan host a quarter of the Knesset at dinner', 6 February 1995

———. 'Sparks fly in Amman', 14 June 1995

———. 'Hussein warned he's moving too fast on normalization with Israel', 1 August 1995

———. 'King Hussein warns local opponents of peace process', 10 November 1995

———. 'Jordanian opponents of normalization with Israel score symbolic victory', 1 November 1996

———. 'Odds for Hebron deal stay the same', 8 January 1997

———. 'New crises with Jordan as Weizman takes gov't plan to Arafat', 6 May 1997

———. 'Is Jordan joining the Israel-Turkey axis?' 7 September 1998

———. 'Is there a dam in Jordan's future?', xiii/89, 12 May 1999

Mideast Mirror (cont.). 'Egypt-Jordan differences over Dead–Red canal', 23 September 2002
———. 'Incident at Wahdat camp', 5 April 2004

Mishal, Shaul; Kuperman, Ranan D.; and Boas, David. *Investment in Peace: The Politics of Economic Cooperation between Israel, Jordan and the Palestinian Authority* (Brighton, 2001)

Nevo, Joseph. 'The Jordanian-Israeli Peace: the View from Amman', in J. Ginat et al. (eds), *The Middle East Peace Process: Vision Versus Reality* (Norman, OK, 2002), pp. 167–77

Noor, Queen. *Leap of Faith: Memoirs of an Unexpected Life* (New York, NY, 2003)

O'Sullivan, Arieh. 'Israelis urged not to travel to Arab countries', *The Jerusalem Post*, 9 August 2001
———. 'Keeping it quiet', *The Jerusalem Post*, 26 December 2001

Pelham, Nicolas. 'Islamists join election contest', *The Financial Times*, 16 June 2003

Petra-JNA News Agency Website. 'Jordanian parliament says Israeli water cut plans "serious threat" to peace', Amman, Arabic, 17 May 1999

Pinkas, Alon. 'Israel, Jordan sign treaty', *The Jerusalem Post*, 27 October 1994

Plotkin, Lori. *Jordan-Israel Peace: Taking Stock, 1994–1997* (The Washington Institute, Washington, DC, 1997)

Prusher, Ilene R. 'Despite peace, Jordan sees tourist no-show', *The Christian Scientist Monitor*, 14 August 1996

Rabin, Eitan (et al.). 'Israel, Jordan in quiet talks: PM attempts to placate Hussein, *The Jerusalem Post*, 17 February 1998

Rodan, Steven. 'Only Jordan is promoting the peace process, says ambassador', *The Jerusalem Post*, 1 April 1997
———. 'Jordanian envoy: no water, no talks, *The Jerusalem Post*, 7 May 1997

Rubinstein, Danny. 'A bridge over troubled waters: how Israel's plan to cut water supplies helped build new ties between Jordan and Syria', *Ha'aretz Daily Newspaper*, 25 May 1999

Rudge, David. 'Children's group are the first Jordanian visitors', *The Jerusalem Post*, 29 November 1994
———. 'Israeli tourist stabbed in Jordan', *The Jerusalem Post*, 1 May 1997

Ryan, Curtis R. *Jordan in Transition: from Hussein to Abdullah* (Boulder, CO, 2002)

Salibi, Kamal. *The Modern History of Jordan* (London, 1993)

Satloff, Robert B. *From Hussein to Abdullah: Jordan in Transition,* (Washington, DC, 1999)

———. 'A US strategic opening: Americans and the Jordan-Israeli peace treaty, five years on' *The Jerusalem Post,* 22 October 1999

———. 'The Jordan-Israel Peace Treaty: A Remarkable Document', *Middle East Quarterly,* http://www.meforum.org/meq/issues/19950 (27 June 2005)

Shamir, Shimon (ed). *Israel-Jordan Relations, Projects, Economics, Business* (Tel Aviv, 2004)

Shapiro, Haim. 'Jordanians say Israel delays visas', *The Jerusalem Post,* 20 November 1994

———. 'Jordan seen as more dangerous for Israelis than Egypt', *The Jerusalem Post,* 9 August 2001

Shlaim, Avi. *Collusion across the Jordan* (New York, NY, 1988)

Sommer, Allison Kaplan. 'Ceremony cancellation shocks, angers Beit Shemesh', *The Jerusalem Post,* 7 May 1997

Starr, Joyce R. and Stoll, Daniel C. *The Politics of Scarcity: Water in the Middle East* (Boulder, CO, 1987)

Steele, Jonathan. 'War in the Gulf: Pressure on the king to denounce invasion: Jordan's leader falls short of direct criticism of the US', *The Guardian* (London), 5 April 2003

Stern, Bazelal. 'Olmert: keep politics and business matters separate', *The Jerusalem Post,* 8 July 2003

Sunday Times (London). 'Jordan Assists Israeli army', 30 December 2001

Susser, Asher. *Jordan: Case Study of a Pivotal State* (Washington, DC, 2000)

Swarns, Rachel. 'Israelis and Jordanians cast an accord upon the Dead Sea's waters', *The New York Times,* 2 September 2002

The Associated Press. 'Jordan declares drought, aid for farmers', 17 January 1999

The Economist. 'Jordan: non-combattant loser', 6 April 1991

———. 'Jordan's new king', 13 February 1999

The Jerusalem Post. 'Peace City to be built, 19 October 1994

———. 'Army brass meet and exchange gifts', 27 October 1994

———. 'Disappointment with peace gains hits Amman stocks', 2 January 1995

———. 'Jordan, Palestinians sign accord', 27 January 1995

———. 'Jordanian guild expels writer for ITV interview', 10 May 1995

The Jerusalem Post (cont.). 'Peace brings Jordan record tourism boom', 10 December 1995

———. 'New Jordanian PM expected to improve ties with Israel', 21 March 1997

———. 'Jordan gunman says girls mocked him', 28 March 1997

———. 'Deaths on the Island of Peace', 3 April 1997

———. 'Foreign Minister pushes "Red–Dead" canal to US Jews', 16 March 2001

The Jerusalem Report. 'People-Peace in the Air', 27 November 1997

The Jordan Times. 'Jordan: Israel plays down Jordan's objection to tunnel issue', 2 October 1996

———. 'Israel: Netanyahu on Ties with Jordan, Other Issues', 17 October 1996

———. 'Jordan to receive U.S. military equipment', 13 December 1996

———. 'Reciprocity is Vital', 17 March 1997

———. 'With slogans left behind' Editorial, 20 November 1997

———. 'Jordan: 47 Jordanian, Israeli Companies Cooperating in Exportations', 16 March 1998

———. 'Jordanian Official: Jordanian Foreign Minister Accepts Sharon Clarifications', 24 March 1998

———. 'Israel: Israel's Mordekhay on Withdrawal, Peace Issues', 15 April 1998

———. 'Jordan: Lawyers to file international lawsuit against Ariel Sharon', 3 May 1998

———. 'Jordan: Jordanian columnist on trade with Israel, PA', 31 May 1998

———. 'Jordan: Jordanian investors try to reduce Israeli interest in zones, 15 July 1998

———. '"New McCarthyism" feared as anti-normalization campaign heightens', 21 July 1998

———. 'Jordan: Jordanians investors urged to have "open mind" on QIZ', 7 August 1998

———. 'Jordan Keen to Expand Trade with Israel, Palestinian Areas', 27 February 1999

———. 'Jordan to unveil water "Emergency Plan" in next few days', 17 March 1999

———. 'Country to receive emergency UN food aid to counter effects of drought', 4 August 1999

———. 'Six years later', 26 October 2000

———. 'Jordan pins high hopes on FTA', 9 November 2000

———. 'Jordan times year end report views "ailing economy"', 20 December 2000

The Jordan Times (cont.). 'Report views projects to boost Jordan's water resources', 25 December 2000

———. 'Israeli firm invests $1.5 million in Jordan factories; 2000 trade figures noted', 22 February 2001

———. 'Jordanian official: trade with Israel "modest in volume", "limited in nature"', 26 October 2001

———. 'Jordan: Government plans to replace foreign workers in QIZ with Jordanians', 7 January 2002

———. 'Jordan: Exports Witness 25% growth in 2001, US largest consumer', 2 February 2002

———. 'Jordan, Israel to lay cornerstone for international science centre', 8 March 2004

The Middle East Red Palm Weevil Program, 5-Year Summary: 1998–2003 (Tel Aviv, 2003)

The Star (Beirut). 'Jordan-Israel Industrial estate faces criticism', 4 December 1997

The Times (London). 'Jordan assists Israeli army', 30 December 2001

The World Bank Group. 'Jordan Data Profile', 'Israel Data Profile', World Development Indicators database, April 2004

Thomas, Evan and Dickey, Christopher. 'Farewell to the King', *Newsweek*, 15 February 1999

Tidwell, Alan. *Conflict Resolved?: A Critical Assessment of Conflict Resolution* (London, 1998)

United Press International. 'Jordan begins new air route to Israel', 6 January 1997

———. 'Jordan's April Fool: Sharon Killed', 1 April 2004

Voice of Israel (Tel Aviv). 'Israeli ministers urge Jordan to make arrests over embassy shooting', in Hebrew, 24 September 1997

Vulliamy, Ed. 'US punishes Jordan by cutting aid', *The Guardian* (London), 12 April 1991

Walker, Christopher. 'Israel has secret Jordan meeting on water crisis', *The Times* (London), 10 May 1997

Wilson, Mary C. *King Abdullah, Great Britain and the Making of Jordan* (New York, NY, 1988)

Wolf, Aaron T. *Hydropolitics along the Jordan River: Scarce Water and its Impact on the Arab-Israeli Conflict* (Tokyo, 1996)

World Economic Forum. 'Jordan and Israel sign trade pact', Press Release, 16 May 2004, http://www.weforum.org

Xinhua News Agency. 'Israel, Jordan, Palestinians to make joint efforts to combat flies', 29 July 1994

———. 'Jordan's premier criticizes Netanyahu', 1 December 1996

———. 'Israeli FM to visit Jordan', 11 December 1996

———. 'Jordan condemns Israel's new settlement plan, 26 July 1997

———. 'Jordan, Israel agree to establish industrial zone', 16 November 1997

———. 'Jordan silent on reported talks with Israel', 9 September 1998

———. 'Syria begins to supply water to Jordan', 15 May 1999

———. 'Israeli firm to sell arms to Jordan', 18 October 1999

———. 'Jordanian businessmen refuse cooperation with Israel in Iraq's reconstruction', 30 June 2003

———. 'Three Israelis indicted for vandalizing Rabin memorial', 4 November 2003

Yudelman, Michal (et al.). 'Hussein, Netanyahu try to resolve water crisis', *The Jerusalem Post*, 7 May 1997

Zacharia, Janine. 'Jordanian foreign minister to "Post": It's safe for Israelis to visit', *The Jerusalem Post*, 22 August 2001

Zak, Moshe. 'Quietly, they talked about water, borders', *The Jerusalem Post*, 21 October 1994

———. 'Crisis proof peace treaty', *The Jerusalem Post*, 10 October 1997

———. 'A missed opportunity', *The Jerusalem Post*, 15 October 1997

———. 'Thirty years of clandestine meetings: the Jordan-Israel peace treaty' *Middle East Quarterly*. Http://www.meforum.org/article/241 (27 June 2005)

Zunes, Stephen. 'The Israeli-Jordanian Agreement: Peace or Pax Americana?', *Middle East Policy* 3.4 (1995), pp. 57–68

INDEX